FEMINISMS AND DEVELOPMENT

Disrupting taken-for-granted assumptions, this expert series redefines issues at the heart of today's feminist contestations in a development context. Bringing together a formidable collective of thinkers from the global South and the North, it explores what it is that can bring about positive changes in women's rights and realities.

These timely and topical collections reposition feminism within development studies, bringing into view substantial commonalities across the countries of the global South that have so far gone unrecognized.

Series editor

Andrea Cornwall

Forthcoming titles

Feminisms and Development for Empowerment:
Towards Women's Political and Economic Autonomy
Andrea Cornwall and Jenny Edwards

Women, Sexuality and the Political Power of Pleasure:
Sex, Gender and Empowerment
Susie Jolly, Andrea Cornwall and Kate Hawkins

About the Editors

Naila Kabeer is Professor of Development Studies at the School of Oriental and African Studies, London University. She has extensive experience in research, teaching and advisory work on gender, poverty, labour markets, livelihoods, social protection and grassroots citizenship. Her publications include *Reversed Realities: Gender Hierarchies in Development Thought*; *The Power to Choose: Bangladeshi Women and Labour Market Decisions in London and Dhaka*; and more recently, *Gender and Social Protection in the Informal Economy*. She has also edited a number of books, including *Inclusive Citizenship: Meanings and Expressions* and *Institutions, Relations and Outcomes: Methodologies for Planning and Case Studies from the Indian Context*, both published by Zed Books.

Ratna Sudarshan is Advisor (Research and Projects) at the Institute of Social Studies Trust, New Delhi, where she was Director from 2003 to 2011. She has researched and published on women in the informal economy, with a special focus on home-based work, social protection and local economic development; gender and education; research and policy linkage; and gender and evaluation. Other recent publications include a co-edited special issue (on 'Evaluating gender and equity') of the *Indian Journal of Gender Studies*, 19, 2 (June 2012).

Kirsty Milward founded and co-manages Suchana Uttor Chandipur Society, an organization offering education focused on social and gender equality amongst the Adivasi communities where she lives in West Bengal, India. She is also a freelance consultant providing writing, editing and evaluation services and specializing in gender and rural development. She has a particular interest in various organizational formations inspiring action to advance social and economic equality. Kirsty has an MA in gender and development from the Institute of Development Studies, University of Sussex.

Organizing Women Workers in the Informal Economy

Beyond the Weapons of the Weak

edited by
Naila Kabeer, Ratna Sudarshan
and Kirsty Milward

Zed Books
LONDON & NEW YORK

Organizing Women Workers in the Informal Economy: Beyond the Weapons of the Weak
was first published in 2013 by Zed Books Ltd, 7 Cynthia Street, London
N1 9JF, UK and Room 400, 175 Fifth Avenue, New York, NY 10010, USA

www.zedbooks.co.uk

Designed and typeset in Bembo with Good display by Kate Kirkwood
Index: John Barker
Cover design: www.alice-marwick.co.uk
Printed and bound by CPI Group (UK) Ltd, Croydon CR0 4YY

Distributed in the USA exclusively by Palgrave Macmillan, a division of
St Martin's Press, LLC, 175 Fifth Avenue, New York, NY 10010, USA

A catalogue record for this book is available from the British Library
Library of Congress Cataloging in Publication Data available

ISBN 978 1 78032 452 4 hb
ISBN 978 1 78032 451 7 pb

Contents

Acknowledgements

● ●

The workshop which brought together the contributors to this book was organized as part of the Pathways of Women's Empowerment programme, and the editors would like to acknowledge the funding by DFID that made this possible. They would also like to thank: ISST, New Delhi, for hosting the workshop and ISST colleagues who assisted with follow up interviews with various contributors; Cath Sluggett for work on a draft of one chapter; the several waste pickers, sex workers and other informal sector women workers who talked to us during visits; the anonymous referees who provided comments on a draft version of the book; and Mike Kirkwood for excellent copy editing. Finally, the editors would like to acknowledge the fruitful nature of the collaboration that made this book possible, but Ratna Sudarshan and Naila Kabeer would also like to extend their special thanks for Kirsty Milward for playing an important co-ordinating role.

Preface

Andrea Cornwall

Women's economic empowerment has gained an ever more prominent place on the international development agenda. Access to an independent income and the ability to determine how that income is spent is well recognized as playing a significant part in women's ability to enjoy greater control over their lives and their choices. And yet for millions of women around the world poor working conditions, lack of recognition and rights, and lack of any sources of security undermine some of the more positive, empowering aspects of entry into paid work. Many of those women work in the informal sector, doing jobs that they themselves may not even recognize as work. Isolated, dispersed and difficult to reach, these are working lives beyond the scope of conventional modes of labour organizing; their location at the intersection of multiple forms of disadvantage makes collective organization of any kind complex and difficult.

Workers in these arenas may experience many dimensions of exploitation, oppression and discrimination not only in the pursuit of their work, but in everyday interactions with society and its institutions. Paid work may bring them few of the life benefits enjoyed by women workers in other sectors of the economy, where regular paid work can build women's self-esteem and negotiating power in their everyday lives (Kabeer 2008). In many of the contexts in which informal sector work absorbs a substantial proportion of the female labour force, women are socialized into compliance. Some of the jobs that these workers undertake lie within the care economy, privatized and occluded from public view, and often subject to stigma and other more symbolic forms of marginalization. Others exist on the very margins of the visible economy, dealing with its detritus and with the symbolic and actual dirt of human existence.

There are powerful barriers to identity-based organizing, as to the recognition of these forms of work as occupations and of the workers within them as human beings with dignity. Exercising agency may be limited to the individualized tactics of resistance that are the 'weapons of the weak' (Scott 1990), rather than the bolder, more combative strategies of traditional labour movements. The risks that these workers may face in engaging in activism of any kind may be so substantial as to threaten their very existence. Domestic workers are at the mercy of their employers in whose private homes they work, where they can be physically abused and subject to peremptory dismissal for the slightest infraction. Sex workers are especially vulnerable to exploitation and abuse at the hands of law-enforcement agents who may deny them both protection and justice. Workers at the margins of agricultural and waste industries have little security of any kind, and much to lose.

This book forms part of a new series dedicated to feminist engagements with development. It arises out of an international research programme, Pathways of Women's Empowerment, that set out to understand women's journeys in diverse settings, sectors and contexts. Focusing on a series of entry points, representing the principal strands of activism and action framed by feminist engagement with the field of gender and development – work, body and voice – Pathways sought to map women's experiences of empowerment, and to seek out 'hidden pathways' beyond the gaze of conventional development strategies through which significant changes might be taking place. In its concern with the domain of women's work, this contribution speaks to a major theme of Pathways' research: the conditions under which work can be empowering for women. But it does much,

much more than this. It addresses issues that have been central preoccupations for gender and development, from the interplay between individual and collective processes of change, to the significance of representation and recognition in the struggle for gender justice. And in the active engagement of activists and organizers in the making and shaping of this book, it offers us new and inspiring ways of thinking about the contribution of women's work to women's empowerment.

The contributors offer a unique window into the struggles of workers in marginalized sectors of the informal economy for rights, recognition and redistribution. Their point of departure is the observation that while paid work can empower individual women, rarely does it offer sufficient emancipatory potential to really transform the structures of constraint that sustain women's subordination and oppression. Recognizing a lack of collective action as a major brake on women's economic empowerment, the book seeks to learn the lessons from examples of successful mobilization by women workers in the informal economy. The way in which it does this is unique, and constitutes a particularly rich and valuable resource. The stories that this book tells are tales from experience, told by people who have played a key part in the struggles that they recount. Many of the authors are themselves activists with long histories of organizing; the book's uniqueness lies in this, and in the coaxing out of narratives in interactions that were able to find form in the written word. Thus they share with us stories that are rarely committed to writing, in the voice of the protagonists themselves. The insights that they bring to the accounts of mobilization and change are born of that experience, and provide us with a deep and detailed account of the specificity of these struggles as they take place in different cultural, social, economic and political contexts.

One of the strongest messages emerging from this synthesis of experience is about the significance of starting with the experience of workers themselves, and being sensitive to the particularities of context. The gains achieved in each of the cases recounted here need to be carefully contextualized against a backdrop of factors that militate against any kind of progress in achieving rights and recognition, as well as those that have fostered or favoured it. A very different politics of representation emerges to that conventionally associated with labour organizing. An understanding of the cultural dimensions of dirt, for example, is vital to make sense of the significance of the mobilization of domestic workers in India – and of the symbolic gains represented by, for example, the celebration of Vishwa Karma puja in Karnataka with 'broom worship' rituals. It is equally important to understand the political context. A driving factor that made it possible for domestic workers in Brazil to achieve such substantial gains, for example, was their presence within a broader union movement that had brought the former leader of the metalworkers union, Luiz Ignácio Lula da Silva, to the presidency.

The book offers a powerful testament to the long-argued case for seeing 'development' not as a series of short-run, results-oriented projects but as a longer-term process that may take unpredictable turns and in which the most important role for external actors – funders, as well as facilitators – is that of supportive accompaniment. The gains we see here are fruits of long, difficult processes through which workers' organizations have evolved their own ways of working, their own strategies and their own goals. These modes of organizing are practical as well as political, engaging tangible as well as symbolic resources in the process of building movements that slowly, softly, move from small acts that reclaim the right to have rights to bigger, more assertive actions.

At the heart of these processes lies the struggle not just for better working conditions and workers' rights, but above all for recognition as human beings: for dignity and for citizenship. This interplay between recognition and redistribution, and the relationship between workers' mobilization and the pursuit of citizenship, is vital for understanding better what can be done to support processes of empowerment that go beyond individual gains to making a transformative impact on the achievement of gender and social justice. It is here that this book makes such an important and inspiring contribution to understandings of empowerment.

Andrea Cornwall
Director, Pathways of Women's Empowerment RPC

References

Kabeer, N. (2008) 'Paid work, women's empowerment and gender justice: critical pathways of social change', RPC Pathways of Women's Empowerment Working paper No. 3. IDS, Sussex.

Scott, J. C. (1990) *Domination and the Arts of Resistance: Hidden Transcripts,* New Haven, CT: Yale University Press.

INTRODUCTION
Beyond the Weapons of the Weak
Organizing Women Workers in the Informal Economy

Naila Kabeer, Kirsty Milward and Ratna Sudarshan

Women's participation in the labour force has been increasing in many parts of the world, hand in hand with the growth of the informal sector in relation to the formal economy. At the same time, many of the challenges presented to conventional models of workers' organizations by informal sector workers are well known: workers' organizations tend to articulate their strategies, forms and modes of organizing around well-defined workplaces, tasks and employers, and around a model of the worker as a breadwinner man. Informal sector workers, on the other hand, may have physically dispersed workplaces, a wide range of tasks, no identifiable employer, and, increasingly, are women. Nevertheless – and perhaps surprisingly – there are numerous examples across developing economies of organizations which have in fact managed to mobilize around the interests of informal sector women workers, despite the limitations, for them, of conventional models. The question of how they have achieved this has thus become increasingly salient.

This book is part of a larger research project carried out under the auspices of the Research Partners' Consortium on Pathways of Women's Empowerment.[1] Detailed research into the impact of paid work on different aspects of women's lives in a number of different countries[2] found evidence supporting the empowering potential of paid work, but with a number of qualifications (Kabeer 2011).

While paid work did indeed have a positive impact on women's empowerment, as measured by a range of indicators, this was strongest and most consistent for women in formal employment. However, they made up a only a small minority of working women in the countries studied. The overwhelming majority of women in these as in most developing countries are concentrated in informal economic activities characterized by irregular and unpredictable returns for their labour and difficult, often exploitative working conditions. Furthermore, impacts were largely restricted to changes at the level of individual women and their families. There was very little evidence that access to paid work promoted any form of collective action on the part of women to tackle the dense root structure of gender injustices experienced in their daily lives, including their working lives.

The research on the relationship between paid work and empowerment therefore concluded that while access to regular paid work could empower individual women in the sense of enhancing their sense of self-worth and their ability to negotiate important aspects of their own lives and the relationships that mattered to them, its broader emancipatory potential was limited.[3] It did little to enhance their legal status as citizens, enjoying equal rights as women, as workers and as human beings, nor did it promote their organized capacity to struggle for the recognition and realization of these rights.

It was this absence of the organizational capacity to bring about change that appeared to be a major factor curtailing the emancipatory potential of women's access to paid work and condemning so many of them to forms of work that left them economically insecure and politically marginalized.[4] This book therefore shifts the analytical focus from individual women engaged in these informal forms of work to organizations that have set out to work with women in the informal economy. It will explore the rationales that brought these organizations into existence, their strategies for addressing the needs and interests of their constituency, and what this tells us about the processes through which the empowerment of individual women interacts with broader struggles for gender justice.

The organizational challenge of the informal economy

The most famous proponent of the idea that women's engagement in the paid economy could provide the basis for their emancipation was Friedrich Engels ([1884]1942). Writing during an era of mass factory-based production, he argued that women's entry into the public sphere of the market place would free them from the patriarchal constraints of the domestic economy and promote their collective action with male workers around shared class interests. The trade union movement that came into existence during the era of standardized assembly line production certainly engaged in collective action on behalf of its working class membership, but it was, and remained, a male-dominated membership.

The capacity of the trade union movement to defend the interests of its membership rested on both structural and associational power (Silver 2003). The structural power of trade unions is derived from the strategic location occupied by privileged sections of the male working class within the capitalist economic system. As a result of this location, collective strategies – such as the closed shop, collective bargaining and the threat of strike action – were effective in winning gains for their membership. These gains in turn strengthened the organizational capacity of the unions, since they could rely on the loyalty and financial backing of their own membership to pursue further gains.

Trade unionism as an organizational form was transplanted with relative ease to the large public sector enterprises and capital-intensive forms of production that characterized the earlier import-substituting phase of industrialization in developing countries. But the unions failed to reach out to the vast majority of workers, both male and female, in countries where informal activities were characterized by easy entry, low earnings and the absence of a clear-cut employer–employee relationship. In addition, the attitudes of mainstream unions towards informal workers were, and still are, often characterized by fear and hostility, since they perceived such workers as a threat to the privileges they had won through their organized action (Breman 1996, Spooner 2004, Chhachhi and Pittin 1996, Gandhi 1996, Horn 2002). As a result, less than 10 per cent of workers, and considerably lower percentages of women workers, were members of trade unions in most of these countries.

There are a number of reasons why trade union membership was so much lower among women workers than men. Labour markets were highly segmented along gender lines and working women were disproportionately concentrated in the informal activities that trade unions largely overlooked. In any case, the greater limitations of their labour market opportunities and the absence of legal protection and social security in most informal jobs made any form of organized protest by women a high-risk activity. In addition, the male-dominated nature of trade unions, their fight for the 'family wage' for male workers – premised on their purported role as primary breadwinner – and the imposition of various 'protective' restrictions on women's capacity to work, all contributed to the near-absence of women in their ranks.

Since the 1970s, changes in the world economy have eroded the basis of the power of organized labour and reduced the size of its membership. The new hyper-mobility of capital, able to pursue cost-cutting strategies on a global scale, has meant that multinational companies can relocate, or use the threat of re-location, to bring the disciplinary pressure of large pools of unemployed or underemployed workers to bear on the unionized workforce. Moreover, the fragmentation of production processes and the pursuit of flexible labour market strategies have replaced the concentrated and stable workforce of the earlier period with a disaggregated, dispersed, largely informal – and increasingly female – workforce. The structure of such work inhibits the emergence of collective identity and collective interests. The difficulties that women workers face in becoming unionized by virtue of their location in precarious forms of work would therefore appear to have been further compounded by these changes in the environment for organization.

However, there are other changes, some rooted in the pro-cesses of globalization itself, which have opened up new possibilities for organization among sections of the working poor who had hitherto been excluded from the labour movement. The internationalization of the women's movement, its advocacy for women's rights in different spheres, and its ability to make links between grassroots activism, the state and the international development community has been one aspect of this. Another aspect has been the proliferation of organizational efforts of varying scale and orientation that seek to address the needs and interests of women workers in explicit response to the history of neglect by the official trade union movement. In addition, more recently, the declining membership of trade unions has led to the realization on the part of many trade unionists that the future survival of unionism depends on organizing informal workers, a disproportionate percentage of whom are women (Gallin 2001, Chun 2008).

This book is concerned with examples of a sub-set of these latter organizations, dealing primarily with working women who occupy sections of the informal economy that are hardest to reach. As Kanbur (2009) points out, while being informal is to be outside state regulation, informality takes different forms: workers may be part of a formal establishment but one that is not complying with formal regulations; they may be in establishments that choose to be informal in order to avoid regulation; or they may be in establishments that are wholly outside the purview of regulation.

A number of the organizations discussed in this book are engaged with workers who belong to the first category: working for formal establishments, sometimes in global value chains but in informal conditions. The majority of organizations, however, deal with workers in the 'wholly informal' category. Their work may be linked in various ways to the formal economy, but these linkages are generally loose and largely invisible. They are concentrated in casual, dispersed, isolated, part-time, irregular and often home-based activities in the invisible margins of the urban informal economy or in remote rural areas. They are often self-employed or lack any obvious employer. They may be in direct competition with each other – for work, for orders for their products, for space to sell their goods and services. And they are frequently located at the intersections of different kinds of inequality – class, race, caste, occupation and legal status – so that building a shared identity and interests represents an even greater challenge.

The organizational challenge of the informal economy is further exacerbated in cultures where women are brought up from childhood to comply with cultural norms about female docility, and where their lives may be controlled to a large extent by the decisions of dominant family members, so that there is little in their upbringing to give them the courage to stand up to powerful actors in the public domain. Describing the difficulties that poor working women face in acting collectively on their own behalf in the Indian context, Sinha (2006: 11) suggests that 'one of the most powerful barriers to organizing is fear. Women have been brought up in fear of their men, their employers and their communities. They live in constant fear of losing their livelihoods, of starvation, of losing their children to illness and of being thrown out of their houses.' They have little legal or social protection to help them confront entrenched asymmetries of power both at home and in the wider economy. Any strategies they may pursue in order to increase returns to their labour or improve their working conditions have, by necessity, been confined to the traditional 'weapons of the weak': hidden subversions and individualized resistance (Scott 1990).

Organizations that seek to promote collective action among women in the informal economy clearly face enormous challenges. As the International Labour Organization has noted (ILO 2004: 45), 'the needs and problems of such a diverse work force are as varied as the barriers and constraints they face in organizing'. Yet various kinds of organizations have emerged in recent decades to address precisely these challenges. Some of these have emerged in collaboration with, or as part of, mainstream trade union movements; others operate outside this mainstream but may draw support from their association with trade unions or with social movements, non-government organizations (NGOs), and so on. There is therefore a growing body of experience of organizing hard-to-reach working women in the informal economy, but few attempts to synthesize these experiences and draw out their lessons. That task is undertaken by this book. The following chapters deal with examples of organizations that are working with this category of women workers in order to draw out both common patterns and unique responses to particular circumstances, and thus deepen our understanding of some of the collective pathways to change that might be relevant for different groups of working women in different sectors of the economy. The contributions come from India, South Africa, Thailand and Brazil. Many are first-hand accounts, written by those who are directly involved in the work of organizing. They deal with experiences across the spectrum of informal activities, including domestic work, sex work, waste picking, international migration for casual factory work, agricultural wage labour for global and local markets, work in the fishing sector and natural resource management.

In this introduction, we draw out themes from the chapters in order to address some key questions. What gave these precarious workers the impetus and courage to organize? What were the main obstacles faced by their organizations in efforts to address what Nancy Fraser (1997, 2005) calls the injustices of redistribution, recognition and representation? These relate to the unfairness of the economic system and the exploitative relations of work that it generates; the denial of respect and dignity to certain groups of workers on the basis of their identity and the work they do; and the absence of an organized voice that can articulate their needs and rights as women, as workers and as citizens. In addition, we are interested in what is distinctive about the strategies they drew on in order to transcend the structurally disadvantaged position of women workers within the economy. What emerges from our analysis is a range of different strategies that straddle decisions about organizational form, nurturing a common identity across the many inequalities that divide women workers: cultural appropriations, discursive strategies, legal activism, the deployment of information and information technologies, provision of practical support on an everyday basis, the search for social security, engagement in politics and alliance building. Through our analysis of the obstacles faced by organizations in different contexts and for different groups of workers, and the strategies used to overcome them, we begin to discern the emergence of a very different repertoire of weapons among these working women to those they previously relied on: the weapons of the organized.

The strategic choice of organizational models

It is striking – but not surprising – that most of the organizations discussed in this book have their origins in the efforts of actors who come from a different class background to the women workers being organized. Given the struggles for survival and security which dominate the everyday lives of working women drawn from some of the poorest sections of their society, and given their location in forms of work that are denied not merely social recognition, but also self-recognition, the likelihood of spontaneous self-organization among these workers is extremely low. In the absence of some kind of widespread revolutionary momentum, organizational impetus has largely come from the efforts of middle-class actors belonging to NGOs. However, in most cases, the role of these external actors was that of facilitation rather than active organization. The emphasis was on letting women learn to articulate their own priorities and identify their own pathways to change. Crucially, this is a very different approach to that adopted by organizations that work to predetermined goals and are dedicated to the expansion of their memberships.

Examples of these externally initiated efforts include the Women on Farms Project, promoting a trade union of women farm workers in South Africa; the social activists who help to set up Kagad Kach Patra Kashtakari Panchayat (KKPKP) among waste pickers in Pune, India; Stree Jagruti Samiti, the women's organization that set up the Karnataka Domestic Workers' Union (KDWU) in Bangalore; the MAP Foundation that worked with Burmese migrant workers in Thailand; Sampada Grameen Mahila Sanstha (SANGRAM) who initiated Veshya Anyay Mukti Parishad (VAMP), a sex workers' collective in two states in India; and USNPSS (or the Uttarakhand Environmental Education Centre) which helped to organize the Uttarakhand Mahila Parishad (UMP).

There are exceptions, of course: Social Need Education and Human Awareness (SNEHA), the Tamil Nadu fishing women's organization discussed by Rethinam in Chapter 4, was set up by a young man from within the fishing community, inspired by the spirit of community service. In Brazil, it was the Rural Workers' Union that began to recruit women agricultural workers into its membership, although the rural women's movement had been pressing for such inclusion for many years, while the domestic workers' movement was largely led by domestic workers, some of whom had become politicized through their affiliation to the Communist Party.

The decision about organizational form was generally the product of considerable deliberation and reflected what was considered most conducive to the goals of the organization. To some extent, it was also influenced by organizational models that were familiar within the particular context. Trade unions, for instance, are largely associated with wage labour and, at least in the South Asian context, with the urban economy. As discussed in this book's Endnote by its founder, one of the battles that the Self-Employed Women's Association (SEWA) in India had to fight when it was first set up in 1972 was the right to form a trade union with self-employed casual labour associated with the textile industry. The established trade unions argued that the essence of trade unionism lay in collective bargaining between employers and employees – and self-employed women, by definition, had no employers. The SEWA organizers argued that self-employed women did need to engage in collective bargaining – but with a wide range of actors, including local government officials and middlemen. It was this precedent that allowed the organizers of the waste pickers' movement in Pune, KKPKP – described here by Narayan and Chikarmane (Chapter 7) – to register the new organization as a trade union.

There were a number of factors behind their decision. First of all, they wanted to encourage its members to consider themselves as 'workers' rather than as 'people who rummage through garbage' – the common perception shared by the general public and the waste pickers themselves. A trade union, being legally defined as a workers' organization, would promote this identity. Second, it had become clear to the organizers that the waste pickers were not seeking to get out of waste picking as an occupation, but rather to regulate and upgrade their working conditions. Organizing themselves as a trade union acknowledged the 'permanence' of their occupational status and put the issue of working conditions at the top of the agenda.

Solomon's chapter on organizing rural women in South Africa (Chapter 2) also traces the decision by an NGO to work towards a membership-based organization along trade union lines. The Women on Farms Project was initiated by Lawyers for Human Rights, a South African NGO, in order to strengthen the capacity of women living and working on farms to claim their rights. WFP was subsequently registered as an NGO in 1996 and continued this work, giving priority to building the organization of farm women, in the absence of self-organizing initiatives within the farm community. It began by setting up formal groups, called Women's Rights Groups, on the farms in which it worked. The decision to use their organizing efforts to set up a membership-based organization along trade union lines reflected a variety of factors: the need to bring the groups together into a coherent structure, and concern about the continued dependence of the groups on WFP and donor funds. It also reflected awareness on the part of WFP that, as an NGO, it could not represent farm workers in disputes around the widespread labour rights violations that they were experiencing, since the South African Labour Relations Act only allowed workers to be represented by registered trade union representatives. Sikhula Sonke, the union that was formed, had to make some adaptations in order to maintain its identity as an organization of farm women. Union law does not allow the exclusion of members on the basis of gender, but with the technical help of WFP they were able to 'write women's leadership into the Constitution'.

In Brazil, trade unions were an important vehicle for women's struggles for historical reasons. Rural trade unions, organized under the National Confederation of Agricultural Workers (CONTAG), the main trade union body, had been active in Brazil for a number of decades but had been prevented from advocating agrarian reform during the years of military dictatorship. Consequently, they had focused their efforts on extending welfare provision, in the form of pensions and health services, to their membership. While the rural women's movement had as one of its central demands the incorporation of women workers into the rural unions, the unions remained largely resistant to these claims, in some cases arguing that women were already represented within the unions by their husbands. It was only with the rise of 'new unionism', born out of a wave of struggle against military dictatorship, that CONTAG began to instruct its local-level affiliates to recruit women and train them for leadership positions.

The domestic workers' union in Brazil (Chapter 5) also emerged out of the wave of democratization that made it possible for workers to unionize. The formation of a union was significant as a way of formalizing the movement, and in framing their demands to be recognized as workers with rights like every other worker. This was especially important for domestic workers because of the elision of paid work with carrying out what would otherwise be unpaid care work. It helped to assert the identity of worker for women who lived in the homes of their employers and were exploited 'as part of the family'.

The idea of trade unions had little resonance in the rural context in India. Neither of the two rural organizations from the Indian context discussed in this book took trade unions as their model. Instead what has emerged as a common organizational form in rural areas are community-based organizations that evolve in response to the rhythm of local livelihoods. This is exemplified in SNEHA, which was set up as a series of eventually federated village-based community organizations to advance the identity and interests of women working in the fishing community and later, when the government policy of forming self-help groups (SHGs) became widespread, encouraged women to be members of SHGs so as to access government schemes and for savings and credit purposes. Similarly, UMP, discussed by Pande (Chapter 3), came into being with the federation of a number of whole village-based women's groups which had evolved initially as support groups to village *balwadis* (child-care centres) set up by the USNPSS, an (initially) government-funded environmental education NGO.

VAMP – a sex worker organization working in small and large towns in western Maharashtra and northern Karnataka and discussed here in Seshu's contribution (Chapter 8) – made a conscious decision *not* to register as a trade union, but to organize as an informally associated collective. On the face of it, this decision was taken on the basis that many sex workers involved in the activities were not always prepared to be identifiable as sex workers – a requirement for the trade union model. As the organization evolved, it became clear that for the time being, the struggle for recognition – to be treated as human beings with human rights – took priority over issues of worker rights and working conditions that were the primary focus of trade union activity in India.

In Thailand, the option of organizing Burmese migrant workers through trade unions was not on the agenda for a long time. Trade unions had been banned in Burma since 1964, so the workers who sought jobs in Thailand did not have a history of trade union struggles to draw on. Thai law did not allow migrant workers to form their own trade unions but did allow them to join existing unions. However, Thai trade unions showed a considerable degree of hostility towards migrant workers on the grounds that they stole jobs from Thai workers. The Migrant Assistance Program emerged out of the efforts of a number of NGOs working with Burmese migrants, both male and female, in the agriculture and construction sectors who were subject to constant police raids and human rights violations. It was registered as the MAP Foundation in 2003 in order to gain recognition in the eyes of Thai authorities and the public at large as a legitimate Thai-based NGO working on the ground around a recognized set of issues. This was intended to give greater credibility to their work, legitimacy to their advocacy efforts and some degree of security in dealing with the police and other authorities. Its work on gender issues began as the result of a small grant from the International Women's Development Agency in Australia. After consultation with Burmese migrant women, this led to the setting up of informal forums where these women, from different ethnic backgrounds, could come together to discuss issues of common interest. While the MAP Foundation retained its commitment to working with both migrant men and women, Pollock's contribution (Chapter 9) traces the importance that gender-related issues have come to assume in its work, and the gradual road to building alliances with the Thai trade union movement.

Building a shared identity

Essential to the continuity of organizations of the kind covered in this book, and to the effectiveness of their collective actions, is the extent to which members share a sense of identity and interests. The geographically dispersed, socially isolated and frequently casual conditions under which many informal workers operate – the multiplicity of grounds on which they experienced social exclusion – means that a shared identity cannot just be assumed, but most often has to be built. While initially the organizations were cognizant of the multiple identities that characterized their members, their focus on livelihood issues appeared to reflect a pragmatic form of class politics. It recognized that security of livelihoods was a major preoccupation for workers in precarious jobs in the informal economy and that livelihood concerns could exercise the gravitational pull necessary to bring them together. In addition, the emphasis on their identity as workers served to cut across the other identities of race, caste, ethnicity and legal status that divided the working poor and undermined the effectiveness of their struggles to improve their living conditions.

Aside from the multiple forms of exclusion experienced by working women in the informal economy, the other, gender-specific challenge faced by these organizations was that many of these women did not see what they did as 'work' but as part of a looser notion of survival and livelihood activities. There was not necessarily a clear-cut distinction between their market and domestic activities, or between their roles as workers, mothers, wives and members of their community. In addition, many subscribed to broad social perceptions of their work as lacking value.

These chapters describe the different discourses and practices employed by the organizations to build this sense of shared identity and the extent to which processes of identity formation then became the basis of claims-making. For several organizations, raising the status of – or reducing stigma around – the work of their members was an important part of the process of building a shared and valued identity. This was particularly germane in the case of waste pickers, sex workers and domestic workers. Struggling for recognition as human beings with human rights was in some ways more urgent than, or a first step towards, being treated as workers with workers' rights. While waste pickers and sex workers experience pervasive stigma around their occupations as a constant issue to be addressed, for domestic workers their social exclusion derives from two sources. One is the general invisibility and low value attached to domestic work, whether paid or not. The second is the history of their occupations, which have entrenched highly unequal employer–employee relations. For domestic workers in Karnataka, these inequalities have their roots in the feudal agrarian economy in which farm workers were often bonded labour. The marginalized position of domestic workers in Brazil is rooted in the country's history of slavery. Most domestic workers in Brazil are black and racial discrimination pervades all aspects of their life experiences.

For some workers, there was nothing self-evident about their identity as workers taking priority. While KKPKP's decision to constitute itself as a union, and its observance of the formalities of registering members, taking details of their family and work, and issuing identity cards, were all important steps in the construction of a common work-based identity, the process was by no means a straightforward one. Many of their members did not step easily into a work-based identity because they had been brought up primarily to think in terms of their domestic responsibilities: their involvement in waste picking was merely seen as a way of discharging these responsibilities.

Similar considerations applied in the case of domestic workers in Karnataka. As Menon points out in Chapter 6, many women in domestic work, like many women in India and elsewhere, have been brought up to regard motherhood and domesticity as an ideal that rarely includes work outside the home. When this did not materialize for them, their decision to engage in domestic work to earn a living was often seen as a second-best option, a temporary phase in their lives rather than its main focus. It was not a valued aspect of their identity. In addition, there were a number of domestic workers who were concerned that formalizing their status as workers jeopardized aspects of informality that they had valued: some degree of flexibility around work arrangements, such as the ability to take days off when they needed to rather than on regular, predetermined days, and the possibility of getting loans from employers (a practice rooted in older feudal-based employer–employee relations).

Sex workers in VAMP had a different set of issues about the worker identity. They remained in disagreement over whether sex work should or should not come under the remit of labour rights legislation, partly due to the variety of forms which commercial sex work could take, and the various ways in which workers sought to negotiate the stigma of this work. For some of these sex workers, as for some waste pickers and domestic workers, there was an important distinction between being a 'worker' and being a person doing whatever it took to earn a living for themselves and their families. Other members of VAMP resisted a focus on labour conditions because they saw themselves as business women rather than workers.

The MAP Foundation found that it had to work with the multiple identities that migrant women and men from Burma considered important in their lives. Their identities as workers did not provide a clear organizing principle because the kind of work most migrants did was usually a matter of chance, based on the border area through which they had made their crossing into Thailand. Their identities as 'garment workers' or 'fish-processing workers' were therefore not ones to which they related strongly. MAP initially worked with and across other identities, such as ethnicity, which had greater resonance in the women's lives. It is significant that when the MAP Foundation consulted Burmese women migrants about how best to use the funds that had been made available for work on gender issues, it was around questions of their different ethnic identities that women first chose to come together, to get a better sense of what united them as migrants in Thailand as opposed to what had divided them as citizens of Burma. The violence they experienced – as migrants and as women – emerged as one of the first issues around which migrant women were willing to organize. As Pollock points out, the process through which those women came together – around shared interests and identities as workers – took much longer.

The resources of 'soft power'

A major motivation for this book was to explore the kinds of resources drawn on by organizations of, and for, women workers who could not rely on their strategic location in the economy to confront the power of capital. The contributions to the book suggest that, in place of the more confrontational tactics traditionally associated with the trade union movement, these organizations often sought to achieve their goals through the exercise of 'soft power',[5] drawing on the resources offered by culture, discourse, information and communications, and the law.[6]

Cultural appropriations

Organizations have been skilled at choreographing actions around recognized cultural symbols and references in order to subvert or appropriate their meanings for their own members or to gain public attention for their struggles. Domestic workers in Karnataka organized 'broom worship' rituals on the occasion of

Vishwa Karma Puja, when tools of ('male') work , such as vehicles, are worshipped. Since brooms are considered archetypically 'unclean', this action was perceived as particularly provocative.

In similar appropriations, KKPKP organized two actions. Raksha Bandhan is a ritual in which sisters tie thread bracelets on their brothers' wrists to symbolize their bonds, including brothers' duties. Waste pickers in Pune decided to tie a giant 'rakhi' all around the Municipal building, to emphasize that waste pickers were making a large contribution to municipal work to take care of the environment, but received little in return from the Municipality. KKPKP members also organized a *bin chipko andolan* – a reference to the iconic environmental Chipko movement, in which women hugged trees to stop them from being cut down. In this case women hugged the bins in one neighbourhood to stop a waste entrepreneur from removing them in the interests of his new, motorized waste collection service.

KKPKP have also used re-readings of familiar cultural events to illustrate social analysis. The organization has used the image of a popular annual ritual in which a human pyramid is formed to reach a pot of curd and currency notes tied high on a rope to depict hierarchies within the recycling sector as well as gender, caste and class.

In Brazil, CONTAG, the confederation of rural trade unions, chose International Women's Day, 2000, to launch a series of events across the country to publicize its commitment to building its membership of women workers. These events included the Marcha das Margaridas on 10 August, commemorating the day on which north-eastern trade union leader Margarida Alves was killed. This march has now become a regular occasion when thousands of rural women descend on Brasilia to demand justice for working women in rural areas. Also in Brazil, the Domestic Workers' Federation has sought to promote public recognition of the role of Dona Laudelina de Campos Mello, the domestic worker who, in the 1930s, initiated the process of organizing that led to the setting up of the Federation. Such recognition gives the movement a sense of its own history as well as providing an iconic symbol of the quest of black Brazilian women for dignity and rights.

Another example of the imaginative use of cultural symbols was the 'Panty Power campaign', in which Burmese women affiliated to MAP's Women Exchange in Thailand were involved. Coordinated by Lanna Action for Burma, a group of women activists in Thailand, and involving women across the world, the campaign called on women to post their panties to the Burmese embassies in their countries as a statement of women's continued engagement with the struggle for democracy in Burma. Within Burmese culture, contact with women's private garments is considered to have an emasculating effect on men.

Discursive strategies

Along with the use of symbolic objects and events to influence the way work and workers were seen, organizations made skilful use of discursive strategies in order to advance their goals. VAMP has invested a great deal of effort in promoting discourses that could help to transform both public and sex workers' perceptions about their work. They have sought to change the focus of sex worker support organizations in the health-oriented context of HIV/AIDS from the rights of sex workers – to health services, for instance – to the sex workers' right to work. They have argued with registration officials to retain the term 'Veshya' – meaning 'prostitute' – in the organization's official name, rather than opting for a more sanitized version, and changed the organization's name, originally AIDS-focused, to one that included the terms 'Anyay Mukti', meaning 'freedom from injustice'.

Unions in Brazil campaigned vigorously for rural women workers to be recognized as equals to their male colleagues, as professional rather than casual workers. One route to achieving this recognition has been through their efforts to revalue the work of women through discursive strategies, challenging the idea that women's ability to carry out the 'delicate' tasks in grape production was somehow an 'innate' feminine skill – and therefore did not need a monetary reward corresponding to its value-creating contribution.

For KKPKP, it was important to shift public (and self-) perceptions that waste pickers were simply people who rummaged in
the waste. They drew on a variety of discourses – economic,
professional and environmental – to argue that their members
were performing a valuable service in the waste economy,
collecting and trading recyclable commodities, and that theirs
was a far more efficient and sustainable method than other
alternatives on offer. Over time, its language has shifted to that of
service provider within a business model located within the new
economics of waste.

KKPKP, SNEHA and UMP have all drawn on environmental
discourses to steer and shape the organizations. For members of
KKPKP, the articulation of waste pickers' roles as environmental
managers, recyclers and re-users of waste products has shaped
opportunities in which to develop new ways of working in these
roles in the changing economy, rather than being sidelined by the
new entrepreneurial private sector initiatives that also draw on
'green' discourses. It has been active in protesting the inclusion
of incinerators for fuel generation in the Clean Development
Mechanism (CDM) – pointing out that these incinerators
compete for the same waste that waste pickers can recycle.

For SNEHA, part of their focus has been in alliance with groups
protesting against the marine damage implied by unsustainable
levels of large-scale commercial fishing, and environmentally
threatening practices such as aquaculture. Reversing this image,
these protests emphasize the environmental sensitivity and sustainability of local-level fisheries and the role that women play within
them. For UMP, environmental sustainability to support mountain
livelihoods has been a driving force, and particular aspects of this
sustained discussion have brought women together in opposition
to market forces in the context of economic transformation. For
example, UMP has linked discussion and analysis of the experience
of local development interventions – which promote organic
production for sale in cities but, at the same time, the entry into
villages of chemically generated food and the cash to buy it from
organic sales – to women's concerns about children's nutrition:

this has made improving the use value derived from their own natural resources an organizational priority.

Reading across the different discourses deployed by different organizations, it appears that most of them are interested in shifting structural constraints sufficiently – at least in the short run – to increase the 'room for manoeuvre' for their membership, enabling them to gain greater recognition for their work, fairer returns for their labour and greater security of livelihoods. There are a number, however, whose discourses appeal to a different vision of society, one organized along economic, social and governance lines that do not make it necessary to disrupt communities and destroy the environment in order for progress to take place.

The politics of information

The pragmatic and political use of information, and of information technology, have also featured prominently in the strategies of these organizations. Organizations have collected information to learn more about their own membership. WFP carried out a survey to ascertain the incidence of domestic violence among farm women; as a means of challenging widespread prejudice, KKPKP conducted an informal study into how many waste pickers had been accused of theft (a common charge against them) and how many cases were conclusive; KDWU used a survey into hours of work and earnings of domestic workers in order to estimate what the 'living wage' should be.

Information has also been used to educate the membership about the value of their work. The Rural Workers' Union (STR) in Brazil, for instance, kept its members informed about the price at which the grapes they helped to cultivate were selling in export markets, in order to give them some idea of their role in generating wealth for the nation. In Chapter 1 Selwyn also notes the stress placed by the trade unions on the importance of women workers educating themselves, with a clause written into contracts to allow workers who are also students to leave the farms at 5 p.m. in order to attend school. An official from the Ministry of Labour interviewed by Selwyn commented on how the union efforts to keep its membership informed about their rights and about the value of their products had combined with workers' growing access to the internet to make them far more aware and able to speak up for their rights than had been the case twenty years ago.

Information and communication technology has been utilized to reach out to isolated and dispersed workers. In Thailand, for example, MAP experimented with a number of different methods for reaching out to migrant domestic workers. These are mostly full-time, live-in workers who are not entitled to regular days off, and with whom it is therefore difficult to make regular contact. MAP arranged for contact points at festival sites where domestic workers might attend; arranged a phone line and a PO Box address to make the organization accessible; but eventually found broadcasting a phone-in programme on local radio was the most effective route. For the Brazil Domestic Workers' Union, local radio has been an important tool for reaching out to members and was instrumental in attracting the attention of Creuza Oliveira, who subsequently became a leader of FENATRAD, the National Federation of Domestic Workers.

Along with this inward-turned use of information, organizations have also used information as a means to draw public attention to their cause and to support their demands. For instance, members of KKPKP used street theatre to educate generators of waste about source segregation. This represented a reversal of the more common purpose of street theatre, which was to educate the poor about various issues. In addition, KKPKP sought to quantify the waste pickers' contribution to the local economy, initially on the basis of simple extrapolation methods and later on the basis of more formal research in collaboration with the ILO. This provided the basis on which they made a variety of claims to the municipal government.

The migrant domestic workers in Thailand, together with their Thai counterparts, organized a postcard campaign, getting supporters to sign postcards that they sent to the Ministry of

Labour on the International Day of Solidarity with Domestic Workers, 28 August. Over 6,000 postcards were signed and handed to a representative of the Parliamentary Committee on Labour at a national consultation on domestic workers.

WFP worked closely with Sikhula Sonke to bring the conditions under which farm women were working in the South African context to the attention of the wider public. WFP became extremely skilled over the years in conducting high-profile public campaigns, making use of the mainstream media. An excellent example of the use of information politics to advance the interests of the farm women was the decision to send a representative of Sikhula Sonke to Tesco's Annual General Meeting to testify in person to the violations of labour rights that had been repeatedly documented in reports compiled by WFP and presented to Tesco's management. The direct testimony of a woman who worked as a fruit picker on a Tesco supplying farm had a powerful impact on many shareholders, who declared themselves willing to take a cut in their dividends if it helped to improve working conditions for these women.

Legal activism

While most of the organizations that feature in this book stressed the importance of educating their members about their rights under the law, for some organizations, legal activism was a central core of their organizational strategies. The MAP Foundation in Thailand, for instance, backed up its regular training of migrant workers with the services of a legal team that could provide them with support in making use of the law.

One of their first opportunities to test this strategy related to the rape of two migrant women by Thai rangers. In Chapter 9 Pollock recounts the resistance and difficulties they met along the way, including lack of cooperation from the local UN High Commissioner for Refugees (UNHCR) office. 'Bulldozing' their way through these barriers, they succeeded in getting the rapists convicted. They used this experience to develop a set of guidelines to help women to get justice in cases of sexual violence.

An important finding that emerges from Pollock's chapter is that giving workers knowledge of the law and their rights as workers led to a decline in reliance on spontaneous, but largely ineffectual strikes that they had resorted to in the face of working conditions that, as she points out, 'even migrant workers found impossible to tolerate'. Instead, workers began increasingly to resort to the law. Whereas previously, making legal complaints had proved time-consuming and often fruitless, MAP provided members with information, not only about labour laws, but also about legal mechanisms for arbitration. It was a group of women workers from a knitting factory who first attempted to navigate these mechanisms rather than go out on strike. While they did not succeed in getting their full demands, their partial success proved to be a moment of revelation: 'migrant workers could go to court, migrant workers could deliberate on the verdicts they received and make their voices heard. The courts had to listen to migrants, the employers had to go through a legal process.'

Another organization that appeared to make the law central to its strategies was WFP. Begun as a project by a legal rights NGO, it set out to provide rights-based education for women living and working on farms and started its organizational activities by setting up Women's Rights Groups among these women. Its decision to consolidate these groups as a trade union reflected the fact that the Labour Relations Act in South Africa only allowed registered trade union representatives to represent workers. As we noted earlier, one of its most high-profile attempts to improve the working conditions of farm workers relied on its ability to provide evidence that farms supplying Tesco were failing to comply with the labour laws. However, like MAP, it did not confine its legal activism to workers' rights. From the outset it recognized domestic violence as a major problem in the lives of farm women and helped its members with information on relevant legislation and guidance on obtaining an interdict against an abusive partner.

For VAMP, on the other hand, issues regarding the law have provoked some ambivalence – partly because, as Seshu writes, 'In most settings including India, prostitution is neither legal nor illegal; it has no status'. This, combined with the 'moral discourse' which surrounds sex work, means that what constituted legal justice for sex workers could be at odds with what other groups perceived as justice. A proposed amendment to the Immoral Trafficking Prevention Act that would make sex workers' clients liable for prosecution had been welcomed as justice, for example, by HIV-positive women in Chennai, but, for sex workers, it threatened to drive their work into an even more vulnerable underground context. The lack of legal status for sex work has made it difficult for sex workers to resist being treated as criminals by the police, but through their *mohalla* (neighbourhood) committees, and armed with knowledge of their rights as citizens, VAMP members have been able to negotiate certain changes in police behaviour: that women are not treated in a violent manner during raids, that raids are conducted without the use of truncheons, that no one is beaten or pulled by their hair, and that only female officers can touch a sex worker during the raid.

Everyday practical support

The deployment of the resources of soft power often had practical gains as their ultimate objective. When the STR sought to educate women workers in grape cultivation about the value of their contributions to company profits, when the MAP Foundation helped migrant workers take employers to court, or WFP educated farm workers about their labour rights, it was in order to achieve improvements in wages and working conditions. However, these strategies did not necessarily have immediate pay-offs. Given the insecurity of informal livelihoods, the meagreness of the returns and the overriding preoccupation with the exigencies of survival, it was essential that organizations addressed the everyday practical concerns of their memberships. The support in question took a variety of different forms, as might be expected, given both the different contexts and forms of work in which informal workers are engaged, and also that, for women workers in particular, practical support may have to straddle both family and working life.

In some cases, the provision of practical support had a tactical objective. In Chapter 9, for instance, Pollock notes that the MAP Foundation used health education as a relatively uncontroversial entry point through which to visit migrant workers at their worksites. For others, providing practical support that had more immediate and visible returns helped to demonstrate the relevance of the organization to the lives of its membership, as well as providing that membership with the 'breathing space' it needed to take on longer-term goals.

In Chapter 2 Solomon points out that WFP's concentration on farm women's immediate practical gender needs allowed it to later develop its strategy to include an explicitly feminist agenda that addressed their strategic gender interests. Its earliest activities included the distribution of information among its membership about new social security grants to which they were entitled, especially the Child Support Grant, and assisting them in accessing these entitlements. It also cooperated with Sikhula Sonke around a number of campaigns, including for toilets for farm workers in the orchards and fields. Over time, as it took on issues of gender-based violence, it provided farm women with information on relevant legislation, such as how to obtain an interdict against an abusive partner, and available resources, such as women's shelters and counselling services.

KKPKP set up a number of cooperative scrap shops for its membership, the profits from which are shared by members. It also set up a credit cooperative that looked after its members' savings and provided them with loans, and ran a 'gold loan scheme' that allowed members to pawn their jewellery to the union at lower interest rates relative to money lenders. It has also engaged very systematically with the police to address the harassment of its members and police attempts to extort money from them. This has paid off: extortion demands have almost ceased and waste pickers are now much more able to stand up for themselves if they encounter harassment.

For VAMP, it was the practical processes involved in regular condom distribution in the course of HIV prevention work that not only gave the sex workers their first organizing principle, but also grew into community-based spaces for addressing much wider issues of injustice and solidarity: the *mohalla* grievance committees.

Stree Jagruti Samiti had struggled for an extended period to cope with the challenges of making and maintaining contact with domestic workers, initiating all kinds of local meetings, observation points and discussion venues. They only began to succeed when they decided to open and manage their own placement agency – run by domestic workers for domestic workers – thus maintaining contact with workers as they changed jobs, while also gaining some purchase in negotiating contracts and better worker conditions. Providing domestic workers with an identity card has also proved to be of practical help, as the worker can draw upon the support of other members of the union. So in case they are wrongly accused of some misdemeanour, or if an employer withholds salary, other members accompany the worker to ensure she gets her due. The KDWU had tried out a skill-upgrading programme, but found that these practical inputs were insufficient to reach some of the most vulnerable workers, who are live-in, full-time workers.

USNPSS began its work with rural women whose livelihoods depended on natural resources by addressing the long working days imposed by their multiple responsibilities. Their response was to set up *balwadis* – child-care centres for three- to six-year-old children, which not only relieved women of some of their daily child-care responsibilities but also served as a focal point to initiate work around women's health, expanding choices within and through education, for example. Over time, practical support extended to the promotion of new agricultural techniques through collective planning and experimentation: activities included afforestation programmes, water and soil conservation techniques, and gaining access to niche markets for local produce.

Rural trade unions in Brazil succeeded in winning a number

of practical gender-specific gains for women agricultural workers, including provision of crèche facilities, a paid day per month to visit the doctor, the right of women with babies in the crèche to breastfeed for an hour per day over and above the lunch hour, and two months maternity leave with the right to return to employment. They have also campaigned for improved transport conditions in recognition of the sexual harassment that women workers often face on overcrowded buses.

The struggle for social security

Along with addressing the more immediate concerns of everyday life – which varied across different groups of workers and different contexts – there was one set of livelihood concerns that seemed to cut across many of these differences. This was the concern with social security. While there is clearly a practical element to this concern, it also had longer-term strategic implications. For those in precarious forms of work, returns to which may be unpredictable from day to day, month to month or season to season, access to some form of social protection may be a necessary precondition for taking the risks associated with strategies for longer-term change. In addition, for those whose work, and status as workers, had been largely overlooked by the state, the struggle for social security was also, to some extent, a struggle to gain recognition of their status as citizens.

This concern with social protection was manifested in a variety of ways. For some, this was a right that had been won after an extended period of struggle, sometimes in the context of a larger struggle for democracy. In Brazil, we noted how rural unions, denied the right to organize around overtly political demands by the authoritarian regimes in power, had turned their attention to obtaining social security benefits for their membership. In Chapter 1 Selwyn relates how the rural women's movement had mobilized in the 1980s around the demand that rural women be incorporated into trade unions, as this would enable them to access social security benefits, including paid maternity leave and retirement. He cites Deere's point that attaining social security rights was an issue that united all rural women, whether they were temporary or permanent wage workers, landless or in family farming regimes (Deere 2003). The 1988 Brazilian constitution, the culmination of the prolonged struggle for democracy, also established social protection provisions that extended to previously marginalized workers. Trade union efforts have now shifted to campaigns to register women agricultural workers to ensure that they are included in state benefits.

The Brazilian constitution also extended a number of basic rights to domestic workers, including the right to a worker's card, which formalized their status and rights as employees to a minimum wage, advance notice and, since 2000, to unemployment compensation. For the domestic workers' union, the struggle has been to get these rights realized in practice. As the statistics cited in Chapter 5 by Cornwall with Oliveira and Gonçalves show, there is still a long way to go. The union has invested a great deal of its efforts in publicizing these rights, working closely with a succession of progressive governments to urge domestic workers to get their workers' cards and claim their legal due. It has also been collaborating with the state on a state-sponsored programme (the Domestic Workers' Citizenship programme) – in operation in several cities in Brazil since 2006 – to promote the professionalization of domestic work and to educate workers in organizing for their rights.

In South Africa, too, the post-apartheid government extended a range of progressive laws, rights and entitlements to previously marginalized and disadvantaged groups. WFP prioritized social security, seen as a key livelihood issue, in its work with farm women. Since the right to various forms of social protection was already on the books, it chose the social security issue to initiate its work, informing farm women about their entitlements under the new dispensation and assisting them to make claims.

KKPKP, by contrast, was active in attempting to win state recognition for its members' right to social protection. It deployed various information-gathering exercises and discursive strategies to argue to the municipal government that waste pickers provided a valued service to the community. It also made strategic use of the fact that municipal governments in India have constitutional responsibility for waste management to demand medical insurance for waste pickers, pointing to the health costs of their work, such as musculo-skeletal problems and respiratory or gastro-intestinal ailments. This demand was eventually granted in 2002–3. In addition, KKPKP mobilized as part of the struggle of the Alliance of Indian Waste Pickers for inclusion in the social protection measures offered by the 2008 Unorganized Sector Workers' Social Security Bill.

SNEHA has put constant pressure on the state government to extend social security provision to its members. While some existing measures helped male members of the fishing community through the off-season, women were excluded. Recent legislation has extended comprehensive social security to the fishing community. As a result of SNEHA's efforts, women are included as members of the Fisheries Welfare Board that administers the various provisions.

Some organizations are at an earlier stage of their struggle on this issue. For KDWU, a primary aim is to lobby for employers and government to recognize domestic workers as having the same entitlements to social security as other workers. It has also sought to reach out to male construction workers, many of whom are married to domestic workers, by informing them of the existence of social welfare provisions to which they were entitled. This was seen as one means of winning their support for women's efforts to organize.

In the meantime, KDWU has been active in monitoring social protection measures for low-income households. Its members mobilized to protest the poor performance of the Public Distribution System (PDS), an important social protection measure that provided poor families with access to subsidized grains and kerosene through Fair Price Shops. They sustained this protest until action was taken against the shopkeepers who were flouting the regulations. Some of the domestic workers were invited to become members of a vigilance committee appointed by the government to keep a check on the operation of the PDS in that area.

Then there are those groups of workers for whom access to social security is still some way off. In Thailand, where migrant domestic workers are considered to be outside labour laws, the MAP Foundation started its work of organizing them with the very minimal demand that they have at least one day off every week. For VAMP, on the other hand, the priority is to reduce the stigma, and raise the status, of sex work. It is only when this struggle has been won that it will be able to turn its attention to specific benefits for its membership.

Participating in politics

The focus on rights, the engagement with law and the struggle for social protection have, not surprisingly, led a number of organizations into the domain of formal politics. In Brazil, engagement with political processes has been fundamental to the successes of the Domestic Workers' Union. Growing out of class struggles, the domestic workers' struggles built spaces amongst the many organizations initiated during the flowering of democratic energy towards the end of the military dictatorship in 1985. During this period, the union began to join up with other movements, especially the feminist and black movements, all of which were engaging with the articulation of the Federal Constitution of 1988. Since then, the Union has built alliances with politicians to take their issues into the legislative arena and build accountability, and has put representatives on the Councils created by Lula's administration as civil society accountability structures. More recently, the Union has also supported Creuza Oliveira, at that time President of FENATRAD, as a candidate in four successive elections, although she has not yet been successful.

UMP groups have had a profound impact on local politics through their engagement with decision making around forests and other natural resources. As the group became more experienced, a large number of women have been elected to the *panchayati raj* institutions,[7] and a significant attempt was made to enter mainstream politics by fielding a candidate for the state assembly elections. So far, this political activity has not meant joining any established political party.

VAMP's experiences with efforts to participate in local politics are reminders that some informal workers are far less equal than others. In one case, a sex worker who attempted to stand for local elections under reservations for the Scheduled Castes in a constituency where many sex workers lived was disqualified on the grounds that her caste certificate was from a different state. Further proof of her identity was required but would have been too complex a process to arrange in time. In another case, a sex worker was denied the right to stand because she did not possess proof of her father's caste status. Women from the Devadasi community, as she was, do not marry as they are figuratively married to a deity. Hence their children have no identifiable father or the paperwork related to paternity. In response to the refusal of her candidacy, VAMP decided to boycott the election, leading to the ousting of the sitting municipal councillor.

Dealing with inequalities

Divisions between workers

That gender inequalities divide workers is of course one of the main reasons why women have been so poorly represented within the mainstream trade unions and why other kinds of organizations have evolved. However, these inequalities do not disappear with the advent of women's organizations but continue to affect the ways in which men and women interact around struggles by women workers. We see evidence of this in the case of the fisherwomen in SNEHA, whose men supported them when their fight was focused on livelihood issues, but opposed them when they sought to challenge the patriarchal authority of the caste *panchayats* or gender roles within the fishing industry. We see it also in the reluctance of male waste pickers to accept a union logo that featured women – even when women were the founders and overwhelming majority of members of that union. In women's personal lives, we see it in the reluctance of men to share in household work with working wives; in husbands who take over their wives' earnings even when they themselves are unemployed; and in the gender-based violence reported by women workers in almost every context discussed in this book.

However, gender inequalities are not the only ones that divide workers. Organizations that seek to build shared identities and collective interests among the women workers have had to confront the challenge of dealing with the other hierarchies that divide workers from each other as well as from the organizations. In some cases, divisions stem from the organization of work. Within the waste collection sector in Pune, for example, there are many different kinds of tasks, with different social and material implications: there are itinerant buyers who use pushcarts and are mostly men, and female itinerant buyers who use baskets. The worst off are those who collect scrap from dumps or landfills, who are nearly all women; bin collectors are slightly better off and have established rights over certain bins.

For the KDWU, caste issues have been significant, leading workers to refuse certain tasks because of the status they imply – such as cleaning bathrooms; prompting employers to 'purify' crockery washed by certain workers and keep separate utensils for their use; and causing employers to request workers of certain castes when they apply to the recruitment agency. Stree Jagruiti Samiti has responded to these issues by focusing on measures that the workers can realistically take themselves to reject degrading conditions, such as refusing the tea provided in a special cup.

Inequalities between local and migrant workers have proved a divisive factor in certain contexts. In Thailand, MAP is explicitly concerned with this issue among Burmese migrants. One response has been to carefully negotiate and challenge the negative identities attributed to migrants, such as 'alien' status and the association of migrants with specific cross-border political issues. MAP's Women's Exchange programme is directly concerned with building bridges across ethnic identities amongst women who, through migration, found themselves with various issues in common. MAP has also worked with Thai organizations to raise the profile of migrant workers and recognition of their contributions as workers, and encouraged linkages to such Thai workers' unions as exist.

Some members of the VAMP collective have found themselves variously discriminated against on the basis of non-Maharashtrian identity; in their neighbouring state, Goa, sex workers have been widely evicted on the basis that they were not of Goan origin, despite the fact that many had lived there for decades. And when VAMP members considered the possibility of supporting the struggles of bar girls in Mumbai, who were protesting against the 2005 ban on bar dancing by the state government, they found that most bar girls did not identify as sex workers – indeed, it was on the basis of their difference from sex workers that they were arguing against government repression.

KKPKP has experienced tension over the years between 'old' and 'new' migrants to Pune. Most waste pickers were migrants at some point, but KKPKP's original constituency was 'old' migrants who had been in the area for several decades. Hostility within the organization towards more recent migrants, drawn in by pressures in other states was, however, carefully circumscibed by the issue of membership legitimacy and effectively dealt with by charging membership dues – to be paid in instalments – from the time of KKPKP's inception, instead of from the time of enrolment. It has also sought to overcome divisions and prejudices among the lower castes by organizing mixed community weddings that bring these different groups together, and by drawing on the history of the Dalit struggle and the anti-caste movement in the area.

Not surprisingly, some of the inequalities that the Women on Farms Project had to deal with reflected the legacy of apartheid and surfaced in their initial difficulties building solidarity between the mainly coloured (mixed race) farm workers and the black (African) working class in other sectors. This proved a setback to early efforts to promote a 'worker' identity amongst farm workers. By building carefully on work-related issues such as the minimum wage review process during 2008, and on supply chain and value chain analyses which place farm workers firmly in 'worker' categories, this identity issue has been effectively addressed and links to other unions strengthened.

In Brazil, strong linkages with black and feminist movements have had a positive impact on the Domestic Workers' Union, not only by gaining strength and visibility from these strong movements, but also by aligning the Union's vision and principles with the commitment to gender and racial equality that these movements articulate.

Class inequalities: 'leadership' and members

The fact that many of these organizations have been initiated by middle-class activists makes class divisions within their ranks a challenge that has to be negotiated. This is well illustrated in Solomon's account of the relationship between WFP and Sikhula Sonke, which reached a moment of crisis and introspection when Sikhula Sonke began to articulate its need for independence after several years of close cooperation. While WFP had the 'advantages' of an urban, middle-class, and educated workforce, bringing competencies to conceptualize the organization and the expertise to put it into action, these advantages were sources of unequal power relations between the two organizations – and eventually this was resented. An initial assumption of 'sisterhood' between WFP workers and farm workers had masked what Solomon suggests may have been the essentially maternalistic role played by WFP and suppressed some of the differences between the organizers and the membership. 'Surfacing' issues of internal inequalities in organizations so that they are recognized and subjected to scrutiny from the outset, and a space opened up for the evolution of strategies to address them, may be an important condition for such partnerships to flourish.

In some ways VAMP had begun with a similar organizational structure: the 'parent' organization, SANGRAM, that formally initiated VAMP is a health and rights NGO with a middle-class leadership. Today, SANGRAM continues to work in informal partnership with VAMP, and under a single banner for direct action, as well as amongst a broader set of marginalized communities. Nevertheless, this mode of working together has not been without its tensions. Although strategies to deal with the potential divisions caused by differences in life situations of the sex workers and SANGRAM's leadership included explicit efforts by this leadership to discuss, understand and represent the world view of VAMP's membership, the relationship has also involved some periods of separation, and processes of renegotiating the nature of interdependence between the two groups.

The initiators of the KDWU were middle-class women, imbued with a left-wing ideology, and motivated to change society, with equality and the dignity of all work as guiding intentions. Their world view is in contrast to those they are seeking to unionize. In fact, their initial strategy — which was to address the government and influence policy through the strong voice of a Union — has had to be modified to one of seeking to influence the community to change their attitudes from being accepting of semi-feudal, flexible and verbal relationships with their employers, to actively seeking a written, contractual relationship.

Although the Whole Village Groups of UMP are, as the name denotes, formed by bringing together all the women in a village, the USNPSS which initiated the environmental education agenda was started by a group of persons who were 'local' in that they were of the state and lived there, and through their education and work experience brought high levels of expertise into the work. This has allowed an element of external mediation to be introduced into the women's groups, for example to resolve disputes around caste.

The 'outsider' activists involved from the outset in KKPKP have consciously tried to disperse leadership, partly by developing a deliberative, discursive organizational culture, and partly structurally, by vesting decision making in the interactions between a governing board and a large number of members of the waste pickers' Representatives' Council. Nevertheless, their situations bring into focus the tension between the need for strong and visible leaders – 'organization icons' – for the purposes of wider visibility as well as for organizational focus, and the need to avoid 'concentrations of power'.

Building alliances: global and local

As we noted in the introductory section of this chapter, the same processes of globalization that promoted the pursuit of flexible labour and the expansion of the informal economy have also opened up new possibilities for organization among sections of the working poor that had hitherto been excluded from the labour movement. It is no coincidence that it is largely in the last quarter of the twentieth century, when this phase of globalization began, that organizations of informal workers began to emerge (Bonner and Spooner 2012). Even more recent is the organization of informal workers at the global level. These organizations mainly take the form of networks and include Women in Informal Employment: Globalizing and Organizing (WIEGO, founded in 1997);[9] networks of home-based workers (mid-1990s); of street vendors (2002); and the International Domestic Workers' Network (2011) (Bonner and Spooner 2012: 18). Interestingly, the international networks of informal workers are largely led by associations of women workers.

Organizations represented in these international networks have been able to find common ground across countries, for example in advocacy for social protection. Despite the heterogeneity in the situation between informal workers in developing countries and those in precarious situations in the developed world, such joint advocacy has proved to be an effective technique. As Chandhoke points out, even democratic states are 'imperfectly just' and such collective action enables justice to be 'wrested' from a powerful state, as the social protection discourse has, to some extent, shown (Chandhoke 2012: 153–4).

While this is not a measure of their influence, these global networks represent only a fraction of the workers in the informal economy. Particularly in larger economies – like Brazil or India – substantial sections of the labour force may be producing for the domestic market. And even those who produce for global markets may be linked only weakly. While global value chains have a long and deep reach into economies, only small proportions of workers and production form a direct part of their production structure. The bottom end of global value chains often disintegrates into an invisible, fluid and unrecorded informality – home-based work can embellish garments for a global market without the worker ever knowing any other actor in the value chain apart from the local subcontractor who supplies the order. In addition, of course, there is substantial informality beyond and outside the reach of global value chains.

The workers who feature in this book are variously positioned in relation to the forces of globalization. The farm workers in South Africa, the grape producers in Brazil and migrant workers in Thailand are all producing directly for global markets but in varying conditions of informality. Others are very clearly oriented to the domestic market: domestic workers in Brazil and India, sex workers and waste pickers in India. Still others find their livelihoods threatened by global forces, such as the fishing community in India.

Alliances with others are an important means by which these organizations have sought to overcome the marginalized location of their membership, but they vary in the alliances they have sought. Some are more locally oriented than others. There is, too, a difference between an issue or a stream of thought that has global resonance, and the search for locally relevant and meaningful strategies. Both UMP and SNEHA are participants in the development of a gendered ecological world view, and both focus on the problem as locally manifested. The size of the organization and the nature of its issues may make this an obvious and conscious choice. For instance, UMP's evolution, in the remote mountainous areas of Uttarakhand, has been shaped by people living within the locality around issues of concern to them and at a pace that accommodates careful analysis and the balancing of old and new methods and opportunities.

For some organizations, 'the global' often impinges on their constituencies as a threat rather than an opportunity. As related by Seshu in Chapter 8, VAMP has had very negative experiences of the global in the form of (US-based) evangelical NGOs which, on the back of the Bush Administrations' President's Emergency Plan for AIDS Relief (PEPFAR) clause limiting how HIV/AIDS work can engage with sex workers, have carried out raids in the area seeking out minor sex workers. These raids are conducted in the framework of a discourse on trafficking which denies agency *per se* to women, and to which the VAMP women are increasingly articulating their opposition. Similarly, while SNEHA has had positive alliances with global fisheries movements, its experience of internationally coordinated relief and development work after the 2006 Asian tsunami was at least partly negative. Many international NGOs chose to work in partnership with the caste *panchayats*, whose power already represented the most intractable challenge for the women fish workers; some movements attempted to bypass fisheries altogether as a viable livelihood; and others ignored women's active roles in fish production. Through both these interactions involving national and international networks, SNEHA has developed its advocacy agenda, and also made an important contribution by sensitizing its network partners to the significance of community fisheries and to gender issues within the fisheries sector.

Most of the organizations in this book combine a local orientation with some engagement at regional or international level. Narayan and Chikarmane make the point in Chapter 7 that international networks are useful mainly for the 'local effects' they can have. Too great a focus on the ways in which issues are framed and understood at the global level may actually hamper the evolution of a locally grounded articulation of issues at stake. KKPKP has an active and fruitful connection with the Global Alliance of Waste Pickers, which has provided solidarity, support and information about the processes and issues of waste pickers on a broader canvas. Yet it is cautious about what to expect from such alliances, suggesting that the greatest benefit arises from the local-level visibility – and therefore pressure on local or national governments – that can be gained from these relationships. It has found that practical issues, reflecting, for example, differences in the nature and value of waste in India in comparison to other countries, influence the extent to which it can usefully engage with waste picker organizations at global levels. Not surprisingly, it has been far more active in state-based alliances – with other organizations of the lower castes, and more recently with the Alliance of Indian Waste Pickers, particularly in relation to lobbying the central government.

Other organizations have drawn selectively and creatively on the opportunities that international connections and alliances offer for the wider dissemination of issues and networks of solidarity. WFP's joint action with ActionAid, for example, in which a representative from Sikula Sonkhe spoke out at a Tesco AGM, created enduring reverberations in discussions of ethical sourcing and supply chain conditions.

For the MAP Foundation, a major focus of their efforts to promote the rights of migrant workers has been to find an organizational space within Thai civil society that would allow the workers to feel more secure. Consequently, they have invested a great deal of effort in working with other Thai NGOs that take on issues relevant to migrant workers. It has also sought to engage with the Thai trade union movement, an effort that is only recently beginning to pay off as Thai unionists have begun to accept that migrants do not represent the greatest threat to jobs for Thai workers. MAP has also sought to link its small group of domestic workers to the regional campaign, United For Domestic Workers' Rights, and facilitated their meetings with inspiring domestic workers who have led successful campaigns in places such as Hong Kong. The decision by the ILO to develop a Convention on Decent Work for Domestic Workers has been a major source of energy for these migrants, since they now know that there is international legislation that recognizes their work as work and their rights as workers.

In Brazil, national-level networking and alliances – for example with the National Council for the Promotion of Racial Equality and the National Council for Women's Rights (Conselho Nacional dos Direitos da Mulher) – have been a significant feature of the establishment and development of FENATRAD, the domestic workers' federation. But international alliances, in the form of partnerships with international bodies such as the ILO, the United Nations Development Fund for Women (UNIFEM) and feminist NGOs have been instrumental in generating enough visibility to vest power in those national alliances to drive change in policy and legislation.

Conclusion: some broad lessons

The efforts of organizations to promote the collective capabilities of some of the most disadvantaged sections of the working poor offer both inspiration and lessons for those concerned with the injustices of redistribution, recognition and representation as they bear on workers in the informal economy. The failure of most mainstream trade unions to represent the interests of these workers is a reflection not only of the greater numerical presence of men in their leadership and membership, but also of the extent to which patriarchal interests have influenced their evolution and shaped their organizations and strategies. In this concluding section, we draw out some broad lessons from our discussion.

One critical lesson that comes out of our analysis is the impor-tance of starting with the experiences and realities of the workers themselves. This means a very different politics of representation to that customarily practised by trade unions across the world who had developed a common set of strategies around a common agenda, largely based on economic demands. It is evident from the chapters in this book that organizing working women in the informal economy has to straddle two very distinct sets of issues. One converges with standard trade union concerns with wages and working conditions – although for the most margin-alized workers (waste pickers, domestic workers, sex workers, migrants), the concern is as much about dignity as it is about income.

The other set of issues is around identity, the constraints that the members of these organizations faced as women, often from very marginalized groups, and the institutions and practices they have to contend with in daily life as a result. Among some of the gender-specific constraints that feature in these chapters are women's primary responsibility for domestic chores and care of children and family; the secondary status attached to their earnings (frequently internalized by them); the resistance they face from male family members, often taking the form of physical violence; cultural restrictions on their mobility in the public domain; the sexual harassment they frequently encountered on their way to and from work; and the lack of recognition, both social and in their own perceptions, that what they do counts as 'work'. The politics of building voice and representation among these groups of women workers must thus combine the politics of recognition *and* redistribution – simultaneously or sequentially as dictated by the realities on the ground.

Structures of gender inequality differ considerably from one geographical location to the next, meaning that processes of organizing, the ways in which groups evolve, the strategies they use and the issues they prioritize will have a strong local dimension and are best understood in relation to local contexts. Therefore – as distinct from sectoral trade unions – women's groups are often geographically located and develop within localities. They may subsequently be federated and acquire presence regionally, nationally, or even globally, but the local base is extremely important to understand.

Furthermore, the willingness to be responsive to local context rather than working to a predetermined agenda means that the process of organization occurs at a much slower pace than organizing around more standardized forms of work. As we have seen, there are many different elements involved in the process of organizing hard-to-reach groups of women in the informal economy: it takes time to build social acknowledgement and self-recognition of the value of the work that these women do; to organize them and retain their loyalty; to build common identities and interests across women otherwise divided by their location in the economic structure and the social hierarchy; to become a collective force able to win the smaller or larger gains that would give members a stake in the organization and the commitment to further change. In terms of pace and scale, organizations that work at the local level and around local issues are likely to be very different from those that emerge under pressure from external agencies such as the government, donor agencies, trade unions or NGOs. This does not mean that external facilitation is not needed – organizing for change in the kinds of conditions we are talking about does often require an external catalyst to introduce or nurture ideas of change. But it does mean that groups evolve at their own pace and around their own emerging agendas.

And, third, strategies evolve and change over time. The 'long feedback loop' entailed in efforts to address the structural aspects of women's positions in their communities – and society more generally – means that highly politicized demands are unlikely to bring women together in the first instance. As women come together around the more practical concerns of their daily lives, however, as their collective identity starts to grow and strengthen, they appear to become more willing to take on these more political issues. Thus it may be that initial strategies are gentler, less confrontational, with continued affinity with the 'weapons of the weak'. Over time, a greater willingness emerges to engage in open conflict, to take legal action against those in power who violate their rights, and to use their organization's clout to influence political and policy processes and to assert themselves as citizens.

Structure, we know, influences strategy (Chandler 1962). Although different models of organizing are discussed in this book, including trade unions and other forms of association, all of them have prioritized women's perceived realities and needs. This has required organizational structures that are loose enough to accommodate the range of different strategies that have evolved in response to this overarching priority. At the core of these strategies is building a shared identity, and enabling active participation through practical everyday support. Using the resources of 'soft power' to negotiate and influence is one notable difference from the more direct forms of confrontation traditionally pursued by the industrial trade unions. It reflects the very real difference in the location of different sets of workers and the insecurities endemic to the condition of informality. Thus the subversive use of familiar cultural symbols can be seen as an effort on the part of informal workers to bring about change on the basis of continuity rather than disruption, a way of engaging the past that is less threatening to the established order.

Engagement with political processes emerged as an outcome of their struggle rather than an organizing strategy. The priority given to accessing social security entitlements had to combine the politics of recognition, the self- and social acknowledgement of a worker identity, with the demand for redistribution. These organizations have had to start with an acknowledgement of the multiple and intersecting inequalities – of class, gender, social identity and legal status – that divide workers, and find their way to a shared identity and set of goals: they could not assume that a shared class position transcended these differences. Worth noting is the fact that although most of these organizations have a primary focus on the local, many have gained strength from global discourse with or without being actively a part of any global movement.

To sum up, what these chapters tell us – and it is further spelt out in the Endnote on SEWA by Ela Bhatt – is that, despite tremendous challenges, working women on the margins of the informal economy *have* been able to organize. They have been able to work collectively in ways that are still largely absent from the lives of most women in the informal economy (as the Pathways study cited earlier showed). Their strategies have been carefully crafted on the basis of intimate knowledge of local context acquired over extended periods of time, sometimes over many years.

These are stories of change that do not sit easily with 'project cycle thinking', with its logical frameworks, its short time frame, its managed approach to change and its need for predictable and measurable outcomes that currently dominates the mainstream donor community. One of the assumptions, implicit or explicit, behind a project approach, is that the 'tipping point' of change can be identified fairly quickly; thereafter, the challenge remains one of implementation and upscaling, and can be left to the routine funding of governments. But changes in the lives of women are contingent on the shifting or redefining of social norms, and what the stories in this volume tell us is that 'tipping points' are not easily identified, nor are the pathways of change linear or smooth. Consequently, continuous innovation and long-term support is necessary for these efforts at change to bear fruit. The successes achieved are often quite small, representing gains that in the lives of other less marginal groups would perhaps not warrant counting: 80 women members of MAP's Domestic Worker Exchange in Thailand; a few domestic workers fairly placed by KDWU's women-run placement agency in Karnataka; a handful of young women from waste picker families trained to drive waste trucks in Pune; a change in police attitudes towards sex workers in Sangli. There are, eventually, enough examples of changes in legislation, expansion of political possibilities and injustice successfully challenged to suggest that the organizational processes involved can win their members meaningful benefits, the kind of benefits that might eventually result in significant shifts in the structures of gender and other inequalities. But it is often far from clear at the time when these smaller gains are achieved, whether they represent isolated moments in an essentially unchanging history of oppression or are significant precursors to the larger changes to come. It is, in short, a true struggle with no ready-made, predesigned strategies, prone to wrong turns and false starts, with few ways to predict long-term outcomes. It takes enormous commitment on the part of all involved − women workers, founders and activist members − as well as a dogged persistence to persevere in the face of meagre resources and intransigent structures.[8]

While the donor community is not well-disposed to such unpredictable strategies for social change, such strategies are also unlikely to be welcomed by those for whom the old heroic struggles of the organized working class directly confronting the power of capital provides the central paradigm for the structural transformation of society (see, for instance, Priyadarshini 2011). The fact that the struggle against capital appears to have less relevance for these workers than the struggle for rights can be interpreted as conceding defeat on the larger more important issues, including the ongoing informalization of work, in favour of securing some improvements in the conditions of labour (Lerche 2010). Alternatively, it can be interpreted as reflecting the priorities that begin to surface when some of the most marginalized sections of the working classes, those overlooked in the classic trade union confrontations with the owners of capital, become actively engaged around the politics of redistribution, recognition and representation. Their politics are not framed by the confrontations of labour and capital – indeed many have only an indirect relationship to capital – but by their struggle for a more responsive state and an expanded notion of citizenship. It is perhaps significant that the demand for social security that appears to be a priority for workers across the very differing contexts described in this book combines the politics of redistribution with the demand for recognition from the state of their identity as workers. This can be seen as constituting a first step in their journey towards citizenship. It helps to explain the importance attached to formalities such as worker registration and identity cards by those who have hitherto been denied even this basic recognition: the slogan used by the rural workers' unions in Brazil to persuade women workers in agriculture to register was: 'To have personal documents and those of workers is but one step in the conquest of our citizenship'. Despite variations in the contexts in which they work and in the situations of the workers they work with, the organizations described in this book can thus be seen to share a common goal: to democratize the struggle for structural transformation from the bottom up, opening it up to those who were overlooked, marginalized or simply forgotten by the official labour movement so that they too are a part of the larger processes through which new visions of society are forged, advanced and defended.

Notes

1 The research programme, funded by DfID, the Norwegian Ministry of Foreign Affairs and others, brings together research partners from the Institute of Development Studies (University of Sussex), the School of Oriental and African Studies (University of London), the Centre for Gender and Social Transformation (BRAC Development Institute, BRAC University, Bangladesh), the Social Research Centre (American University of Cairo), the Federal University of Bahia (Brazil), and the Centre for Gender Studies and Advocacy (University of Ghana). See www.pathways empowerment.org for further information.

2 These were Bangladesh, Ghana, Egypt, Brazil, Pakistan, Afghanistan, Palestine, Nigeria and Sierra Leone.

3 For a discussion of the distinction between empowerment and emancipation, see a thematic overview of the transformative potential of paid work carried out by Kabeer (2008).

4 While some of the women in our studies were affiliated to organizations, these were primarily church-based organizations and microfinance NGOs, none of which were engaged in promoting women's collective capability to struggle for their rights.

5 A term coined by Joseph Nye to refer to the ability to attract, persuade and co-opt rather than use force or money.

6 We have drawn here on the work of Keck and Sikkink (1998).

7 *Panchayati raj* is a three-tier system of local governance in rural areas, created following a constitutional amendment in 1992, within which there is a 33 per cent reservation for women since 1993 (now enhanced to 50 per cent in many states). The system comprises elected councils at village level (*panchayats*), as well as intermediate and district levels, with five-year terms. The *gram sabha* (village assembly) consists of all persons on the village electoral rolls. The constitutionally mandated PRI system is to be distinguished from 'caste *panchayats*' that exist in some areas, have no legal status and concern themselves with prescribing norms of social intercourse.

8 Engaging with organizations like these, therefore – either as 'editors', as we did, or as other kinds of individuals and organizations offering support – means engagement on their own terms. For us, sometimes these terms meant using approaches at the margins of regular editorial work: piecing together information from interviews; visiting organizations to be able to add texture; updating texts after phone discussions; meetings around kitchen tables to find a 'writing moment'. As these organizations have

themselves constantly blended, adapted and invented methods for continuing their journey, perhaps those working with them need to meet this adaptability with their own.

9 Since it was established in 1997, the global network Women in Informal Employment: Globalizing and Organizing (WIEGO) has promoted organizing in the informal economy with a special focus on women members and leaders and has helped to build and strengthen sector-specific national, regional and international networks of organizations of informal workers in four sectors: domestic workers, home-based workers, street vendors and waste pickers. For more details, see http://wiego.org/wiego/core-pro grammes/organization-representation.

References

Bonner, Christine and Dave Spooner (eds) (2012) 'The only school we have: learning from organizing experiences across the informal economy', Women in Informal Employment: Globalizing and Organizing (WIEGO), April, http://wiego.org/sites/wiego.org/files/resources/files/Bonner_Spooner_The_Only_School_We_Have. pdf, p. 18 (accessed 4 August 2012).

Breman, J. (1996) *Footloose Labour: Working in India's Informal Economy*, Cambridge: Cambridge University Press.

Chandhoke, Neera (2012) 'Who owes whom, why and to what effect?' in Sebastiano Maffettone and Aakash Singh Rathore (eds) *Global Justice: Critical Perspectives*, London: Routledge, pp. 143–62.

Chandler, Alfred D. (1962) *Strategy and Structure: Chapters in the History of the Industrial Enterprise*, Cambridge, MA: MIT Press.

Chhachhi, A. and R. Pittin (1996) 'Introduction', in A. Chhachhi and R. Pittin (eds), *Confronting State, Capital and Patriarchy: Women Organising in the Process of Industrialisation*, London: Macmillan Press.

Chun, J. J. (2008) 'The limits of labour exclusion: redefining the politic of split labour markets under globalisation', *Critical Sociology*, 34, 3: 433–52.

Deere, C.D. (2003) 'Women's land rights and rural social movements in the Brazilian agrarian reform', *Journal of Agrarian Change*, 3, 1: 257–88.

Engels, F. ([1884]1942). *The Origin of the Family, Private Property and the State*, New York: International Publishers.

Fraser, N. (1997) *Justice Interruptus: Critical Reflections on the 'Post-Socialist' Condition*, London: Routledge.

—— (2005) 'Reframing justice in a globalizing world', *New Left Review*, 36: 1–19.

Gallin, D. (2001) 'Propositions on trade unions and informal employment in times of globalisation', *Antipode*, 33, 3: 531–49.

Gandhi, N. (1996) 'Purple and red banners. joint strategies for women workers in the informal sector' in A. Chhachhi and R. Pittin (eds), *Confronting State, Capital and Patriarchy: Women Organising in the Process of Industrialisation*, London: Macmillan Press.

Horn, P. (2002) 'Voice regulation and the informal economy', paper presented at the Informal Consultation on Re-Conceptualising Work, InFocus Programme on Socio-economic Security, International Labour Organization, Geneva.

ILO (2004) 'Organising for social justice', prepared for International Labour Conference, 92nd Session, Geneva: International Labour Organization.

Kabeer, N. (2008) 'Paid work, women's empowerment and gender justice: critical pathways to social change', Pathways Working Paper 3, available online at www.pathwaysofempowerment.org/PathwaysWP3-website.pdf (accessed 6 October 2012).

—— (2011) 'Contextualising economic pathways to women's empowerment: findings from a multi-country research programme', Pathways policy paper, October, available online at www.pathways ofempowerment.org/Economic_Pathways_to_Womens_Em power ment.pdf (accessed 6 October 2012).

Kanbur, Ravi (2009) 'Conceptualising informality: regulation and enforcement', *Indian Journal of Labour Economics*, 52, 1: 33–42.

Keck, M. and K. Sikkink (1998) *Activists Beyond Borders: Advocacy Networks in International Politics*, Ithaca, NY: Cornell University Press.

Lerche, J. (2010) 'From "rural labour" to "classes of labour": class fragmentation, class and caste struggle at the bottom of the Indian labour hierarchy' in B. Harriss-White and J. Heyer (eds), *The Comparative Political Economy of Development: Africa and South Asia*, London: Routledge.

Priyadarshini, A. (2011) 'The "quiet revolution" and women's proletarianization', *Economic and Political Weekly*, 46, 6: 73–8.

Scott, J. C. (1990) *Domination and the Arts of Resistance: Hidden Transcripts*, New Haven, CT: Yale University Press.

Silver, B. J. (2003) *Forces of Labour. Workers' Movements and Globalisation since 1870*, Cambridge: Cambridge University Press.

Sinha, S. (2006) 'Building visibility and voice: documenting lesson and learnings in home-based workers', report prepared for United Nations Development Programme (UNDP), New Delhi.

Spooner, D. (2004) 'Trade unions and NGOs: the need for co-operation', *Development in Practice*, 14, 1 and 2: 19–33.

1
Women and Rural Trade Unions in North-East Brazil[1]

Ben Selwyn

In recent years globalization has made capital increasingly mobile, bringing opportunities for firms to seek out cheap labour wherever it may be found. In discussions of the implications of this situation, it is often assumed, or concluded, that labour is at a greater disadvantage in the current situation than it was prior to globalization because of its relative immobility. For women workers – a significant group in many of these new, globalized production processes – this disadvantage may be compounded by the difficulties they face in achieving adequate representation through trade unions – iconic symbols of worker struggle and power, but usually built and managed around a male breadwinner model which presents many challenges for women.

One form of increasing capital mobility is the unfolding retail revolution (Reardon *et al.* 2001; Humphrey 2007) occurring over the last quarter-century, first in the global North and now, increasingly in the global South, and involving new technologies, production systems and supply chains connecting geographically distant producers with economically powerful northern supermarkets. This revolution involves not just increasingly wide global sourcing, but also the setting/imposition of ever-stricter requirements on producers (Dolan and Humphrey 2000). In tandem with the expansion of non-traditional agricultural exports to supply global retailers, the 'feminization of agriculture' has been documented widely. Simply put, this refers to a situation where there is an absolute increase in women's participation in the agricultural wage labour force and/or where there is an increase in the percentage of women workers relative to men in the sector (Deere 2005: 17; Katz 2003: 33). The double subordination of women workers (as workers and as women) is often observed in globalized export agriculture. Hence, Raynolds argues that 'employers manipulate gender ideologies and institutions to depress wages, to increase labour discipline, and to maximize labour extraction from both women and men' (2001: 25). And 'women are seen as an apt group for the implementation of flexible and precarious kinds of work, given their higher levels of socioeconomic vulnerability' (Spulveda, quoted in Ferm 2008: 23).

Whilst there are numerous cases where women workers experience such a regressive double marginalization (Thrupp 1995; Deere 2005), it is also important to investigate cases where gendered working practices have given rise to more complicated and, possibly, more progressive outcomes. This chapter takes the case of women workers in export horticulture in north-east Brazil to explore what these new sites might sometimes offer women workers, and whether they have been able to increase their bargaining power. The study looks at the context in which the rural trade union was operating, the ways in which women workers have engaged with the union, and the extent to which they have won benefits as workers through this engagement.

In the São Francisco Valley's export horticulture (specifically table grape) sector, by 2008 there were around 120,000 irrigated hectares of fruiticulture (VALEXPORT 2008). By the mid-2000s, table grapes had become the region's principal export crop; between 1997 and 2007 export volumes and earnings increased from 3,700 tons and US$4.7 million to over 78,000 tons and over US$170 million (*ibid.*). Half-way through the first decade, there were more than 50,000 workers employed in the grape sector alone.[2] Production has expanded rapidly, from approximately 4,500 hectares of vineyards in 2001 to around 12,100 hectares by

2007 (Selwyn 2007b; VALEXPORT 2008). The valley accounts for over 90 per cent of Brazilian grape exports (*ibid.*) because it is able to organize production to take advantage of periods of low supply in Europe. National and international capital has located and relocated to the region to take advantage of the boom (Selwyn 2010a).

The chapter is structured as follows: the following section places this case study in the broader Brazilian context. The next sections explain the reasons for and extent of women's employment in the São Francisco Valley, documenting how women have become increasingly active in the valley's rural trade union and how this, in turn, has resulted in important changes both within the trade union and to women's working conditions in the grape sector. The final section offers some preliminary conclusions to this study.

Methodology

Too often academic literature conceptualizes labour as if it were simply an input or a cost of production (to be reduced), but it is important to resist this approach. Kabeer notes, in her study of women workers in Bangladesh:

> Allowing women's own accounts to inform an analysis ... has the advantage of including a set of 'voices' which are often missing from both policy and academic discussions ... the 'subjective' insights provided ... offer a valuable tool for interpreting the more 'objective' hypotheses formulated by researchers and policymakers. (1999: 262)

The account that follows is based on research conducted along the São Francisco Valley, in the states of Pernambuco and Bahia, north-east Brazil, in the summer of 2008. I recorded open-ended, semi-structured interviews in Portuguese with women workers on farms and at the trade union headquarters in Petrolina (Pernambuco). The open-ended approach enabled interviewees to introduce issues that they thought relevant, even if they were not part of my list of questions.

Women in Brazilian agriculture: the broader context

This chapter, whilst concentrating on women in the São Francisco Valley in the interior of the Brazilian north-east, exists within a broader national (and of course international) context. As Deere and León (2001) note, in most countries the achievement of progressive, pro-women legislation has often depended on the participation of women in social movements organized to achieve such legislation and regulation. In the Brazilian context the crucial decade for rural women was the 1980s.

The 1964 coup, following elite fears of lack of strategic direction by state planners (Kohli 2004) and of unrest in both urban and rural settings, ushered in 21 years of military dictatorship (Cardoso 2001) and derailed attempts by the peasant leagues, communist parties and other organizations to advance the cause of land reform and enhanced livelihoods for the masses of Brazil's rural dwellers. Political decompression (Cummings 1989), driven in part by major industrial unrest in and around São Paulo (which gave rise to the formation of the workers' party) created space for new rural social movements to begin, once again, campaigning for rural justice. Whilst the academic focus has been on issues surrounding agrarian reform, and in particular the activities of the Landless Labourers Movement (MST), Deere (2003) also notes that the 1980s witnessed the beginnings of heightened participation by women within rural trade unions.[3]

During the military dictatorship, rural trade unions were organized within CONTAG (Confederação Nacional dos Trabalhadores na Agricultura), which, whilst prevented by the military from campaigning for agrarian reform, provided its members with services such as pensions and health care. Cappellin (1997) notes how, during the 1970s, the Comissão Pastoral da Terra (CPT) played an important role in raising the consciousness of rural women, who went on to question social injustices. However, Deere (2003: 263), following Siqueira (1991) notes how, in the 1980s, 'The rural women's movement developed around two central demands: the incorporation of women into the unions and the extension of social security benefits, including paid maternity leave and retirement, to rural women workers.' The context within which these demands emerged added to their potentially radical content because many local trade unions were male-dominated and unconcerned with rural women's welfare or their potential role in their organizations. Deere recounts how in the north-eastern states of Paraíba, union leaders argued that women were not rural workers, and that as dependants of their husbands they had no need to join the union because they already had guaranteed benefits.

This ignorance of rural women's welfare and participation was challenged from the mid-1980s onwards, with male trade union leaders and representatives within CONTAG emphasizing the need to increase female membership. Subsequently, CONTAG began instructing its local-level affiliates to encourage women's participation and train women for positions of leadership. Deere (2003: 264–5) explains this shift by CONTAG with reference to the 'new unionism' of the more militant CUT union (Central Unica dos Trabalhadores). Indeed, in the mid-1990s CONTAG affiliated to CUT, itself founded in 1983 out of the wave of struggle against the military dictatorship. This continued a process of reorientation of regional rural trade unions previously accustomed to acting as effective welfare networks. In addition, the increasingly large and influential MST was campaigning for extensive agrarian reform, keeping rural issues close to the centre of the Brazilian political agenda.

By 1987 women represented around 29 per cent of the membership of the trade unions affiliated to CONTAG (*ibid.*). Campaigning by trade unions, in the context of a newly established civilian government keen to legitimate itself by distinguishing its actions from those of the prior dictatorship, contributed to the 1988 constitution, subject to enabling presidential legislation. The constitution established equal rights for urban and rural men and women with respect to social security benefits and labour legislation. The benefits included rights to unemployment and disability insurance, and 120 days of paid maternity leave for women.

The election of Collor as President in 1989 dampened the potentially progressive impacts of this constitution, as in 1991 he vetoed the legislation for paid maternity leave for women in family agriculture, which in turn encouraged employers of rural wage labourers to ignore the broader legislation as well. However, as Deere notes (*ibid.*: 268), 'Since attaining effective social security rights was an issue that united more rural women (whether temporary or permanent wage workers, landless or in the family farming regime), it is not surprising that these rights would constitute the most important arena of struggle for the rural women's movement in subsequent years . . . .'

Not only did subsequent rural social movements campaign around these issues, but Siqueira (1991) notes how, within the context of a rising feminist discourse, issues such as women's sexual freedoms also became prominent within the rural trade unions' agenda. In 1991, a major campaign was launched by numerous social movements, including CUT, to better the position of women in agriculture. A range of demands included (1) overturning Collor's veto of paid maternity leave; (2) that state benefits be provided immediately to rural workers; and (3) that women workers be provided with child-care centres and integrated health care. The campaign also highlighted the prevalence of violence against rural women. In 1993, as part of its agenda to incorporate women into its organization, CUT adopted a quota system whereby 30 per cent of national, regional and state trade union leaders would be women.

The trade unions' campaigns for rural women's welfare continued into the 1990s, including raising awareness of the prevalence of the use of unregistered women workers who were thus ineligible for the state benefits. The campaign for the registration of women workers was carried out under the slogan, 'To have personal documents and those of workers is but one step in the conquest of our citizenship' (cited in Deere 2003: 276). In 2000, CONTAG launched a series of events across Brazil in association with the celebration of International Women's Day. These events included the Marcha das Margaridas on 10 August, the anniversary of the murder of north-eastern trade union leader Margarida Alves. This march is now a regular occasion when thousands of rural women descend on Brasilia to demand rural justice through an end to rural poverty, hunger and violence. These issues were raised and supported by vigorous campaigns by rural trade unions from the late 1980s onwards. The following discussions illustrate the particular forms of representation, participation and mobilization of women workers in Brazil's São Francisco Valley.

Women workers in the São Francisco Valley grape sector

The principal trade union in the São Francisco Valley is the Sindicato dos Trabalhadores Rurais (STR, Rural Workers' Union). This union, and the increasing importance of women workers and trade union representatives, are discussed in detail below. First, this section provides an overview of the grape sector in which the majority of women workers in the valley are employed. Within the grape sector women comprise the overwhelming majority of the labour force. They are employed, increasingly, on temporary contracts. While during the mid- to late 1990s women comprised the majority of permanently employed workers, by the early 2000s they made up only between 40 and 50 per cent (Selwyn 2010b). This is still significantly more than in other world regions of grape production. For example, Barrientos (2001: 86) shows that in Chile and South Africa women comprise 5 per cent and 26 per cent of the permanent labour force and 52 per cent and 69 per cent of the temporary labour force respectively.

There are several reasons for the initial gender division of labour and its change over the last decade or so. Referring specifically to the São Francisco grape sector, Collins (1993) provides four reasons why the employment of women helps farms reduce their labour costs. First, managers tend to grade women's skills differently from men's: 'What would ordinarily be construed as skill, grafting of grape vines, is coded instead as manual dexterity, delicacy and nimbleness of fingers.' Hence, skilled work is redefined as 'natural' to women workers – therefore not a skill *per se*, but an attribute, thus reducing pressures on farms to remunerate skilled workers more favourably. Second, women are relatively easily classified as temporary workers because they are assumed to have primary responsibility for looking after their families. Third, in the 1980s and early 1990s women were perceived to be less active politically in the São Francisco Valley. Fourth, women are also perceived by firms to be less bothered by the close supervision exercised by the field managers.

However, whilst large numbers of women were initially employed on permanent contracts, there are at least two reasons why increasingly they are being employed temporarily.[4] The intensity of work on exporting farms is increasing. Whereas farms initially employed workers based on daily task targets, most have moved to combining such targets with piece rate systems – thus seeking (mostly successfully) to maximize workers' productivity (Selwyn 2007b). Under these conditions, managers often consider male workers to be stronger and able to work for longer periods in the heat, and have subsequently begun to employ increasing numbers of male workers on permanent contracts.

A second reason is that whilst non-wage costs of employing women may be relatively lower than for male workers under conditions of flexible labour contracts (Standing 1989), once women workers win rights, such as crèche care facilities and maternity leave, non-wage costs may become higher than for male workers. One manager explained how

> The problem with hiring women under Brazilian law is that they have the right to stay at home for three months per year when they are pregnant. If you add another month for holidays, then she is away from work for four months of the year … but we are changing and many men are already doing the bunch pruning process. Since they only have one month of holidays, it is better for us to hire them.[5]

Employers on many farms thus recognize (and exaggerate) the potential disadvantages associated with hiring large numbers of women on permanent contracts. Consequently, many farms across the valley employ women workers neither on a permanent nor a temporary basis: the former would entail higher costs and the latter would prevent managers guaranteeing recruitment of the necessarily skilled workers to carry out the detailed work in grape production. Instead they hire women increasingly on 'permanent temporary' contracts.[6] On the one hand, this strategy enables farms to 'retain' skilled workers for the seventeen-week production cycle twice a year whilst laying them off during the intervening periods. In addition, this strategy places pressure upon women workers to maintain a reputation as 'good' workers – achieving productivity objectives set by managers, and not 'causing trouble' – in order to be re-employed the following season. On the other hand, it also means that they have significant experience of the grape sector, know many of their co-workers, and have experience of working in or at least coming into contact with the region's rural trade union, as discussed below.

Rural trade unions and women workers

Some literature concerned with women's employment in developing countries observes how trade unions are often male-dominated and unresponsive to the specificity of women workers' conditions. For example, Mitter (1994) argues that most trade unions in the global South focus on organizing workers in the formal sector, and that their cultures and procedures usually assume a male bias by, for example, failing to take account of the real experiences and lives of women workers.

Clearly there are many cases of such male bias. However, Standing (1992) provides important evidence from numerous cases to show that where industries and firms are unionized, the gender gap in wages tends to be narrower. This raises the question of how unionization and trade union activity can lead, under certain circumstances, to significant improvements in women worker's wages, conditions and ability to participate in and influence trade unions. Whilst male bias exists in many trade unions, it would be erroneous to reject *a priori* the possibility of such organizations changing in ways that benefit women workers. Indeed, Hyman (2007: 198) suggests that different trade unions by definition possess stronger or weaker organizational capacities, which can be better or worse suited to meeting the challenges faced by their memberships, and which should be understood as 'the ability to assess opportunities for intervention [and] to anticipate, rather than merely react to changing circumstances'. Their effectiveness in formulating and pursuing such strategies requires 'the capacity to interpret, decipher, sustain, and redefine the demands of the represented, so as to evoke the broadest possible consensus and approval' (Regalia 1988: 351). Hence, the quality of a trade union's bureaucratic organization will determine to an important degree its ability to respond to new challenges. However, it is not just at the upper leadership levels that the ability to anticipate, interpret and decipher changing circumstances is important. Crucially, Barker *et al.* (2001: 15–17) argue for distinguishing between authoritarian and authoritative trade union leaderships, suggesting that for the latter 'leadership is exercised at all manner of levels and locations . . . and not only by those obviously designated as "leaders"'. And Hyman (2007) observes that Gramsci's notion of 'organic intellectual' is relevant in situations where leadership is not simply an activity performed by the formal trade union bureaucracy: 'Grass-roots activists may develop a breadth of information and analytical capacity which distinguish without distancing them from their colleagues. Hence there can, and must, be a complex dialectic between leadership and democracy.'

Paulo Freire's (1970) attempts to develop an emancipatory educational praxis are particularly relevant here. Like Gramsci, Freire stressed the dangers of a strong dichotomy between educators and educated, and instead argued for dynamic reciprocity in order that education becomes the 'practice of freedom' and 'the means by which men and women deal critically with reality and discover how to participate in the transformation of their world' (cited in Mayo 1999: 5). His concept of 'conscientization' (critical consciousness or consciousness raising) stresses the ability of educators to assist the oppressed to develop new levels of awareness and move from viewing themselves as objects of broader forces to becoming self-determining subjects. Trade unions that aim at a radical reshaping of the political–economic terrain on which they operate often attempt to engage in such practices in order (1) to change the balance of forces between employers and employed; and (2) to change the way the employed (workers) view their role in the transformative process (from being recipients of benefits to being active participants in the winning of benefits).

If it is accepted that trade unions are potentially flexible and can learn and incorporate new practices into their routines, and that membership can inform these practices, then it is also possible to envision a situation where women workers, in particular in economic sectors where they predominate, may stand a chance not just of gaining better representation from such organizations, but also of playing a significant part in their evolution.

Trade union strategies

The STR was originally formed in 1963 to represent small-scale farmers in the São Francisco Valley. We have seen that, as in the rest of Brazil, the 1964 military coup and subsequent 21 years of military rule heavily influenced trade union activity until the return of democracy in the mid-1980s. However, in the context of a revived trade union movement from the early 1990s, and co-terminously with the early expansion of the valley's horticulture sector, the STR began campaigning vigorously for improvements in rural workers' rights. Its leadership soon identified sources of workers' structural power on export grape farms. These farms employ precise scientific production practices to produce high-quality fruit, including a complex harvest calendar comprising over 30 operations such as berry and bunch pruning. The intense heat of the valley accelerates plant growth and operations must be performed at specific times to facilitate production. If they are delayed the fruit quality quickly deteriorates. The trade union leadership realized that short suspensions of work would severely reduce fruit quality. The STR was able to use actual and threatened strikes to disrupt fruit quality and so push employers to make concessions to the sector's labour force. Consequently, workers have experienced significantly improved conditions over the last two decades. Initial gains included pay rates above the minimum wage, established overtime wages, the right for workers to have the use of protective clothing, and the right of trade union representatives to enter farms at lunch breaks to communicate with members.

Despite this reorientation towards rural wage workers, Collins (1993) observed how initially women were largely ignored by the STR. But this did not last long. From the mid- to late 1990s, in response to campaigns for women workers' rights led by trade unions elsewhere in Brazil, and at the prompting of the Regional Confederation of Rural Trade Unions (FETAPE), the STR began campaigning on women workers' issues and recruiting women into its leadership. The trade union's women's officer describes how the trade union reorientated itself towards women workers: 'We wanted to gain influence amongst the workers and help them improve their lives and working conditions and we realized that to win their leadership we needed to appeal to women workers in a special way. How could we be considered the leaders of the valley's workers if we only fought to improve conditions for men?'[7]

Through its ability to mobilize workers, the trade union has been able to win victories and improve women's working conditions significantly. Gains include provision of crèche facilities; a paid day per month for women workers to visit doctors; the right for women with babies in the crèche to breastfeed for an hour per day, over and above the lunch hour; and a two-month period of paid maternity leave, with the right to return to employment following such leave. Significantly, it has also campaigned vigorously for improved transport conditions. Initially workers often experienced overcrowded transport to work and women complained about sexual harassment (groping) on buses. A recent gain included in the collective agreement is that all workers have sufficient seating space on company-provided transport, thus giving women workers valuable personal space and dignity.

Alongside these gains women workers have experienced important changes to their lives, often seeing themselves in new ways. The following section uses interviews with women workers, most of whom were members of the STR, to provide an image of how women workers have emerged to play a central role in the trade union – the São Francisco Valley's largest civil society organization. In contributing to the amelioration of working conditions, they simultaneously transform their own perceptions about their roles in domestic and civil society.

The experience of work

Work on grape farms is hard. Male and female workers work for around eight hours a day in temperatures often above 30°C, and are subject to increasingly scientific management designed to raise labour productivity (Selwyn 2007a). Managers tell of how buyers, importers and quality inspectors from northern countries, when visiting the farms, often faint from the heat! Aldemira highlights how starkly different conditions of work prior to and within the grape sector often are:

> We had easy working conditions on my father's farm, but we had very little income. When I started working on the grape farms, the work became much harder, but my income also increased. It was a big difference from working for my family – we [the workers] were told what to do – sometimes the managers were rude to us and humiliated us – this never happened on my father's farm.[8]

Similarly, referring to the valley's employers generally, Simone describes how

> They make us work harder every year, and not all of them provide us with the basics that are agreed in the collective agreement. Some farms' basic standard [Daily Task Target] pruning rate is 2,000 bunches per day. Some women can prune 2,500 bunches a day, but

that is too much work! If we don't achieve these targets they move us to another job and demand that we meet these targets. ... If we are on temporary contracts and want to be invited back to work for the following harvest, then we have to meet these targets.[9]

Despite tough conditions, women workers are overwhelmingly proud of their work and of the opportunities it gives them, which, as noted above, in turn reflects campaigns by Brazilian rural trade unions more generally to valorize the work of their members. For example, Francisca is 23, has two young children, and works on Timbauba, the largest farm in the region, with over 3,000 employees during the harvest cycle. She explains how 'It is good to work here, we have few opportunities to work so this is a good place for us. ... This is the first time I've worked here, and I like it. I study, I live alone with my two children, and I rent the house for BR$60 per month in Novo Descoberta, near Lagoa Grande.'[10] Women often have to negotiate their new status as wage earners with their husbands. An STR official explained that

> We have women members who work, but their husbands do not work. When they get home they have to prepare the food and look after the house, and at the end of the month some husbands tell them, "Give me the money." Women accept this because they are scared of fighting for their rights and many of them are afraid because their husbands beat them when they complain.[11]

However, despite many men's initial resistance to women's entering the workforce, it is also often the case that the former become more accepting of their partner's role as familial bread-winner. Magda-Adriana explains how

> In the beginning it was difficult. My husband was not happy about me working like this; he was jealous and he thought that other men would chase after me on the grape farms. At the start he was embarrassed by my working and not having a proper job himself. But I fought against his doubts and worries and started working and earning a wage for the first time. Today he accepts my work. Men never accept that a woman has to work, because they are afraid that women will become independent of them, and will not 'remain

under their thumb' – but once we show them we can do it, they are OK about it.[12]

Clearly women have different experiences of the impact their employment has upon intra-household relations, ranging from relative empowerment through the gaining of a disposable income to increased workload and the double burden of wage and domestic labour. Yet positive domestic outcomes resulting from employment – that some women experience improvements in their domestic lives, and that the trade union acts as a forum for workers' interaction and communication – at least present the possibility that women will share these experiences, and that a more assertive culture of pushing for greater equality in the home will emerge. Whether this occurs will depend partly on the actions of the women workers themselves in conjunction with the trade union leadership and wider membership.

Women in the rural workers' union

Before working in the grape sector many women had no experience of trade unions, but once employed they quickly come into contact with trade union representatives. The current salaried workers' secretary of the STR's story of initial encounter, increasing involvement and eventual election to a position of influence in the trade union is instructive when considering the potential for women's activity within the STR. She explains how when she started working, 'The *delegado sindical* [trade union representative] began talking to us, and organizing us to go to meetings about the conditions of work in the valley, and how the rural workers' union had a vision of improving our lives as workers. With the campaign around the collective agreement I learned more about our rights and I joined the trade union.'[13] She recounts how she became increasingly involved in trade union activities: 'I began working in the union when I learned about our rights in the convention. Every time the employer did something wrong, or failed to implement an agreement within the convention I got in contact with the *delegado sindical* and the trade union to try and rectify the situation.'

Distinguishing between grape production and the rest of the fruiticulture sector, she argues that women workers fulfil important tasks at work and, consequently, have the possibility of engaging in collective action to improve their conditions both as workers and as women: 'We have a conception that women need to be at the front of the political process in the STR. The STR leadership at the moment is four men and three women. It wasn't always like this, but women have become more important in the STR as we have continued to represent wage workers.'

As part of its continuing attempts to mobilize the rural labour force, since the early 2000s the STR has been engaged increasingly in consciousness raising among its membership. This entails STR leaders visiting farms and explaining to workers their role in the grape production process, while simultaneously encouraging STR members to become increasingly active within the trade union, in particular through the reporting of employer abuses to trade union *delegados* and/or to the union leadership. One development in this educational work is the trade union's emphasis on women's abilities to perform delicate tasks in grape production. As already mentioned, managers initially employed women on the basis that their ability to carry out delicate operations made them particularly suited to the job of grape production – but, as noted by Collins (1993), since this ability was considered innate rather than an acquired skill it did not attract higher wages or special working conditions. This made it easier for employers to play down the importance of women's work, thus attempting to preclude any claim from women workers for preferential remuneration through, for example, bonuses or better conditions. However, the trade union is attempting to subvert this ideology. The waged workers' secretary tells how

> We tell the women, 'Look at your contribution to the wealth of the SF valley. If it were not for you the farms would not be able to produce these high quality grapes, export them, and make such huge profits. In reality the dynamism of the valley is in your hands,

it is you that produce and you deserve better conditions.' In this way we educate them about the importance of their work and why it is important to become active in the trade union.

There is a feedback mechanism operating here: increased awareness of their rights and employers' responsibilities enables women workers to identify abuses and mobilize the trade union, which in turn works in conjunction with other organizations such as the Ministry of Labour in order to rectify such abuses. This leads to a situation where increasingly aware women workers are able to orientate the trade union towards campaigning around their interests. A labour inspector from the Ministry of Labour explained how

> Today workers know a lot more than when I started here (about twenty years ago). They all have TVs. They have access to the internet. Their trade union tells them about their rights. They know how much grapes sell for in Europe. The trade union makes a big effort to teach them about their rights and how they have been achieved. When you have better information you are better placed to speak up for and fight for your rights. Many of them study in their spare time. So they are much more aware than previously.[14]

The trade union's stress upon the importance of women workers educating themselves is notable. A trade union lawyer explained how one of the important gains established and written into the collective agreement is a clause related to workers who are also students. According to the clause, workers must be free to leave farms at 5 p.m. in order to attend school. Hence, they cannot be 'forced' to do overtime:

> This was a major achievement by the trade union. Not only did we win it, we have defended it, and we impress upon the workers the importance of their studying. That is why so many of them are in education at the same time as working on the grape farms. Previously workers would work until six, seven or eight in the evening. Generally, a worker who studies does so in the evening, and so they have to be free to leave work at 5 p.m. in order to get

home, have a shower, and get ready for and go to school. And if there is an exam that they need to take during the day, farms are required to allow them to take the day off.[15]

The lawyer estimates that worker literacy levels have increased over the last decade, with over 70 per cent literate by the late 2000s, and the impact on women workers' political consciousness was noticeable to the author throughout the interviews. This is a significant achievement, because, as Diane Elson argues, organizations seeking to represent women workers should be concerned with 'enhancing the skills and education of those workers, so that if workers lose their jobs, they have acquired something of permanence – more self-confidence, more organizational and advocacy skills, more knowledge of how their society works' (1996: 50). The policy is also widely supported by women as it guarantees them the ability to leave farms relatively early to care for their children, a tacit understanding which is shared by farm managers.

The struggle for recognition

As noted earlier, since the late 1980s and early 1990s, Brazilian rural trade unions have been campaigning vigorously for women workers to be recognized as equals to their male colleagues, and as professional, rather than casual, workers. This form of consciousness raising is echoed by Sonja who emphasizes that, 'We are workers and professionals, we know our work very well, we are proud of our work.... The trade union is our only point of support.'[16] As this and other quoted interviews suggest, these sentiments are increasingly widespread within the female section of the valley's labour force.

Whilst this sentiment echoes broader tendencies within Brazilian agriculture, there are also specific local factors that enable the STR to pursue such a strategy. The trade union lawyer explains how

The big *coroneis* [oligarchic rural bosses] used to rule this valley. ... They forced those under their influence to vote in the ways that they wanted. That is changing now, in particular because of the higher level of education … and also because workers have wages and are not dependent on them in anything like the way they used to be.

The decline in the power of these bosses and the rise in influence of rural trade unions has enabled the latter to widen their horizons and diversify their strategies. The trade union lawyer notes that: 'We see that European and US workers have better conditions than here, and we want to emulate them because, after all, a worker is a worker wherever he is. The difference is in the level of consciousness.'[17]

In an interview, Elizabeth elaborated on the trade union's campaigns to gain recognition of the value of women's work:

> Those beautiful grapes that you eat in your country, they are the result of our work, women's work. You've seen how nicely they are prepared. The majority of that work is done by skilled, professional women, like us. We have the delicate touch that enables us to produce these beautiful grapes.

She concluded:

> We need to be more highly valued.… In your country, who knows about how we work and live? We work on the farm, then we get home and have another battle. We go back home and tidy it up, we get to bed at eleven thirty or twelve and then need to get up at 4 a.m. to prepare our packed lunch and get to the collection point for around 6 a.m. to start work at seven. … People who eat these grapes need to know what our lives are like.[18]

Interaction between the STR and other social movements

It was noted earlier that following the end of the military regime, the Brazilian rural trade unions were not the only social movements campaigning for enhanced livelihoods for their members. In addition, the MST has become increasingly well known in its struggle for meaningful and sustainable land reform. Whilst there are not always obvious connections between rural workers' campaigns for better wages and conditions and the struggle for land reform, in this particular case the two campaigns are often intimately connected. In 2008, for example, over 2,000 women from Pernambuco went on the Marcha das Margaridas in Brasilia, organized in Pernambuco by FETAPE. The STR organized a delegation from the São Francisco valley, and sent about 120 of its members and supporters, with about 50 from Petrolina, including rural wage workers, family agriculture workers and landless workers campaigning for agrarian reform. This suggests how radicalization in one part of the agrarian sector can complement (perhaps even feed into) radicalization elsewhere in the sector.

Conclusions

This chapter began by noting briefly that many commentators on the capital mobility brought by globalization posit a general trend of the deterioration of the relative position of labour. However, the analysis of the evolution of the STR's role *vis-à-vis* women workers, and in particular the latter's ability to influence the trade union, reveals a case of positive interaction between a rural workers' union, initially orientated to and run by men, and its expanding number of (both flexibly and permanently employed) women workers. There is no particular reason, given its earlier history of representing male-led family farmers and then male wage workers, why the STR would not simply have continued to focus on issues concerning male workers. However, the broader mobilizations by Brazilian trade unions to enhance the position of rural women workers certainly contributed to a situation where the STR was encouraged to reorientate its priorities and strategies. In addition, the positive impacts of first including and then increasing the numbers of women occupying leadership positions within the STR, on the one hand, and the trade union's strategy of consciousness raising on the other, have further strengthened women's positions within the union, raising the possibility of future campaigns to further enhance the livelihoods of the valley's female workforce.

What this case study also reveals is a process whereby the

struggle to gain recognition of the worth of women's work is connected, quite intimately, to the specific nature of the economic sector within which they are employed. In the São Francisco Valley grape sector women were initially employed because their ability to carry out 'delicate' tasks was portrayed by employers as a natural attribute, and thus not deserving of any additional remuneration or provision of enhanced working conditions. The STR has begun to subvert this dominant conception, aiming to replace it with an emphasis upon the importance of women's work in generating the valley's wealth. This is, in short, a struggle about women workers' ability to organize within trade unions, and a broader recognition of women workers' contribution to economic development.

Notes

1 The account that follows is based on research conducted in the São Francisco Valley, in the states of Pernambuco and Bahia, north-east Brazil, in 2002 and 2003 (for my PhD) and follow-up research in August and September 2008. All the interviews cited below were conducted by the author.

2 Estimates provided by STR and the Ministry of Labour.

3 The rest of this section draws heavily on Deere (2003).

4 For a fuller analysis of the changing gender division of labour in the valley's export grape sector see Selwyn (2010b).

5 Interview with manager, JMM farm, Petrolina, 3 June 2002.

6 See also Barrientos (1999) and Bee and Vogel (1997) for a similar analysis.

7 Interview, Petrolina, 8 June 2002.

8 Interview, Petrolina, 3 September 2008.

9 Interview, Petrolina, 4 September 2008.

10 Interview, Petrolina, 4 September 2008. In August 2008 BR$60 exchanged for about US$40.

11 Interview, Petrolina, 19 August 2008.

12 Interview, Petrolina, 16 August 2008.

13 These and the following quotes are based on an interview, Petrolina, 12 September 2008.

14 Interview, Petrolina, 27 August 2008.

15 Interview, 21 August 2008.
16 Interview, Petrolina, 21 August 2008.
17 Interview, Petrolina, 27 August 2008.
18 Interview, Petrolina, 21 August 2008.

References

Barker, C., A. Johnson and M. Lavalette (2001) 'Leadership matters: an introduction', in C. Barker, A. Johnson and M. Lavalette (eds), *Leadership and Social Movements*, Manchester: Manchester University Press.

Barrientos, Stephanie (1999) *Women and Agribusiness: Working Miracles in the Chilean Fruit Export Sector*, Basingstoke: Macmillan.

—— (2001) 'Gender, flexibility and global value chains', *IDS Bulletin*, 32, 3: 83–93.

Bee, Anne and I. Vogel (1997) 'Temporeras and household relations: seasonal employment in Chile's agro-export sector', *Bulletin of Latin American Research*, 16, 1: 83–95.

Cappellin, Paola (1997) 'Os Movimentos de Trabalhadoras e a Sociedade Brasileira' in Maria Del Priore (ed.), *História das Mulheres no Brasil*, São Paulo: Ed. Contextoe Editora UNESP, pp. 640–66.

Cardoso, Fernando Henrique (2001) 'A política externa do Brasil no início de um novo século: uma mensagem do Presidente da República', *Revista Brasileira de Política Internacional*, 44, 1: 5-12.

Collins, Jane (1993) 'Gender, contracts and wage work: agricultural restructuring in Brazil's São Francisco Valley', *Development and Change*, 24, 1: 53–82.

Cummings, Bruce (1989) 'The abortive abertura: South Korea in the light of Latin American experience', *New Left Review*, I/173: 5-32.

Deere, C. D. (2003) 'Women's land rights and rural social movements in the Brazilian agrarian reform', *Journal of Agrarian Change*, 3, 1: 257–88.

—— (2005) 'The feminization of agriculture? Economic restructuring in rural Latin America', Occasional Paper 1, United Nations Institute for Social Development, www.unrisd.org/publications/opgp1 (accessed 5 July 2007).

Deere, C. D. and M. León (2001) *Empowering Women: Land and Property Rights in Latin America*, Pittsburgh, PA: University of Pittsburgh.

Dolan, Catherine and John Humphrey (2000) 'Governance and trade in fresh vegetables: the impact of UK supermarkets on the African horticulture industry', *Journal of Development Studies*, 37, 2: 147–76.

Elson, D. (1996) 'Appraising recent developments in the world market for nimble fingers' in A. Chhachhi and R. Pittin (eds), *Confronting State, Capital and Patriarchy: Women Organising in the Process of Industrialisation*, Basingstoke: Macmillan, in association with the Institute of Social Studies.

Ferm, N. (2008) 'Non-traditional agricultural export industries: conditions for women workers in Colombia and Peru', *Gender and Development*, 16, 1: 3–26.

Freire, P. (1970) *Pedagogy of the Oppressed*, New York: Continuum.

Humphrey, J. (2007) 'The supermarket revolution in developing countries: tidal wave or tough competitive struggle?', *Journal of Economic Geography*, 7, 4: 433–50.

Hyman, Richard (2007) 'How can trade unions act strategically?', *Transfer*, 13, 2.

Kabeer, N. (1999) 'Globalization, labour standards, and women's rights: dilemmas of collective (in)action in an independent world', *Feminist Economics*, 10, 1: 3–35.

Katz, E. (2003) 'The changing role of women in the rural economies of Latin America' in *CUREMIS 2*, Vol. 1 – *Latin America and the Caribbean*, Rome: Food and Agriculture Organization (FAO).

Kohli, A. (2004) *State-Directed Development: Political Power and Industrialization in the Global Periphery*, Cambridge: Cambridge University Press.

Mayo, P. (1999) *Gramsci, Freire, and Adult Education: Possibilities for Transformative Action*, London: Zed Books.

Mitter, S. (1994) 'A comparative survey' in M. H. Martens and S. Mitter (eds), *Women in Trade Unions: Organising the Unorganised*, Geneva: International Labour Organization (ILO).

Raynolds, L. (2001) 'New plantations, new workers: gender and production politics in the Dominican Republic', *Gender and Society*, 15, 1: 7–28.

Reardon, T., J. M. Codron, L. Busch, J. Bingen and C. Harris (2001) 'Global change in agrifood grade and standards: agribusiness strategic responses in developing countries', *International Food and Agribusiness Management Review*, 2, 3: 421–35.

Regalia, I. (1988) 'Democracy and unions: towards a critical appraisal', *Economic and Industrial Democracy*, 9, 3: 345–71.

Selwyn, Ben (2007a) 'Export Grape Production and Development in North East Brazil', PhD Thesis, University of London.

—— (2007b) 'Labor process and workers' bargaining power in export grape production, North East Brazil', *Journal of Agrarian Change, 7*, 4: 526–53.

—— (2010a) 'Globalized horticulture: the formation and global integration of export grape production in North East Brazil', *Journal of Agrarian Change*, 10, 4: 537–63.

—— (2010b) 'Gender, wage work and development in North East Brazil', *Bulletin of Latin American Research,* 29, 1: 51–70.

Siqueira, D. (1991) 'A organização das mulheres trabalhadoras rurais: o cruzamento de gênero e de classe social' in D. Siqueira, J. Teixeira and M. Porto (eds), *Technologia Agropecuaria e a Organização dos Trabalhadores Rurais*, 57–90, Brasilia: UNB.

Standing, G. (1989) 'Global feminisation through flexible labour', *World Development*, 17, 7: 1077–95.

—— (1992) 'Do unions impede or accelerate structural adjustment? Industrial versus company unions in an industrialising labour market', *Cambridge Journal of Economics*, 16: 327–54.

Thrupp, L. (1995) *Bitter-Sweet Harvests for Global Supermarkets*, Washington, DC: World Resource Institute.

VALEXPORT (2008) 'Há 20 Anos Unindo Forças Para O Desenvolvimento Do Vale Do São Francisco E Da Fruticultura Brasileira', Petrolina: VALEXPORT.

2

Understanding the Dynamics of an NGO/MBO Partnership

Organizing and Working with Farm Women in South Africa

● ●

Colette Solomon[1]

This chapter addresses the power dynamics and inequalities in the relationship between a South African non-government organization (NGO), Women on Farms Project (WFP) and the membership-based organization (MBO), Sikhula Sonke, which it established. In particular, it focuses on the genesis and evolution of the relationship between the two organizations and how unanticipated and initially unarticulated tensions led to a shift in power and a new phase in the relationship between them.

First I provide a short background to WFP, including the key discourses that have informed the understanding and approach of WFP's work with farm women. Then I contextualize the living and working conditions of farm women in post-apartheid South Africa that led WFP to form Sikhula Sonke. In the third part of the chapter I analyse the various phases of the relationship between WFP and Sikhula Sonke. As the author of this contribution I am aware of and declare my own positionality as a WFP staff member who was also very intimately involved in the changing relationship with Sikhula Sonke. Finally I provide a reflection on the specificities of this relationship but also draw broader lessons about the potential and limits of NGOs and MBOs working together in organizing women workers in the informal sector.

73

Overview of WFP

Women on Farms Project (WFP) is a registered South African NGO working with women who live and work on commercial farms, mainly in the Western and Northern Cape provinces. It started in 1992 as a project of another NGO, Lawyers for Human Rights (LHR). WFP's mission is to empower and strengthen the capacity of women who live and work on farms to claim their rights and fulfil their needs. Within this mission, the building of farm women's organizations is prioritized, given the virtual absence of self-organization initiatives within the farm worker community. Formally established as an NGO in 1996 shortly after South Africa's first democratic elections, WFP set out to address the specific socio-economic needs of farm women through the provision of rights-based education and assistance to address the discrimination they experienced within the home, workplace and community. Through its structure and organization-building work, the project is working towards a rural landscape in which women are organized, confident and assertive in representing their own interests and playing prominent leadership roles.

WFP implements the following programmes to address the key livelihood challenges of farm women: Cooperatives; Health and Empowerment; Labour Rights; Land and Housing; and Social Security. Within each programme, the project undertakes rights-based capacity building; advocacy, lobbying and campaigns; human rights case work; research; and – importantly – building organizations/structures of farm women. Until 2008, the latter was primarily focused on building the farm women's social movement, Sikhula Sonke. Indeed, as outlined further below, all of WFP's programmes were directed at Sikhula Sonke's members.

While WFP has recently become explicitly feminist in its political agenda, historically its work and orientation has also been underpinned by the values and discourses of struggle, class awareness as workers, and women's empowerment.

Struggle

At least since 1912, when what would become the African National Congress (ANC) was formed, the black majority in South Africa has been involved in a struggle for equal rights and citizenship. After the formal introduction of apartheid in 1948, the struggle became directed against the apartheid state. As a broad-based movement, it not only comprised an armed struggle waged from neighbouring countries, but significantly also consisted of civil society formations engaging in various campaigns of civil disobedience such as consumer and student boycotts and demonstrations aimed at collectively weakening the state and rendering the country ungovernable. While the struggle was for a non-racist, non-sexist South Africa, there have been critiques that the non-sexist dimension was always subordinated to the non-racist agenda. Notwithstanding this valid critique, women played various critical roles in the struggle, including as soldiers in the liberation armies. Women's active participation in the mass democratic movement both emerged from and developed a social consciousness, and provided women with an opportunity to develop leadership. Furthermore, when the mostly male leadership of various progressive organizations was detained during the states of emergency in the 1980s, it was women who filled the resulting vacuum.

Class awareness as workers

In apartheid South Africa, (black) workers were largely deprived of any labour rights; indeed, farm workers were actually prohibited from being trade union members. During the turbulent and politically active years of the 1970s and 1980s, workers were also organizing themselves, ultimately resulting in the formation of the powerful trade union federation, the Congress of South African Trade Unions (COSATU), which comprised affiliated trade unions from various sectors, including textile and domestic workers, who were predominantly women. The labour movement was an integral part of the mass democratic movement which became formalized in the tripartite alliance between COSATU, the ANC and the South African Communist Party. As trade union members, workers were aware of their contribution to the national economy as well as their collective strength. Key to trade union organization was the political education of members, which included a sound understanding, analysis and critique of the capitalist mode of production, the role and place of workers, and the development of a workers' consciousness. Again, despite the fact that the trade unions were often patriarchal, sexist and male-dominated, women played key leadership roles as workers.

Women's empowerment

Key concepts in WFP's understanding and approach to women's empowerment are the feminist principle that 'the personal is political'; agency; and patriarchy. In practical terms, this has translated into an approach that necessarily begins with the trans-formation of the individual woman, but must lead to women taking collective action to challenge the (patriarchal) structures of oppression and discrimination. As part of its mission to empower and strengthen the capacity of farm women to claim their rights, WFP regards its role as providing women with rights information, raising their consciousness and confidence so that they become their own agents of change. Thus, WFP's mission prioritizes the building of structures of farm women. These structures have included farm-level agricultural cooperatives, health teams, and land rights forums – as well as Sikhula Sonke, the trade union and social movement.

The following section discusses the main contextual factors and precipitating reasons which led to the need to organize women farm workers, from small farm-level groups and ultimately to the mass-based trade union, Sikhula Sonke.

Circumstances giving rise to the formation of Sikhula Sonke

The formal end of apartheid in South Africa marked the abolition of a range of laws and policies that systematically discriminated against the black majority population. Many of these laws were specifically targeted at black workers and controlled and limited their labour, land access, tenure and mobility in towns, cities and white-owned farms. Post-democratic South Africa also saw the introduction and extension of a range of progressive laws, rights and entitlements to previously marginalized and disadvantaged groups, including workers and farm workers in particular. For example, in addition to general labour laws such as the Basic Conditions of Employment Act (BCEA) which protected all workers, there were also laws which afforded specific rights to farm workers, such as the Sectoral Determination for Farm Workers (SDFW). However, given farm workers' physical isolation, their lack of history of organization during the mass democratic struggle and their low post-democracy rates of unionization (less than 5 per cent), it was not surprising that farm workers did not know their (new) rights. Farmers, on the other hand, took advantage of farm workers' ignorance, resulting in widespread non-compliance to laws. It was this particular set of circumstances that provided a major impetus for organizing farm workers.

It is important to understand contemporary agriculture and the position of farm workers, especially farm women, in the historical context of agriculture in South Africa. Commercial agriculture has its roots in the slavery plantations of the seventeenth and eighteenth centuries. Indeed, many farm workers are able to trace their ancestry to slaves. With the formalization of apartheid in 1948, South African agriculture became legally underpinned by a system of racial segregation and oppression. Like other black South Africans, farm workers were discriminated against in terms of race; but there also existed a specific relationship of paternalism between the farmer and his workers, which largely derived from its origins in slavery. For generations, farmers have effectively inherited the workers from their fathers and have treated them, at best, as minors or children to be taken care of or, at worst, as possessions. Women farm workers have also lived within a strongly patriarchal system in which men are regarded as the head of the household and the main breadwinner. These related systems of patriarchy and paternalism have directly and indirectly had a number of social and economic outcomes at both household and farm levels, which have resulted in specific forms of marginalization for farm women.

At the household level, farm women experience high levels of gender-based violence. As discussed later in this chapter, gender-based violence has been a priority focus of WFP's legal rights work since its early years.[2] In WFP's Cooperatives Programme, 80 per cent of cooperative members reported that they were, or had been, in physically abusive relationships. Similarly, in a small survey of 200 farm women undertaken by WFP during its Sixteen Days of Activism to End Violence Against Women and Children in 2008, it was found that 28 per cent of respondents were, or had been, in abusive relationships. A direct legacy of centuries of the so-called 'tot system'[3] is the endemic alcoholism among farm workers. Alcohol consumption by farm workers is reported to be twice that of the urban poor. South Africa has the highest rate of foetal alcohol syndrome in the world, with the highest incidence recorded among farm worker communities in the Western and Northern Cape. While obviously not a justification for violence against women, alcohol abuse is usually implicated in the majority of reported domestic violence cases involving farm workers.

The most significant and changing factor in the lives and circumstances of farm workers is the increased casualization and feminization of agricultural labour. With the advent of democracy in 1994, various progressive laws were introduced, many of which extended legal rights and protections to farm workers for the first time. Moreover, this period also saw the opening and deregulation of the export market. In an effort to avoid compliance to the new labour laws and to respond to increased competition, requirements and escalating costs, farmers steadily reduced their permanent male workforce, opting instead to employ casual and seasonal workers, who are mainly female. Between 2002 and 2007, nearly 150,000 jobs were lost in agriculture. In 1994 alone, the year of South Africa's first democratic elections, there was a decline of

19 per cent in the number of permanent jobs in agriculture (du Toit and Ally 2003).

Despite the fact that, in absolute numbers, more women are represented in the agricultural labour force, the strongly patriarchal system means that they still experience systematic discrimination. First, there is an established gendered division of labour, with women generally occupying lower-paying jobs such as picking and sorting, based on the belief that they are 'nimble-fingered', while higher-paying jobs, such as drivers, are effectively reserved for men. Second, there is a gendered wage hierarchy by which women are paid less for the same work, arising from the historical perception of men as breadwinners and women as working for 'supplementary' income, although the reality is that a large number of women are the primary or only income earners in the household.

Given the historical marginalization of farm women, as well as their post-apartheid circumstances described above, their living and working conditions clearly needed to be addressed. The following sections discuss the formation of WFP and Sikhula Sonke and trace specific changes in WFP's organizational strategies, which were always informed by farm women's priorities and needs.

Stages in the relationship between WFP and Sikhula Sonke

Labour pains

Work in the agricultural sector is highly gendered, with women generally clustered in the lowest-paying jobs, earning less than men for the same work, and increasingly employed on casual terms without the protection and rights enjoyed by mainly male permanent workers.

Since the advent of democracy in South Africa in 1994, and the introduction of a raft of progressive laws and entitlements that had direct implications for previously disadvantaged groups, including farm workers, WFP was focused primarily on rights-based education and capacity building among farm women. Informing women of their various new rights and entitlements, and enabling them to access and realize these rights would remain a mainstay of WFP's work in all its programmes. The initial strategy was to focus on farm women's practical gender needs: for example, it informed them about the new social security grants, especially the Child Support Grant, and the various eligibility criteria and means tests, and assisted them in accessing these entitlements. After working with women on a relatively safe and uncontroversial issue such as social security, and thus gaining their trust and confidence, WFP's strategy evolved to become more 'political' when it responded to the widespread labour rights violations reported by farm women. While new labour legislation such as the Labour Relations Act of 1995 and the Basic Conditions of Employment Act 1997 placed the relationship between farmer and farm worker within a legal framework for the first time, they did not transform history overnight. Farm workers' historical vulnerability and isolation, their dependence on and fear of the farmer, and their lack of unionization meant that they did not know their labour rights and were afraid to assert them.

WFP's early work with farm women's immediate priorities allowed it later to develop its strategy to include an explicit feminist agenda and address farm women's strategic gender interests. Thus, it broadened the issues it tackled to include the so-called 'personal' or 'private' aspects of women's lives. In a context of patriarchal gender relations and significant socio-economic inequalities, farm women experience high levels of gender-based violence, as noted above. WFP helped women to make the connection between the personal and the political as they addressed this widespread violence. On a practical level, the project provided farm women with information on relevant legislation, how to obtain an interdict against an abusive partner, and available resources such as women's shelters or counselling services. Thus, from its very beginning, WFP's changing strategy was always informed by the changing priorities of farm women.

In the process, it moved from rights-awareness training to developing organizations.

Central to this changing focus was the belief that agency and organization building are key elements in empowerment interventions. Thus, on all the farms on which WFP worked, it started establishing formal groups which became known as *Vroue Regte Groepe* (Women's Rights Groups/WRGs). Through the WRGs, it was able to provide rights awareness and education to farm women, especially around the issue of gender-based violence. WFP staff visited farms, made personal contact with women and provided information about the work of the organization. After contact had been made with one or two women on a farm, they were asked to recruit other women on their farm, inviting them to attend meetings, discussion sessions and workshops on women's rights and needs. This strategy became an important organizing and mobilizing tool. WRGs also served the additional function of being a support structure for the women involved, where they derived comfort and strength from each other. For the first time, they realized the importance of a collective. These WRGs later became farm committees, which signalled another shift in organizational strategy – from providing rights-awareness training through WRGs to building community structures. It also coincided with a shift in focusing exclusively on raising awareness to actually tackling labour rights violations experienced by farm women.

A number of critical issues were coalescing to inform WFP's (policy) choice to establish a membership-based organization. First, although these WRGs and farm committees were grassroots structures of farm women, they were completely dependent on WFP for inputs, training and organization; they had limited reach, and no linkages to other structures. The groups remained atomized and isolated, with no capacity to tackle issues beyond their immediate farm gate. Their struggles remained isolated, both geographically and politically. Nonetheless, the significance and contribution of the early Women's Rights Groups cannot be underestimated: they represented the first opportunity for farm women to learn about their rights and entitlements as workers, citizens and women, and to make the connections between the 'personal' and 'political'. Apart from conservative church groups for women, they also represented farm women's first experience of political organization and consciousness raising. Most significantly, the WRGs were the precursors of what would become Sikhula Sonke.

Second, while it was becoming apparent that farm women were experiencing widespread labour rights violations, WFP was unable, as an NGO, to represent farm workers in labour disputes: the Labour Relations Act of 1996 stipulates that workers can only be represented by a registered trade union representative. Third, WFP realized that it was still intervening in only a few individual, isolated cases, with no impact on the broader constituency of farm workers. There was thus recognition that workers' collective action needed to be strengthened, as well as their organizational ownership and control. Fourth – a related issue – WFP realized the importance of building a strong rural civil society to lobby and hold government responsible for ensuring the rights and needs of rural women. WFP thus took a decision to change its strategy: it would now seek to organize and mobilize farm women into a collective through farm committees and district committees. An organizational structure was thus developing, even though WFP did not have a clear idea of the final shape of this structure.

Finally, WFP was also asking questions about its own dependence on donor funds and its long-term sustainability. Specifically, what would WFP leave behind should donor funds dry up? This resulted in discussions, debates and workshops with farm women about the need for and form of a membership organization – that is, about the various alternative structures that might be formed (such as a voluntary association or a trade union). After thorough and extensive research and consultation with farm women, it was collectively decided to establish a trade union/social movement.

Giving birth: Sikhula Sonke is born

In 2004, the farm committees and WRGs were collapsed into the new trade union, Sikhula Sonke. This effectively meant that

WFP's broad membership base now shifted to the trade union and broader social movement. This also entailed a reorientation of WFP's activities to that of an NGO servicing the members of the trade union. In practice, this translated into Sikhula Sonke members becoming the main beneficiaries of WFP's programmes and activities.

With Sikhula Sonke growing directly from WFP's farm-level micro-mobilization of the late 1990s, a unique relationship existed between the two organizations from the beginning. This was formalized in a Memorandum of Understanding (MoU) which described the respective roles and responsibilities of the two organizations and also determined WFP's strategy for the next five years. In terms of the MoU, WFP undertook to actively build, capacitate and skill Sikhula Sonke – both its farm women members as well as its salaried staff, who were all former farm workers themselves – to realize full independence by 2009. WFP committed to providing the following support to Sikhula Sonke:

- building the capacity and skills, including political and ideological education, of both Sikhula Sonke staff and members;
- conceptualization and strategic thinking – for example, for campaigns, advocacy and lobbying;
- providing financial support, including raising funds on behalf of Sikhula Sonke, assisting with setting up financial systems of accountability, developing a self-sufficiency plan, as well as paying staff salaries;
- setting up administrative and human resource systems and procedures;
- providing office space, motor vehicles and other necessary resources and infrastructure;
- assisting in establishing branches and recruiting members for Sikhula Sonke.

Sikhula Sonke committed itself to representing farm workers in labour disputes, collecting joining fees from members, negotiating with employers, building its membership, ensuring members' participation in training workshops facilitated by WFP, hosting fundraising events to contribute to their financial needs, and so on. Significantly, the MoU set out lines of accountability for Sikhula Sonke staff to ensure collective accountability to both Sikhula Sonke as their employer and WFP, who effectively paid their salaries. In other words, Sikhula Sonke staff had an employment contract with WFP (the NGO) while subscribing to the code of conduct and constitution of Sikhula Sonke (the MBO). This duality of responsibility would later prove to be a major source of tension and conflict between WFP and Sikhula Sonke.

Thus, for the first three to four years, WFP and Sikhula Sonke shared a resource base, including funding and office space. In consultation with Sikhula Sonke, WFP wrote the funding proposals to undertake activities and interventions with and for Sikhula Sonke members. For WFP, this arrangement entailed focusing and directing all its programme activities to the members of the new emerging organization. In other words, between 2004 and 2008 WFP's programme activities represented the interface of the WFP and Sikhula Sonke relationship.

Growing up: comparative advantages in working together

In the first phase of the formal working relationship between WFP and Sikhula Sonke, WFP's primary strategy was to build the capacity of Sikhula Sonke so that it would be able increasingly to function independently. Thus in the early years WFP and Sikhula Sonke forged a cooperative working relationship around both training and capacity building, as well as campaigns. It was mainly through WFP's Labour Rights Programme that the two organizations interfaced: the programme trained Sikhula Sonke organizers on labour rights issues, enabling them to address cases of labour rights violations experienced by their members. This synergy represented the ideal working relationship in so far as WFP, being unable to represent workers directly, trained Sikhula Sonke staff to do so. As Sikhula Sonke members started reporting other cases such as evictions, poor health and safety conditions, poor housing conditions, difficulties in accessing social grants, and domestic violence, WFP started facilitating other relevant training, including casework management, for both Sikhula Sonke staff and members through its other programmes. WFP's strategy for building Sikhula Sonke's knowledge of various rights and increasing their ability to intervene on behalf of members was clearly proving effective.

In addition to training, WFP and Sikhula Sonke also cooperated around campaigns, such as a joint 'toilets in the vineyards' campaign. On the majority of farms, farmers did not provide toilets for farm workers in the orchards and vineyards, meaning that workers were simply forced to use the fields. The issue was of greater importance for women than men because they reported adverse health impacts as well sexual harassment and assault as a result of having to strip down to their underwear, removing their overalls. Armed with the relevant labour rights information (provided through WFP training), Sikhula Sonke organizers were able to negotiate successfully with farmers for the provision of toilets on the farms on which they had members.

A clear division of roles and responsibilities was emerging between the two organizations, largely as a result of their respective capacities, at least in the early years. Indeed, a few months after its registration as a trade union in 2004, WFP and Sikhula Sonke reflected on the principles and practices existing between the two organizations. Although there was agreement that the formal distinction between the two organizations be maintained – WFP as the NGO and Sikhula Sonke as the trade union – there was also recognition that Sikhula Sonke actually operated more like one of the WFP programmes than as an independent organization.

In the years during which the two organizations worked and operated cooperatively, there was an implicit recognition of their complementary roles. Each organization acknowledged the other's comparative advantage, respected its distinctiveness, and recognized the fact that the sum was greater than the parts. However, there were four main areas of difference which, while initially serving as complementary features, would later become critical sources of tension and conflict in the evolving relationship.

First, and fundamental, was the fact that WFP 'gave birth to' or 'established' Sikhula Sonke, or Sikhula Sonke was 'born out of' WFP. This gave rise to a basic inequality between the two organizations from the very beginning, with Sikhula Sonke (and its members) initially being the beneficiaries of WFP. A related aspect of this inequality between the two organizations was the recognition of Sikhula Sonke's need for skills development and WFP's undertaking to build the capacity of Sikhula Sonke.

Second, WFP was an NGO while Sikhula Sonke was a trade union/social movement. As an NGO, WFP comprised university-educated staff who were variously and appropriately skilled, while, as a social movement, Sikhula Sonke had staff who, as former farm workers themselves, had first-hand experience of the lives and priorities of their membership base. Furthermore, as an NGO, WFP was accountable to its funders and Board, while Sikhula Sonke's first line of accountability was to its members and National Executive Committee (NEC).

A third element of difference (and inequality) arose from WFP's role as fundraiser for both organizations, a role it undertook because of its staff's ability to develop and write funding proposals and narrative and financial reports to funders. All proposals were joint proposals in which WFP essentially directed all its programmatic activities, especially training and capacity building, at Sikhula Sonke members. Thus, proposals were premised on a synergistic relationship between WFP and Sikhula Sonke, with WFP contributing its expertise and Sikhula Sonke providing its members. Comprising urban, middle-class and university-educated feminist professionals, WFP also significantly provided a solid feminist ideological and political agenda and content to Sikhula Sonke, as well as relevant thinking and analysis about gender and models of women's empowerment. However, it is important to note that WFP staff were not 'theoretical' or 'ivory tower' feminists, but were all black women who came from backgrounds of political and student activism. Thus, the feminism of WFP was deeply grounded in South Africa's realities and histories, particularly the changing priorities of farm women. As noted earlier, examples of WFP's explicit feminist agenda included first tackling women's practical gender needs (accessing child support grants, for example) and then moving on to their strategic gender interests (such as gender-based violence).

A fourth set of differences related to the relative strengths of both organizations. With their education, expertise and skills, WFP staff were able to conceptualize and strategize the substance and content of campaigns and advocacy strategies, for example. Meanwhile, Sikhula Sonke staff, as union members, were not only able to mobilize other members for demonstrations organized as part of these campaigns, but also brought to them their lived experience of the issues they addressed. As the following example illustrates (Box 2.1), this complementarity proved highly effective in this early period of cooperation, when it was successfully employed in a campaign strategy.

By 2008, Sikhula Sonke had not only acquired a membership of 4,000; its staff had also acquired the necessary skills, which increasingly enhanced its capacities and ability to function independently of WFP. Thus, one of the fundamental premises of the initial relationship between WFP and Sikhula Sonke – Sikhula Sonke's comparative lack of skills – had significantly changed. This, together with other roles changing and the relationship between the two organizations evolving, led to the emergence of tensions and conflicts between the two organizations, despite the existence of the MoU and a vision of operating as 'sister' organizations.

Leaving home: tensions and power shifts

As in many parent–child relationships, rapport between the two organizations was uncomplicated in the beginning when respective roles and boundaries were straightforward – when, crudely stated, Sikhula Sonke was almost completely dependent on WFP (for finances, capacity building, skills development and so on) and WFP was making nearly all the key strategic and conceptual decisions. However, with the passage of time, differences that previously had been complementary became areas of contestation, and consensus yielded to diverging interests.

Ironically, it was the very basis of the WFP–Sikhula Sonke relationship – Sikhula Sonke's growing capacitation by WFP – that expedited the shift in power. Between 2004 and 2008, WFP invested its entire programme of work and *raison d'être* in building Sikhula Sonke. This included not only technical capacity building in areas such as setting up administration and financial systems, but also political and ideological thinking and planning. It was thus actually a testimony to WFP's successful capacity building that Sikhula Sonke felt ready to function independently by 2008, a year ahead of schedule. However, Sikhula Sonke's proposed exit from WFP also marked the culmination of a period of increased tensions between the two organizations.

A first area of tension arose around the issue of *accountability*. As an NGO, WFP was accountable to its funders and Board of Directors, while Sikhula Sonke was accountable to its members and National Executive Committee (NEC). WFP had undertaken all fundraising efforts on behalf of both organizations; specifically, all funding proposals were written so that WFP's activities were targeted at Sikhula Sonke members. As Sikhula Sonke became stronger and more assertive, tensions and differences now arose around lines and priorities of accountability.

In its most tangible form, the issue was manifested during the annual organizational planning process, which took place at the beginning of every year. Staff of both organizations participated in a three-day workshop in which the work plan for the coming year was jointly developed. For WFP, with its primary accountability to its funders, the first consideration in the development of work plans is existing contractual obligations to funders – thus activities for which funding has been secured are prioritized in work plans. In the early years of the partnership, Sikhula Sonke implicitly subscribed to this line of accountability and thus also prioritized funding agreements in developing the work plan. However, as Sikhula Sonke grew and strengthened as a trade union, it increasingly asserted that its primary accountability,

Box 2.1   Strategic complementarities: a case study

The large UK retailer, Tesco, is one of the main European buyers of South African fruit. Tesco has always boasted that it sources all its produce and products from suppliers who subscribe to ethical standards. Between 2003 and 2006, WFP had informed Tesco of widespread labour rights abuses on many of its fruit-supplying farms in the Western Cape, citing reports received from farm women. It asked Tesco to intervene and ensure labour law compliance on their farms. Tesco effectively dismissed the NGO's claims, asking WFP to name specific workers and farms. WFP explained that farm workers would face severe reprisals from farmers if named, with the risk of losing their jobs and on-farm housing.

In 2006, working with the British NGO ActionAid, WFP reconceptualized the issue into an international campaign, which entailed attending Tesco's Annual General Meeting (AGM) in London. The campaign was predicated on the involvement of a farm worker, and WFP enlisted the assistance of Sikhula Sonke in this regard. One of its members, Gertruida Baartman, a fruit picker on a Tesco-supplying farm, expressed her willingness to participate in the campaign. Thus, in July 2006, in a London hall full of hundreds of Tesco shareholders, Gertruida stood up and described the labour and housing conditions on her Tesco-supplying farm. She reported that members working with pesticides were not provided with mandatory protective clothes; that women workers earned less than men for the same work; and that housing conditions were poor. Shareholders, many of whom were female retirees, were shocked to hear Gertruida's story and said they would be prepared to take a decrease in their dividends if it meant an improvement in the living and working conditions of farm workers like her. Tesco's CEO requested a meeting with Gertruida (and WFP and Sikhula Sonke) immediately after the AGM. A direct result of this meeting was an undertaking by Tesco to have all its supplying farms audited through a multi-disciplinary and developmental audit, which not only described labour and social conditions, but also included an action plan that outlined any remedial actions and a timeline for addressing areas of non-compliance.

Apart from the clear and immediate benefits to farm women, this campaign also demonstrated the efficacy of the complementary working relationship of WFP and Sikhula Sonke, where the NGO successfully conceptualized the campaign strategy while the MBO enabled the involvement of a farm woman. The campaign was only successful because of the relative contributions of both organizations; without either, it could not have been possible. The Tesco example typifies the way in which WFP and Sikhula Sonke worked together in the early phase of the relationship – this complementarity was acknowledged as the basis of their successful cooperation.

according to its constitution, was to its members and not to funders. Furthermore, the changing or immediate priorities of farm workers did not always converge with existing funder contracts, which often had a two- or three-year cycle. In other words, Sikhula Sonke wanted or needed the flexibility to be more reactive than funder contracts allowed. However, as the fundraiser with ultimate responsibility for implementation and delivery of the funding agreement, for WFP this issue was not negotiable. By January 2008, this impasse resulted in Sikhula Sonke's non-participation in the joint annual work plan development.

A second and related area of contestation involved *decision making*. In addition to Sikhula Sonke's accountability to its members, it is also constitutionally accountable to the NEC, which is the highest decision-making structure of the organization. However, in the early years of the partnership, Sikhula Sonke staff were paid by WFP and the WFP Board effectively had decision-making power within Sikhula Sonke, largely because WFP was responsible for fundraising and overseeing the implementation of the terms of funding contracts. This meant that Sikhula Sonke was actually accountable to both WFP (management and Board) and Sikhula Sonke (members and NEC). While this worked during the initial period, it later led to confusion and tension within Sikhula Sonke, which started questioning its accountability to the WFP Board and emphasizing accountability to its NEC and members. Because of the intrinsically unequal power relations between the two organizations, WFP asserted its relative authority while, as a (junior) partner in the funding agreements and largely financially dependent on WFP, Sikhula Sonke was obliged to comply with the dual decision-making structure.

A third area of contention revolved around the issue of *public profile/credit and recognition*, especially for high-profile public events such as pickets and demonstrations. Simply and crudely speaking, the division of labour for such events between the two organizations generally entailed WFP conceptualizing and strategizing for the event, including writing press releases and contacting the media, while Sikhula Sonke was responsible for mobilizing farm workers to participate in the event.

Since its establishment in 1996, WFP had built a sound reputation as a leader in the sector. Over the years, its effective and successful public campaigns, with consummate use of the mainstream media (press releases, press conferences, radio interviews, ensuring that its public events were covered by the press) had earned it a high media profile. Given its established public and media reputation and relationship, it was hardly surprising, then, that WFP, and not the virtually unknown Sikhula Sonke, received wide coverage in the press, even when the two organizations embarked on joint campaigns. Generally, only WFP staff were interviewed and quoted, events were reported as 'WFP events', and often Sikhula Sonke was not even mentioned.

Resentment grew within Sikhula Sonke, whose staff and members felt overlooked and overshadowed by WFP, even though WFP was clearly not responsible for how or what the press chose to report. As relations between the two organizations deteriorated, Sikhula Sonke increasingly raised reservations and set conditions to hosting joint public events. It felt that it was denied rightful recognition or credit in the media, although the mass participation of its members was the main element in the success of these events. In protesting this neglect, Sikhula Sonke had, in fact, unwittingly hit on WFP's Achilles' heel – that it did not have an independent base of farm women, but relied on Sikhula Sonke members.

By 2008, Sikhula Sonke felt that WFP was using it to mobilize the necessary numbers for successful demonstrations and pickets. By the time Sikhula Sonke actually exited from WFP in late 2008, the two organizations had not embarked on a joint campaign in nearly a year. Sikhula Sonke believed that, although it had come of age, its close partnership with WFP precluded it from receiving the media coverage that it deserved. Thus, from Sikhula Sonke's perspective, it became necessary to forge its own path and become independent of WFP. For WFP, the issue of its dependence on Sikhula Sonke's members had been raised for the first time, marking a subtle shift in power relations. Until then, WFP had been the senior, more powerful partner and Sikhula Sonke wholly dependent. Now the issue of WFP's dependence on Sikhula Sonke was being raised.

A fourth and related issue concerned *legitimacy and authenticity*. What distinguished WFP from other NGOs in the sector was the fact that its campaigns, lobbying and advocacy initiatives had always been directly informed – and, therefore, legitimated – by its close relationship with farm women. In other words, unlike many other NGOs, WFP never spoke or acted in the abstract or from a theoretical basis; rather, it prided itself on being thoroughly grounded in the conditions and experiences of farm women, first in the Women's Rights Groups, then in the farm committees and ultimately in the Sikhula Sonke membership. This conferred a definite degree of legitimacy on WFP's work, a fact of which the organization was acutely aware. As noted above, Sikhula Sonke's members had become an issue of contestation with respect to joint WFP-Sikhula Sonke campaigns – where Sikhula Sonke believed that it was supplying the farm women, while WFP was receiving all the recognition in the media. Thus, as tensions between the two organizations increased, WFP's access to farm women, specifically Sikhula Sonke's members, was increasingly mediated by Sikhula Sonke. In other words, for the first time since its establishment, WFP no longer had unfettered access to farm women, thus threatening its earlier legitimacy. Again, this reflected the power shift between the two organizations, with Sikhula Sonke increasingly asserting its growing power, primarily located in its membership base of thousands of farm women. Indeed, with time, Sikhula Sonke played a gatekeeping role in respect of its members. Whereas, in the past, WFP had always contacted Sikhula Sonke members directly to invite them to training workshops, now Sikhula Sonke demanded that WFP first obtain permission (from it) before inviting any members. WFP was now realizing that it had effectively handed over and lost to Sikhula Sonke the constituency that it had built up and invested in for over a decade. As noted earlier, since the formation of Sikhula Sonke, WFP had directed all its programmes, especially its education, capacity building and campaigns, entirely at Sikhula Sonke's members. Thus, at the same time that Sikhula Sonke's membership was growing, WFP's access to those members was increasingly tenuous and indirect.

While, in the earlier years of the partnership, WFP's comparative advantage and strength had rested on the education and skills of its staff, in later years this was counterbalanced by Sikhula Sonke's own comparative strength and advantage – the lived experience of its staff, who were all former farm workers. Whereas WFP could boast sound ideological, strategic and conceptual strengths, Sikhula Sonke could lay claim to grounded, lived experience of farm work. Whereas, in the past, these differences had complemented each other, when relations soured, this difference fed the growing tensions and conflict between the two organizations.

Issues of positionality also intervened when class became a further dimension of difference. As two organizations comprising black women staff members, the implications of class had never been discussed. Implicit assumptions had been made about the unifying force of the race and gender commonalities, to the exclusion of a consciousness of class differences. In other words, the fact that some staff members (WFP) were university-educated, middle-class and urban, while others (Sikhula Sonke) often did not have secondary school education, and were working-class and rural, was never explicitly and openly addressed in the partnership. Even when (class) difference had been raised, this was usually done to inspire other farm women by showing the leadership and other skills that former farm workers (Sikhula Sonke staff) had acquired. However, at the height of tensions between the two organizations, just before Sikhula Sonke exited, it became apparent that this had not been the most effective way of dealing with the issue. For WFP, it had been 'positive messaging' when it consistently and publicly acknowledged the fact that Sikhula Sonke staff were all former farm workers who had 'come through its ranks'; WFP believed that it was affirming staff's successful journeys of personal empowerment. While Sikhula Sonke had not initially objected to these public declarations, as relations deteriorated, they now expressed a decidedly negative interpretation, arguing that it was evidence of WFP always reminding Sikhula Sonke staff that they were once farm workers. This shows how the two organizations had very different (class) perspectives about the same incident.

With relations steadily deteriorating throughout 2008, Sikhula Sonke finally exited from the offices it had shared with WFP in October, more than a year ahead of its planned and scheduled departure. For example, in May, the Director of WFP and the General Secretary of Sikhula Sonke engaged in a joint conflict mediation process with an external mediator. While not personally responsible for the tensions, the two leaders of the organizations were the inevitable locus of the rift. With insufficient and unequal trust between the two women, the process was not completed and did not result in any resolution of the conflict. In June, Sikhula Sonke formed an External Reference Group comprising a number of relevant 'experts' such as unionists, labour researchers and academics. In the preceding months, Sikhula Sonke had given WFP a strong indication that it would be asked to serve on the Group. However, when the Group was finally formed in June, Sikhula Sonke did not invite WFP. For WFP, feeling sidelined and undermined was only a part of its concern; it also believed that, in the long term, this was not the most strategic decision that Sikhula Sonke could have taken – given their shared vision and the fact that they were the only two organizations working with farm women. Despite any existing differences, WFP believed that it had a continued contribution to make to Sikhula Sonke in terms of ideology, feminist thought, empowerment strategies, advocacy and lobbying. In September, both organizations agreed to participate in a discussion about their post-exit relationship. However, shortly before the scheduled meeting, Sikhula Sonke informed WFP that it would not be available. In early October, Sikhula Sonke moved out of the offices without informing WFP of its intention to do so. Symbolically, this was arguably the lowest point in the relationship.

Empty nest syndrome: reflections on the post-exit relationship

With Sikhula Sonke's strained and early departure, both organizations were faced with a contemplation of the nature and implications of the post-exit phase of the relationship. Although both organizations had agreed to a post-exit workshop to discuss this issue, Sikhula Sonke never agreed to a date, despite numerous efforts from WFP. Again, this reflected the different priorities of the two organizations. WFP was, in many respects, more vulnerable: with a less certain post-Sikhula Sonke future, it had a definite stake in defining this new phase of the relationship. Sikhula Sonke, on the other hand, was coming into its own, with a growing membership and a growing independent profile. It did not need WFP.

For WFP, there were three main considerations during this period, which largely arose as a result of how the relationship had evolved. First, its *raison d'être* had become the building and strengthening of Sikhula Sonke, while its entire implementation strategy had been premised on having a relationship of cooperation and complementarity with Sikhula Sonke. Second, WFP had built its reputational strength on being conceptually and strategically strong, but also on having a solid grassroots base of farm women. Without Sikhula Sonke members, the central challenge for WFP going forward would therefore be (re)building its own base if it was to maintain its legitimacy and authority. Third, as an independent organization, Sikhula Sonke now potentially became one of WFP's competitors for donor funding. As the only women–led social movement of farm workers in South Africa, Sikhula Sonke was unique and thus potentially more fundable than an NGO like WFP.

While Sikhula Sonke is certainly in an enviable position, with an increasing membership, a growing reputation and profile, and independent sources of funding, it nonetheless also faces a number of critical challenges in this post–exit phase. First, Sikhula Sonke might lose its feminist orientation, which was largely developed and articulated by WFP during their close association. While most WFP staff are schooled in feminist theory and have identified themselves as feminists for many years, feminism was a new ideology for Sikhula Sonke staff. It was WFP that drove the feminist agenda. It remains to be seen how deeply internalized a feminist orientation is within Sikhula Sonke. Second, as Sikhula Sonke increasingly asserts its credentials as a trade union (operating independently of an NGO) that needs to be respected and taken seriously (by other trade unions), it could risk replicating the patriarchal norms and practices of traditional, male–dominated trade unions. For example, there is an increasing tendency to centralize power and authority in the position and person of the General Secretary. Moreover, in trying to distance itself from the (parent) NGO, WFP, and gain greater acceptance from other trade unions, Sikhula Sonke might become more self-conscious about expressing a feminist orientation and, inadvertently, lose one of its distinctive characteristics. Third, unlike all trade unions which are dependent on their members for funding and are thus financially vulnerable, Sikhula Sonke has secured independent donor funding for the next few years. This is a significant achievement and provides Sikhula Sonke with a degree of security and sustainability. However, such funding could also constrain Sikhula Sonke's independence, radicalism and dynamism as a (independent) social movement. While donor funding cycles dictate that the recipient organization (only) delivers on what the proposal and contract spell out, a social movement needs to be responsive to the changing realities and challenges of its members on the ground.

Conclusions

Given the histories of many countries in the South, and the rural–urban inequalities that have generally provided urban women with greater educational opportunities, there is clearly a role for NGOs to play as animators and capacitators in partnerships with MBOs. This chapter study has raised a number of issues and lessons regarding the relationship between NGOs and MBOs (or social movements).

First, there needs to be explicit recognition of the specific synergies and comparative advantages between the two types of organizations and an explicit definition of respective roles. Second, the issues of accountability and decision making also serve to illustrate some of the practical limits of cooperation between NGOs and MBOs given their respective origins, evolution and *raison d'être*. While there are clearly areas of collaboration, such as campaigns, the parameters need to be defined and delimited. Third, there should be a flexibility that consciously and consistently allows the partnership to respond to changing realities (for example, the increased capacity of the MBO). If this does not happen, it is easy for the very areas of complementarity to develop into areas of tension and contestation. Fourth, it is imperative that class and power relations between the two organizations should be explicitly and consistently recognized and addressed. It is not enough to have a common vision, a shared agenda; as necessary is an explicit acknowledgement and articulation of class differences, and the nature and implications of (shifting) power inequalities. Finally, the partnership of NGOs and MBOs may have a finite shelf life, beyond which it becomes destructive and counter-productive for both partners.

For WFP and Sikhula Sonke, and other NGO–MBO relationships, the challenge is to build a partnership that reflects a sisterhood of equality rather than an unequal mother–child relationship.

Notes

1 Colette Solomon was Deputy Director of Women on Farms Project when she wrote this chapter. However, she writes in her personal capacity and the views expressed do not necessarily reflect those of Women on Farms Project.

2 Nearly half of all South African women murdered in 1999 were killed by intimate partners. This translated into a prevalence rate of 8.8 per 100,000 women, or one woman killed every six hours – the highest rate ever reported by research anywhere in the world (Mathews et al. 2004). For the period April to December 2007, 36,190 rapes were reported (Tshwaranang 2009). However, given that research has found that only one in nine rapes are reported, the actual number was probably closer to 325,710.

3 Through the 'tot system', farm workers were paid part of their wage in wine. The system can be traced back to the colonial and slavery era of the 1600s, but was still pervasive on many wine farms into the 1990s. Through the system, farmers made and kept farm workers dependent on alcohol, and thus docile and unlikely to agitate for their rights. While officially outlawed for decades, the 'tot system' has now taken on a new and insidious form in which farmers sell poor quality wine at inflated prices on credit to farm workers. Workers are often left with little money for food and other household necessities after they settle their alcohol debt with the farmer at the end of the month.

References

du Toit, A. and Ally, F. (2003) 'The externalization and casualization of farm labour in Western Cape horticulture', Programme for Land and Agrarian Studies and Centre for Rural Legal Studies (PLAAS), Research Report 16.

Mathews, S., N. Abrahams, L. J. Martin, L. Vetten, L. van der Merwe and R. Jewkes (2004) '"Every six hours a woman is killed by her intimate partner": a national study of female homicide in South Africa', MRC Policy Brief 5.

Tshwaranang Legal Advocacy Centre (2009) 'Violence against women in South Africa fact sheet'.

3

Organizing for Life and Livelihoods in the Mountains of Uttarakhand

The Experience of Uttarakhand Mahila Parishad

•••

Anuradha Pande

This chapter shares insights from the place-based, women-centred programme of Uttarakhand Mahila Parishad (Uttarakhand Women's Federation), a network of around 16,000 rural women in the hill villages of the state of Uttarakhand in India. There are 465 whole village women's groups (WVGs) spread over seven districts of the state, which constitute the federation. In particular, I highlight the point that the dynamics of local livelihoods are governed by a gender dynamic embedded in the community way of life. However, with increasing awareness about gender issues and with the extending reach of global market forces into villages, this dynamic of community life is changing. The process of change is complex because it demands a complete reorganization from traditional ways of life to communities embracing new livelihood options based on the requirements of globalization. The chapter also shows how process-based, holistic approaches to gender can build the capacities of rural women to create and sustain social relationships and networks – and so address the challenges emerging from women's changing positions in rural societies.

Uttarakhand, a small state in the Indian Himalayas, is bounded by Nepal in the east and China (Tibet) in the north. It covers an area of 53,483 square kilometres, with rural people constituting more than 70 per cent of the total population of eight million. The land is dissected by high mountains (7,817 metres above sea level) and low valleys (210 metres). Out of the total land area, about 46 per cent is covered by forests and about 14 per cent is under cultivation. The work of Uttarakhand Mahila Parishad is located in the mid-altitude zone (1,000–3,500 metres) called the Central Himalayas.

Agriculture is the main source of livelihood for rural communities in the Central Himalayas. The cycle of cultivation is the outcome of women's interactions with fields, forests, livestock and water. Although women play a central role in the provision of livelihoods and in sustaining the local food production systems, their contribution is not valued as an important aspect of the community's economic life. Their work in the fields, in forests and at home is viewed as an extension of their gender-specific responsibilities, and has become institutionalized within the gender division of labour in household livelihood systems: men's work revolves around activities that produce cash income while women contribute to social reproduction through their subsistence-oriented work.

As elsewhere, in Uttarakhand women's economic contribution is governed by the complex intersection of caste, age, class and gender relations, and the resulting inequalities in the distribution of resources and power. There are restrictions on women's physical mobility, although these are not as severe as those that operate in the northern plains of India. However, a tradition of women's exclusion from decision making in community and household matters bestows power on men. The result is the subordinate positioning of women within a complex hierarchy constituted by these intersecting inequalities.

Over the years, it is the picture of the rural hill woman carrying a head load of fuel wood or fodder that has come to symbolize Himalayan agriculture. Rural women have continued to work in close proximity with their environment to meet their survival needs. This relationship has been the shaping force in the gradual evolution of varied land-based livelihood systems as well as the particular beliefs and practices that make up the culture of the Himalayas.

The current rapid pace of socio-economic change in India, particularly with the onset of economic liberalization policies, has not occurred evenly across the country. It has been slow to reach the remote mountain villages of Uttarakhand and the old agricultural systems that sustain its population. This is now changing. The effect of global market forces appears to be eroding these systems and replacing them with a new ecological order based on the commoditization of natural resources for use in the global economy. Large-scale construction activities – dams, roads, recreational areas – have threatened indigenous livelihood systems, often displacing communities from their native habitats, or forcing them into greater reliance on degraded ecological resources.

New forms of socio-economic associations are confusing to communities, especially to the elderly people in villages, who still believe in traditional forms of community life. For example, conflicts may occur between the elderly women and their young daughters-in-law on the issue of application of chemical fertilizers in agricultural fields. The older generation of women prefer to use compost and for that matter do not mind keeping cattle at home, whilst the younger generation insist on chemical-based agriculture. Similarly, the young girls attending schools are sold the idea of computer literacy as a means of getting employment in the cities, but their mothers at home know that a computer cannot produce water or food. Further, experience has also shown them that a few top students will get decent employment in the cities, but the rest of their children will either continue to live in the village or be forced to spend their lives in slums in the cities. This is why a major concern for many older women is to conserve and protect the common resources for use in future by their children.

The ecological consequences of changes in local livelihood patterns are deeply experienced by women. The process of environmental degradation in the Himalayas has exposed the fragility of women's livelihoods and the challenges they face in sustaining agriculture. As men migrate to the cities in search of paid jobs, it is women who have had to deal with ecological problems and related livelihood dislocations brought about by deforestation, soil erosion and shortage of water. Poor rural women spend more time and energy in meeting basic survival needs while collective impoverishment translates into intensification of ailments like anaemia, malnutrition, tuberculosis, leucorrhoea and water-borne diseases.

The organization

USNPSS (Uttarakhand Seva Nidhi Paryavaran Shiksha Sansthan, or the Uttarakhand Environmental Education Centre) is an Indian NGO that has been working with rural communities since 1987 to enable them to restore the ecological, social and economic balance of their environment.[1] A major focus of our work has been the creation of and extension of support to rural people's networks, including networks of community-based organizations (CBOs), women's groups, teachers, children, youth and adolescents across the hill districts of the state of Uttarakhand. These networks are mobilized to challenge gender stereotypes and to demystify the myths that dominate the mainstream development practices that have led to the environmentally destructive pursuit of industrialization. For example, the idea of economic development is a myth that is constantly subjected to debates and discussions in meetings organized by USNPSS at various levels. Instead, the issue of ecological poverty is understood as the major challenge of our times. Similarly, ambiguities in the current development discourse, such as labelling elderly rural women as 'illiterate and backward', are countered to promote a sense of confidence among them.

USNPSS started its work in 1987 with financial assistance from the Department of Education, Government of India to act as a nodal agency for organizations and individuals in the state around an environmental education agenda. This required us to travel across the state to track down CBOs and individuals who were working, or might be interested in working, on environmental and educational issues. Many of them were located in villages that were miles away from the road heads,[2] places where no government functionary had ever visited, and where people led a life that was not very different from that of their ancestors. Women and children had never been out of their villages, had never seen a bus or a train, and were not interested in matters of national politics.

USNPSS was ready to support and work with informal CBOs and individuals by exploring and responding to their needs. The early mobilization of women drew upon their knowledge of the land and of biomass production and utilization. It became clear very early on that ways would have to be found to reduce women's long working days, imposed by their multiple responsibilities. This led to the setting up of *balwadis*, or child-care and education centres for three- to six-year-old children. The centre relieved women of some of their daily child-care responsibilities but also served as a focal point in initiating work around girls' education. In the late 1980s, girls as old as fifteen were attending *balwadis*. More than twenty years later, however, the situation has changed completely and all the children now attend school. Further, in collaboration with the Department of Education, Government of India, USNPSS began developing textbooks on environmental education, drawing communities into schools, and enriching the text with knowledge that rural women have cultivated by working on the land for centuries.

Organizing women

Women initially came together around the efforts to provide education to their children. In the early stages, groups were formed to oversee the routine operations of the *balwadis*. The general interest in education led to participation by all women in monthly meetings in villages. The female teachers, supervisors and the heads of the CBOs, responsible for running the *balwadis* in villages, were trained by USNPSS to organize all women of the village as a single group, the WVG. Gradually 'whole village women's groups' (WVGs) began to evolve.

Efforts were made to ensure that the views of women from the lower castes were integrated into the process. However, given the diversity of perspectives in mixed-caste villages and in communities divided by old conflicts, external mediation was required to promote unity. The disjunction between collective (often long-term) and individual (immediate) benefits was reconciled by providing partial assistance for the installation of latrines and cheap water tanks to the most disadvantaged women in the community on a priority basis: these were widows, deserted women and female-headed households. Interlinkages between the provision of safe sanitation, health and livelihoods were discussed in open community meetings to generate knowledge and to promote community ownership of these ideas and activities.

Women's participation in village meetings, *padyatras* (marches on foot) and in regional workshops and seminars was followed later by trips to the USNPSS office in Almora for residential workshops, reviews and follow-up meetings. Through WVGs, the rural women began to connect with the outer world, the mysterious unknown. For the majority of women travelling to attend meetings and workshops at Almora, it was the first journey they had ever made into the world beyond the village. These were not easy journeys. Travelling in a vehicle for the first time in their lives would make them nauseous, their families often resisted their going out, and communities would label them women of 'loose virtue' who had 'no men' in their families to protect their honour. Nevertheless, the women showed immense interest in attending workshops at Almora. This was a place where they were encouraged to speak up and USNPSS staff would listen to their feelings, experiences and sorrows for hours. Regular dialogue between women's groups and USNPSS staff and with the CBOs helped women and the village workers shape and reshape their ideas and activities, and the programme began to grow under a common framework that itself was evolving through experimentation in villages. For example, during discussions at Almora, women repeatedly prioritized the idea of developing oak and other broad-leaf tree forests in villages. However, they had never grown oak seedlings before. They needed support on matters of treatment of seeds and the methods of sowing (right depth, timings for watering, and so on). It was through experimentation in villages that WVGs learnt about the differential growth patterns of vegetation. By actually growing plant nurseries they learnt that − other factors (temperature, climate, water) being the same − both germination and growth rates of oak trees were lower than the other local broad-leaf trees. The best strategy, therefore, was to develop a mixed forest containing different broad-leaf tree species. Since women from different parts of the state were invited to attend meetings at Almora, such lessons were picked up by new groups for immediate application in their own villages.

Similarly, it was through experience that women developed the strategy of not clearing shrubs and herbs from a plantation site in its initial stages of development. Though it was tempting to strip mountain slopes of shrubs to facilitate the growth of grass for immediate use, experience had taught them that in the absence of shrubs, especially thorny bushes, goats and other animals can easily damage small seedlings. The problem was acute in areas where the plantation site had multiple community rights holders and the community vigilance system was weak. The additional insight was that regular harvesting was feasible once oak trees were more than a metre in height.

Since learning from meetings and workshops was translated into collective action, the WVGs began to reintegrate into community life on the basis of new perspectives that they had gained through the programme. Afforestation, nursery raising, conservation of water, protection and preservation of forests and grasslands brought collective benefits to communities and led to restoration of land, but beyond that WVGs began to understand the logic of what they were able to do in relation to the productivity of the land and the patterns of their livelihoods.

The programme had the flexibility to move back and forth between what was learnt and what needed to be recapitulated, thereby allowing WVGs to change, modify and proceed with ideas that were of interest to them. Thus, instead of following a direct, linear path to measurable progress, USNPSS facilitated a dynamic, iterative path that allowed women the time and space to learn and grow at their own pace. For example, afforestation sites and tree nurseries also served as spaces for practical learning in which WVGs could plant seedlings of their own choice. In case of good germination, the work would lead to further action, but high mortality of seedlings would bring the WVGs back to revisit their strategy, develop nurseries again and grow seedlings afresh for further transplantation. As women took on the responsibility for growing trees, something they did not do before, their confidence in their capacity also grew and they provided leadership in developing rules in order to maintain and protect the plantation sites.

Slowly, WVGs began to take up more activities on education, health, natural resource management and livelihoods, alcoholism and violence against women, and addressing the intersecting gender, caste and class disparities that cut across community life and institutions such as the forest protection and management committees, and the village councils (*panchayats*).

Uttarakhand Mahila Parishad

Starting from two villages in 1987, the work with communities, especially women, expanded to about 450 villages in 2000, offering diverse views and experiences from across the state and building an integral, holistic approach to development. In 2001, all the WVGs decided to federate at the state level as the Uttarakhand Mahila Parishad (Uttarakhand Women's Federation or UMP). Currently, around 16,000 rural women represented by 465 WVGs spread over seven districts of the state constitute the federation. It is the largest network of rural women in Uttarakhand.

UMP connects all women within communities in WVGs that diverge in form from village to village, each being valued as unique in itself, but converge to create twenty regional federations (*Kshatriya Mahila Parishad*) that then become part of the state-level federation, the UMP. The lateral and vertical bonds of connectivity among WVGs provide coherence and resilience to UMP as the federation builds from villages to state level.

The UMP head office is in Almora, where it shares infrastructural and other facilities with the parent organization, USNPSS. To avoid hierarchy and to maintain flexibility within the federation, UMP is not registered. Funds come through USNPSS for the federation and are sent to CBOs for utilization through the women's groups.

The executive committee of UMP is constituted by rural women from across the state. Each year, the executive committee meets to review the work and contemplate the future. UMP members also meet regularly in villages and at Almora to share experiences and to learn from each other. An informal advisory committee consists of representatives from CBOs with whom WVGs are associated in villages.

Redefining needs, widening space

There have been gradual transitions over time in women's attitudes and priorities: from wanting to get their children cared for and educated to a shared desire to become educated themselves; from prioritizing road construction as a symbol of development to organizing protests against road constructions which damaged their fields; from demanding provision of water from outside to providing leadership in the development of diverse methods to conserve and use water; and from being an unorganized collection of individuals and families to establishing themselves as powerful village organizations. By taking their concerns from the private domain into the public, WVGs were able to address issues of alcoholism and gambling among men. They began to take strong action against men beating and abusing their wives and children under the influence of alcohol. Examples were set by women punishing their husbands and father-in-laws in public for not abiding with decisions taken in community meetings. Stigma associated with diseases such as tuberculosis, malnutrition, leucorrhoea and other reproductive problems were debated in public, followed by actions to combat the problem.

A number of these struggles centred on women's bodies. For example, during the menstrual cycle, women were required to stay in a separate room and refrain from their usual household activities. In particular, they were required to stay away from the kitchen and the area where deities were kept. It was therefore a radical decision on the part of the UMP to suggest that *balwadi* teachers would continue to run the centres – that their activities would not be interrupted – during their menstrual cycle. It forced communities to start viewing the process of menstruation as part of a natural cycle and to question the tradition of women sitting in isolation for five days. To make the point even more strongly, the UMP staff made visits to villages, entering sacred places, ignoring threats and unpleasant moves by communities. Educational materials, often pictorial, were developed to educate teachers, women and adolescents on issues of human anatomy. Informal interactions in villages led to intensive counselling sessions and, based on these experiences, training programmes and workshops with women's groups and *balwadi* workers were changed and updated regularly.

This transgression of the boundaries that separate 'inside' from 'outside', 'private' from 'public', gave visibility to age-old problems and spearheaded changes in norms about women's mobility and morality. These changes were empowering because women were learning to take full responsibility for themselves and were able to create new ways of being. But these changes did not happen overnight. Efforts to reconfigure women's physical and emotional relationships to themselves and others generated intense emotions in villages. There was considerable resistance from the community and accusations about the morality of WVG members and UMP workers.

Nevertheless, despite setbacks, the process led to the creation of an intellectual and practical space for rural women to learn, innovate, experiment and generate new ways of thinking and being. It enabled women to participate in, and often lead, a movement for change based on their own voices and aspirations. Many women became development workers, were elected as representatives of *panchayats* (village councils) and evolved into community leaders and activists. They used their position to challenge unquestioned assumptions and ill-informed decisions in development programmes and policies. For example, WVGs prioritized adequate staff and improved quality of education in government schools by challenging the practice of teachers spending valuable teaching time managing the midday meals scheme. *Bhiksha nahin, shiksha dou* (Don't give us alms, give us education) was the slogan the WVGs coined to protest against this practice.

Over time, a new development paradigm based on the voices of WVGs has emerged, one that has profound appeal in their villages. WVGs have fostered a collective process of change and worked towards developing solidarity, cooperation, reciprocity and cohesiveness within UMP and beyond. Motivated to make their villages better places to live in, WVGs have sought to make the connections between ecological, social and livelihood issues. The process appeals to rural women because it is holistic and provides space to reflect on their experiences, and thus to develop new ideas for further action. It offers them an opportunity to improve the quality of life in a setting that, while materially deprived in many ways, provides an environment in which they work with nature, protect and manage land and its resources to grow food and, as a village woman said in one of the meetings of WVGs, 'to grow water' (this was in the context of constructing small rainwater infiltration tanks which allow water to percolate in the ground).

The political construction of livelihoods

The WVGs' efforts to maintain and enhance local livelihoods are based on their collective struggle for both economic survival and social recognition of the value of their contributions. Following the core ideas of collective planning, decision making, group ownership and equal distribution of produce among all village residents, WVGs protect and nurture forests, restore old water sources, protect the grasslands from grazing animals and develop new plantation sites. In the process, women assert their rights to decision making in community matters, appropriate space in natural resource management and redefine gender roles and responsibilities.

As UMP organizes rural women to secure their rights over natural resources and to regulate commercial activities in their favour, disputes emerge at home as well as at community and regional levels. While negotiations at home may include several layers of agreements and disagreements, often leading to direct violence against women, it is the conflict at community level that attracts wider attention. For example, the forest could be at the root of multiple disputes within and between communities. In a context of growing population and increasing demand for resources, the destruction of the environment and of traditional livelihoods can set one community against another. Conflicts become sharper in areas where many villages have traditional community rights over a small piece of land. Because all villages are entitled to share in the use of the forest, disputes occur when any of the right holders refuse to accept the decisions of WVGs on land management and protection.

Regulating access to natural resources has often meant a complete change in traditional land management practices. For example, the tradition of allowing cattle to graze in agricultural fields immediately after crop harvesting (*mukhsaar*) has now been changed, though with varying degrees of effectiveness, in all villages where WVGs are functional. Similarly, with women taking up the role of patrolling of forests and of plantation sites on a rotational basis, the old system of appointing a man as a paid guard for vigilance has been abolished in many villages. Further, the traditional all-male forest committees are now replaced by WVGs. As women take decisions in important community matters such as the time and duration of harvesting of wood and fodder from common protected areas and the methods for distribution of produce, the status of a few influential men in communities and the monopoly of institutions like the forest department in decision making is threatened. Women's decisions in community matters are, therefore, not easily accepted by those institutions and men, who have for long exercised authority and control over communities by reserving decision-making power for themselves. In this respect, WVGs have had a profound impact on local village politics.

Important progress towards gender equality in land-based livelihoods has been made as men and conventional institutions have lost patronage over the community and its natural resources. The changes involved in such advances have sometimes led to aggressive responses, which may be mild (disputes in the village and within the women's group, which resolve after some time) or moderate (women from such families not attending monthly meetings, harassment in public places) to strong (filing a legal case against the WVG): UMP has to deal with these from time to time. But through these experiences women have also learnt to shed their fears and prejudices. As Pushpa of Lingurta village says,

> Earlier we did not know that there actually was a difference between a forest guard and a policeman. Many of us would hide in the fields or at home in case a man wearing a *khaki* uniform had entered the village. However, things changed when we began to express our fears and anxieties in women's meetings. Now, we can talk to anyone.

To understand changes in ecological, social and economic systems in villages, and to connect these variations with gender and livelihoods, WVGs from across the state put together their experiences and analysed them collectively. This forms the basis of their own relational framework on livelihoods and development. For example, several large-scale projects on livelihoods run by the government and other development agencies encourage rural women to sell local food as 'organic products' to the cities. At the same time, rural people are given the idea of vitamin pills as the key to a healthy life. While putting together these otherwise separate strands of mainstream development, a collective understanding has emerged among WVGs that the money rural people can earn from feeding organic food to the cities is actually utilized in buying chemically generated, less nutritious food from the same market. Since agricultural produce has never been in surplus in recent times, and men may use money from the sale of organic produce to buy liquor or to gamble, children and women are unable to get nutritious, adequate meals at home. Hence, the priority of WVGs has been to improve the direct use values of their natural resources. A good quality forest near home improves agricultural production because compost, and not chemical fertilizer, is used in the fields. Also, easy access to wood for fuel, to fodder and to water can effectively reduce women's work burdens and improve the quality of life. To enable rural communities, especially women and children, to have nutritious, organic food as part of their own diet, UMP mobilizes teachers, students, men, youth and the CBOs in villages and supports activities to promote the production and consumption of local food. In addition, issues of women's health and the need for proper nutrition are highlighted and subjected to fruitful discussion at various levels.

UMP's approach

The starting premise of the UMP is that all women – whether rural, urban, literate, illiterate, poor, rich, young, old – are intelligent, something that needs to be strongly asserted in a society that treats women as inferior to men and incapable of rational thought. The specific approach towards women of different ages differs according to how the challenge is conceptualized.

The older generation of women, especially those above 50, are largely illiterate. Restoring their confidence is an important feature of UMP because one of the cauterizing effects of intensive government and international campaigns on literacy has been the message that illiterate women know nothing. Yet, time and again, these women have emerged as among the best community leaders and activists. While asserting their rights over forests, grasslands and water, they have developed methods to ensure local control over resources and have mobilized others in communities and in government to follow their decisions.

For example, WVGs have forced the Forest Department to plant broad-leaf tree species of their choice by taking direct action to uproot commercial varieties of trees in the forests. They have organized demonstrations against illegal cutting and selling of trees and in many cases stopped the contractors/agencies accessing the forest for commercial exploitation. They have shown that the grasslands may yield double the quantity of grass after two or three years of protection from free cattle grazing and have devised ways to ensure equal distribution of grass among all community members. They have mobilized against the tapping of water for commercial purposes that would have denied communities their traditional rights over the local water sources. And by reviving indigenous methods of water conservation and storage, they have shown that simple technologies play an important role in developing the livelihood base in villages.

Adolescents and young married girls are encouraged to participate in all activities organized by WVGs. This ensures continuity of concepts and activities from one generation to the next. For example, adolescents are taught to understand and appreciate the contributions of their mothers and aunts in redressing and restoring ecological, social and livelihood-related imbalances in societies. Seedlings planted today by WVGs in village afforestation sites are growing along with these children and will be ready for harvesting by the time the children mature. The adolescent and youth groups are, therefore, exposed to methods of sustainable harvesting. Further, issues of reproductive health, nutrition, education and self-development are emphasized in work related to adolescent groups.

Some of the main features of UMP's approach to organizing and sustaining WVGs are summarized below.

Capacity building

Emphasizing the issue of organizing women as WVGs is important from the point of view of addressing strategic gender interests because, by transforming their villages, women gain the confidence to see potential for transformation of the broader realities of their lives. The philosophy and goals of WVGs, and the activities involved in organizing, revolve around the idea of achieving gender equality, but the underlying values go beyond gender differences to encompass a much wider domain of environmental, social and economic concerns in people's lives, with the aim of developing communities capable of acting from a position of strength.

For UMP to function on a long-term basis, the WVGs and the associated CBOs must have faith in it. Since WVG members are not paid workers of UMP, it is important to nurture alliances and strengthen groups with a sense of solidarity. Conscious efforts are, therefore, made to nurture relationships within and among WVGs. This aspect makes the federation prescient and self-regulating, at least to the point that all members share a common minimal framework and feel that they themselves own the programme. Further, the more closely tied WVGs are by the bonds of a single federation, the more the women emphasize the need for solidarity to facilitate work, especially political activism. Besides working on specific activities in their villages, WVGs organize and participate in experience-sharing and leadership-development programmes at the following levels:

- regular, monthly, meetings organized by WVGs (village level);
- regular, annual, regional congregation of WVGs (at cluster level);
- five yearly congregation of WVGs (state level);

- regular workshops at Almora for WVGs;
- exposure tours and participation in activities outside the village.

For UMP, organizing these events with women and others has never been a formal, routine exercise but a transformative educational framework for thinking about life. Organizing ideas and activities to nurture the work of WVGs are shared, but the deliberations also touch on simple but important matters such as how to ask for permission from men in the family when women are required to go out of the village or how to acquire a piece of the common land for afforestation.

Creating community resources under women's leadership

In remote villages, women's lives are lived in a complex domain of traditional beliefs and practices. To them, restoration of forests and other natural resources is important not only to secure place-based livelihoods but also to maintain harmony in life. The local deities that reside deep in the forest are approached frequently by communities to seek their blessings. Always, the first harvest is offered to them. On a priority basis, communities try to please the local deity and spirits dwelling in forests to chart the course of treatment for sick people. Therefore, many decisions which determine the pace of change in women's lives are influenced by and made within this belief system. Though women are aware of the need for change in certain practices, they do believe in ways that bridge the modern and the traditional value systems. Also, they believe that it is their society, and they should decide what needs to be rejected and what should be changed. Therefore, in promoting transitions in women's lives, UMP is guided by impulses from within the community rather than those externally imposed by donors, development professionals or academicians.

Creating community resources under women's leadership is part of this transition. However, these resources have to be seen as embedded in broader processes of change. For example, the process of eventually creating individual household latrines is necessarily preceded by a process to raise awareness about the benefits and to ensure that the latrine is used by all family members and kept clean. Infrastructure requires reinforcement of ideas and practices that go beyond simple construction work. WVGs look into the condition of the water source so as to get a regular water supply and maintain their sanitation facilities. If degraded, the water source requires restoration. Rainwater harvesting techniques (such as digging trenches or small ponds) provide immediate relief but in view of achieving long-term benefits, broad-leaf tree species that produce humus for quick absorption of rainwater are planted. Saplings, raised by WVGs in carefully managed village nurseries, need to be transplanted, in time, in the catchment area. To ensure proper germination of saplings, the afforestation site needs to be protected – from grazing animals, for example.

Interwoven with processes of creating community resources to strengthen local livelihoods are the challenges of gender and caste-class disparities. In many villages, women and adolescent girls were previously not allowed to use the latrine because of the stigma of impurity attached to female bodies. Changing this has been a long struggle for UMP staff but it has helped dramatically reduce the incidence of water-borne diseases as villages have switched over to latrine use. In addition, having latrines at home, instead of using the fields, has been beneficial to adolescent girls and women, particularly during menstruation and pregnancy.

Another challenge in building collective resources is dealing with the disputes that arise in contexts of extreme scarcity. The reduction of conflict is taken as a development indicator by the WVGs. For example, quarrels are reduced considerably in villages where everyone has a toilet facility and an adequate supply of water to keep it clean. WVG meetings also become the forums for counselling on family matters. Since all women of the village are required to attend meetings, any quarrel that might have happened at home is immediately picked up for collective reflection. Even simple matters of day-to-day life, such as conflicts between women of two generations in a family, are discussed with a view to finding solutions.

Ethics of creating ecological wealth in villages

UMP placed a high value on the ethics of development. The concept is translated into action by WVGs devising different ways of rewarding ethical choices. For example, women making impartial decisions on community matters are not only respected by all in the community but eventually become leaders of their groups. Often, they are invited to other villages to resolve disputes. Also, their work is shared in meetings conducted by UMP at Almora and published for dissemination across the state. On the other hand, people cutting grass or wood on the sly in protected village areas, alcoholic men using abusive language in public places, or using any form of violence against their wives and children, are all forced to pay a fine for their 'wrong deeds'. Although assessing the 'good' and the 'bad' is a subjective exercise, women's judgements are accepted by others in communities because WVGs can ostracize the persons concerned.

As part of their ethical values, the WVGs maintain transparency in financial matters. All members are aware of the financial transactions of their group and each activity is discussed in monthly meetings. When a WVG decides to create a collective fund, all women deposit an equal amount with equal rights on savings. The social implication of this principle is that the relatively affluent members have to agree to deposit the amount that poor women can afford to save every month. Usually, the fund revolves within the village in the form of loans without any linkages to banks. This is done to avoid the risks associated with repayment of loans to banks, but other distinctions between the WVGs' system and current microcredit schemes are also made, the basic point of departure being that the idea of 'we and our money' proliferates, suppressing the feeling of 'me and my betterment' (Pande 2007).

Further, several supplementary activities – such as selling of seedlings from women's nurseries, or renting out utensils and other goods to neighbouring villages for social functions – contribute towards women's collective funds. In addition, in several villages, people donate a small amount to the women's fund as an expression of their appreciation during festivals, and individuals may contribute when there is a wedding or birth in the family.

Over time, women have used money collected in WVG funds in diverse ways. The general trend has been a transition from buying large utensils and other accessories (mats, furniture) for free common use during weddings, childbirth, and other occasions in the village, to supporting education of poor girls by covering their expenses on books and uniform, which provides the basis for greater equity and empowerment of women.

To many, particularly those enamoured of the promise of the market-led economy, UMP's approach may appear 'anti-globalization' in its orientation, in conflict with the rapid change that characterizes modern societies. This view, however, needs to be sensitive to some of the complex issues that remain hidden within the sweeping current of modern development discourse, based as it is on the economic growth paradigm.

The UMP's belief that the attainment of gender equality in rural societies requires long-term and passionate commitment to the cause has led its members to adopt an approach that makes them accountable to communities, to other women, to CBOs and to USNPSS. To this end, UMP has to be open in its dealings and relevant to community concerns. The pursuit of short-term gains tends to gloss over the complexities of people's lives and can deceive communities about long-term costs. The UMP has opted for a more difficult pathway, very different from that being promoted elsewhere, but it is the one that the rural women understand and can associate with, a pathway that they have themselves forged as they began their collective journey towards equality and justice two decades ago.

Valuing each WVG as a unique collective

UMP does not issue any specific guidelines about how to engage in different activities. Women are exposed to new ideas through exposure visits and discussions held at various levels, and try to translate these ideas into action. Take the example of installing a latrine. All decisions are taken in community meetings organized by WVGs. The CBOs and the *balwadi* workers supervise the activity, offering advice on how to dig the 'right pit' and on fitting the seat properly. Depending on their capacity, families erect stone, brick or mud walls or simply cover the structure by a piece of tarpaulin or tin. What results is not a standardized model but a process of experimentation and collective learning which, UMP makes sure, should lead to a change in people's habits from open-air defecation to regular use of the new facility.

Even a small programme of nursery raising and afforestation on community land, though carried out in a similar mountain terrain, throws up different experiences and outcomes for different village clusters. By and large, this diversity in experience and outcome is determined by the social composition of the village, its location in relation to roads and towns, the experiences of CBOs and their motivation. For example, people in a remote village may show greater interest in ecological sustainability issues than people in easily accessible villages that are switching over to multiple off-farm activities. Similarly, traditional rainwater harvesting techniques to recharge springs and rivers and to improve agricultural yields are feasible in villages that own common land. The new habitations developing along the roads depend on the use of fossil fuels and a piped water supply.

This principle of considering each village as a unique entity with its own specific needs has led UMP to deviate from the conventional models of implementing projects under the banner of a 'watershed programme' or of targeting administrative units (such as a block or a district) to guide the selection of villages. Put simply, UMP works without setting targets on coverage, with those women/villages that approach the federation with some idea of work that they want to do in their own village.

Activities

With its strong focus on socio-environmental and political action through collective decision making, UMP provides access to resources, agency and power to those women who are constantly represented as marginal and powerless in the conventional development paradigm. Central to this is the question of who controls the process of development and who benefits the most. Over time, UMP has developed an approach in which the process is controlled by WVGs. Decisions regarding who in the community would get the small support for activities like installing a latrine or a rainwater harvesting tank and on what priority basis, timings of installation, or distribution of money are all taken by WVGs in open meetings. This has led to a strategic shift of power away from government officials and men in communities controlling financial and other matters, to rural women exercising collective choices.

WVGs select a girl from the village to be trained as a teacher to run pre-primary centres in villages and monitor routine work. Progress that children make in the centre is discussed in regular monthly meetings, as are problems and difficulties faced by teachers in running the centres. In addition, WVGs frame the rules on protection and management of forests, grasslands and water sources. They have acquired the courage to question the authorities in local administration and defend their own and their community's rights over resources. Some of the different activities supported by UMP are summarized in Box 3.1.

Political activism

Over the years, WVGs have expanded their activities to address issues of representation and participation of women in the political

Box 3.1   Activities supported by UMP

- Community mobilization to organize and create an enabling environment for women, forming WVGs, connecting with UMP;
- Developing WVGs' capabilities to own and maintain pre-primary centres and undertake other educational activities with children (evening centres, adolescent groups etc.), monitor activities and demand improvements in government schools above pre-primary stages;
- Protecting and nurturing village resources such as forests, water, indigenous varieties of grains and compost to improve the productivity of the land. The nature and scale of activities around ecological restoration impinge on issues of gender-based rights and ownership on land, choices of tree species, the role of commons in securing livelihoods, and the need for natural resources as support systems for the village economy, local governance, etc.
- Running campaigns against alcoholism and gambling prevalent among men; organizing demonstrations against sale of liquor in or near the village, often uprooting outlets; and putting up boundaries against the use of abusive language in public places;
- Organizing campaigns to clean the village paths, the water sources and the houses;
- Demanding equal wages for men and women in state-led schemes, and registering protests against corruption in the public administration;
- Addressing issues of health and nutrition in pre-primary centres, in community meetings, and through regional congregations of women;
- Mapping community health needs, providing information and help to women and adolescent girls on reproductive health, especially on menstruation, child delivery and after care;

- Organizing health camps for women in villages. Facilitating women's access to hospitals, often bearing the expenses of very poor women's (and children's) treatment, including diagnosis and treatment of disease;
- Over the years, more than 7,500 latrines have been installed and in almost all villages, the programme has prompted others to construct latrines and bathrooms on their own, without any external assistance;
- Promoting the idea of involving all women of a village in a single group (WVG), owning and managing their revolving funds by themselves;
- Publishing UMP's booklet, *Nanda*, for circulation to WVGs, CBOs and teachers. Published once a year, *Nanda*'s articles are written by rural women and men, documenting work and providing insights into projects of WVGs that are being tested, rejected and replicated in various parts of Uttarakhand. In addition, educational material is developed and distributed in all villages for use during meetings and in other activities.

sphere. Their increasing participation (and intervention) in formal structures of governance (such as in *panchayats* or village councils) has been a move towards carving out a political space for women by working through issues of representation and resources. UMP optimizes the network of WVGs as a dynamic organization created by women to render visible their changing position in relation to conventional codes of behaviour and practice, and encourages/trains them to stand for *panchayat* elections.

Acting as pressure groups, WVGs have been able to leverage funds available in *panchayats* towards their areas of interest. They have also demanded and received equal wages for their work in government schemes. In addition, WVGs are trying to reorient *panchayat* schemes to address issues of land-based livelihoods. WVGs and their representatives are also raising the point that voting rights and reservations for women in the local committees do not ensure their participation in decision making on livelihood and land management issues. At least, these formal rights have not translated into 'voices' that are heard. For example, women *panchayat* representatives are calling the attention of government functionaries to issues of ecological poverty and related pressure on local livelihoods. In view of the stress laid by the government on economic development, women's concerns about ecological poverty add a new dimension to development practice through *panchayats*.

In addition to their work in *panchayati raj* institutions, WVGs have shown a keen interest in increasing their visibility in formal political processes. For example, in 2006, they had collectively nominated a poor, rural woman to contest for the seat of the member of legislative assembly (MLA) in statewide elections. The campaign ran on donations collected by WVGs from villages. The whole experience of rural women participating freely in state-wide elections to secure their political rights has resulted in more women finding the courage to take part. In the 2008 *panchayat* elections, hundreds of WVG members won the seats of ward members, *gram pradhan* (head of the village), and members of the block development committees and of district councils (see Sara and Pande 2008).

Further, the political parties and the local administration have learnt the hard way that acts of corruption and of injustice to women can trigger uproar in the state, particularly after an incident in August 2008, when a WVG member was murdered in a village. To register their protest, thousands of women (and some men) began to organize demonstrations across the state, followed by a large rally in the district headquarters, ultimately resulting in the arrest of the suspected person. This transition to political activism has had the effect of bringing grassroots democracy to life and given them the motivation to continue in this work with courage and confidence.

Challenges

As UMP tries to bring women together to create an active movement for gender equality around reconstituted notions of community, a number of challenges emerge. A movement built from villages by rural women will invariably, and even voluntarily, experience certain limits on the pace of change, but the values of authenticity and reciprocity could only be nurtured by building on the local ways of life. Rural communities connect to the self and others through their own beliefs and intuitive understanding of the world. Creating a balance between those beliefs and those of the current development discourse is a challenge to UMP, especially because the latter itself has many flaws. The highly dynamic and complex nature of the current globalized economy with its focus on fast economic growth has an in-built potential to create confusion and to exacerbate instability and inequality in remote rural areas where markets are almost non-existent and people depend on subsistence agriculture. It is to contain the damaging effects of these external forces that UMP strives for, and builds on, the values with which it started over two decades ago.

For the last twenty years, WVGs have organized hundreds of demonstrations against indiscriminate use of forests, water and community land to safeguard their social, environmental and economic interests. Actively campaigning against the implementation of large projects that often curtail traditional rights and eschew community access to common resources, women have understood the fact that there is a major gap in the distribution of benefits that requires frugality on the part of communities but ensures abundance for the rich and powerful.

The benefits of the work of UMP also present a challenge because several activities, such as establishing plantations of broad-leaf seedlings in village commons, are likely to come to full fruition after several years of nurture and care. With the current rate of migration of the relatively affluent families from the villages to cities, UMP hopes that saplings planted today will be used by the poor of tomorrow. The abstract ethics of environmentalism, on the other hand, which advocates afforestation to prevent climate change or to minimize the effects of global warming, seems to lack the potential to motivate rural communities to plant and nurture trees for these global benefits.

Conclusion

Originally, UMP worked with the idea of a daily commitment and discipline towards WVGs, creating a holding space for women's concerns with the motivation of providing solutions to collective problems. Over the years, certain patterns have emerged that could be picked up by other groups for use in their own work. The trends of UMP's evolution can be sketched as follows:

- women expressing concern about their children's education and health;
- getting organized;
- learning to plan and prioritize women's needs;
- taking up small projects for their village;
- establishing themselves as strong groups;
- addressing several issues simultaneously;
- gaining the status of community-based institutions;
- learning by intervening in government programmes and policies;
- political activism;
- managing and sustaining work for the last two decades;
- wanting to do more.

This system design helps in understanding how women's concerns change as they learn to prioritize their own needs over others', and with time make various choices presenting a more holistic way of development. It cautions, however, against a rigid structure of activities, advocating instead a flexible approach capable of addressing deeper undercurrents that influence gender concerns in societies.

In the context of the increasing effects of globalization in India, the work of UMP shows that the Himalayan women continue to adopt a way of life that professes the principles of self-reliance and self-regulation through community restoration by reclaiming women's rights. UMP is a network of rural women that enfolds within its gamut a set of tested thoughts and practices that work in villages. However, the views of UMP alone do not hold the power to achieve the goal of gender equality in every society; they can at best provide insights and inform choices to move towards that goal.

Notes

1 For more details about USNPSS, see www.ueec.org.in. This chapter draws on various USNPSS annual reports, available at USNPSS, Almora.
2 'Road head' is widely used in the area to mean the last point that the motorable road goes to, i.e. the point at which mountain footpaths or horse trails connect to motorable road.

References

Pande, A. (2007) 'Nuances of microfinance, gender and development in Uttarakhand', unpublished paper, Uttarakhnad Seva Nidhi Paryavaran Shiksha Sansthan, Almora.
Sara, D. and A. Pande (2008) 'When a woman campaigns, women win', International Museum of Women, online exhibition: 'Women, Power and Politics', www.imow.org/wpp/stories/viewStory?storyid=1827 (accessed 20 September 2011).

4
Negotiating Patriarchies
Women Fisheries Workers Build SNEHA in Tamil Nadu
••
Jesu Rethinam[1]

The fisheries sector is a major source of employment in Asia. This employment extends beyond fishing *per se* to include a range of other activities such as marketing, processing and net making, with roughly three persons working onshore in fisheries-related activities for each person who fishes. Women play an important part in several activities but are less well represented in national or regional fish-worker organizations than in community and local-level organizations. Women's participation, it has been suggested, broadens the agenda of fish-worker organizations to include issues that concern the quality of life, such as access to health, sanitation and education; in particular, women bring a community perspective to the fisheries debate (Sharma 2005).

The experiences of women's participation in local and community-based organizations; the constraints faced; the different perspective they bring; and the ways in which meaningful participation can be strengthened are explored in this chapter through the experiences of one such organization. SNEHA (Social Need Education and Human Awareness) works with women in marine fishing, the dominant sub-sector in the fishing industry, in Tamil Nadu in India. It is active in around 51 marine-fishing villages in the Coromandel coastal area of the state. SNEHA started work in 1984 when there were very few NGOs working with fishing communities, or indeed anywhere on the coast of Tamil Nadu. It was founded by a young man, Christy, who himself came from a fishing community. His aim in setting up SNEHA was to spread the benefits of education, particularly among the women of the community, and to work with them in other ways as needed.

Coastal villages are populated mainly by the fishing community, with a smaller presence of other caste groups.[2] Initially a community-based and community-managed activity, the fishing sector has been changed dramatically by new technologies and trade liberalization. While the impact of these changes was evident from the 1960s, there has been much more rapid change in the post-1980 period, which saw liberalization of economic policies across the Asian region and a new emphasis on increasing trade and foreign exchange earnings. The 'blue revolution', a concerted effort to increase the output of the fisheries sector that has the support of the government, is affecting fishing communities in varying ways. On the one hand, mechanization has opened up new work opportunities for erstwhile non-fishing communities and investment opportunities for capitalists. On the other hand, the situation of small-scale fisheries and those dependent on these as a livelihood is increasingly vulnerable. The coastal villages where SNEHA works are thus in the middle of many changes in methods of fishing and ways of life.

Patriarchy and power in the fishing communities

Fishing communities in Tamil Nadu have long been governed by caste *panchayats* (or *katta panchayats*), which are male-dominated institutions primarily concerned with conserving 'tradition' by prescribing norms of behaviour. These are customary institutions, to be distinguished from the fishermen's cooperatives, which first emerged in the 1960s, or the elected *gram panchayats*, which are constitutionally mandated local governance institutions, collectively known as the '*panchayati raj* institutions', created by the 73rd amendment to the Indian

Constitution and in force since 1993. The caste *panchayat* takes upon itself the role of maintaining social order, celebrating religious festivals, giving rulings on local disputes, and acting as self-appointed custodian of village morality. It plays an explicit role in village politics. Caste *panchayats* have no legal sanction and in many villages membership is a hereditary position. The leaders, or *thalaivars,* were called *Natars* and the baton passed from father to son. Some of this has changed over the years and in many places there is now an informal electoral system for choosing the leaders. Not surprisingly, they are almost always the wealthiest boat owners. For men, power derived from the caste *panchayat* and power derived from participation in economic activity, income and wealth reinforce each other. The situation is different for women. Women are not members of the caste *panchayats,* but are required to conform to their rules – which primarily include rules around marriage and the performance of rituals, but extend beyond that into acceptable norms of behaviour in economic or political life. Thus there is a lack of congruence between women's economic, social and political rights, as enshrined in the law, and the behaviour deemed socially acceptable, as monitored by the caste *panchayats.*

The caste *panchayats* have money at their disposal; they are wealthy because of a system of 'taxation' with which the community complies. Each household makes a contribution, which is intended for management of community affairs. Membership of these *panchayats* in coastal fishing villages of Tamil Nadu requires that one be male, a member of the fishing community, and a local resident. The list of members thus coincides with the list of adult men from the fishing community in the village. Women are not eligible for membership. The *panchayats* argue that women are contained within the household and their welfare is the responsibility of men in the family. They are not required to pay a tax as individuals and, in fact, there is no concept of membership as an individual. The system expects the extended household to include and care for deserted or separated women.

The formal legal system has condemned the actions of the caste *panchayats*. The Madras High Court has directed the government to pass an ordinance to ban them on the Coromandel coast. In a judgement given by Justice M. Karpagavinayagam it is stated that actions of *katta panchayats* amount to a violation of human rights.[3] A Tamil Nadu Government Order issued in December 2003 explicitly states that *katta panchayats* have no legal sanction and that government officers should not participate in nor pay heed to their decisions. Despite these clear statements, the influence of the caste *panchayats* remains strong in the fishing villages.

The gender division of labour within fishing communities

The actual work of fishing is done by men. Both men and women are involved in the pre-harvest activities (such as preparing nets) and post-harvesting work is largely done by women. Women are responsible for household work, including preparing food to be taken on long fishing trips, and care of children and the elderly. Within this division of labour, women are responsible for the marketing of fish. They are therefore less secluded than women in home-based work or within traditional farming households. In addition, a share of the catch retained for home consumption accrues to, and is directly managed by women.

In fishing communities, previously the various activities relating to fishing were performed by different members of the household and the major part of the catch was used for self-consumption. With the increasing commercialization of the sector, wage work has grown and many activities are the task of both paid workers and unpaid household workers, depending on the size of the operation. Women in the fishing villages where small-scale fisheries are still dominant market the fish and have a more important economic role than the women in larger fishing villages, where new technology and larger boats have increased the scale of fishing and output, and where fish merchants dominate.

The paradoxical situation is that in the smaller fishing communities women are expected to comply fully with the caste *panchayats*, yet their traditional role within the fishing community gives them the right to sell the fish, receive the money, and decide whether the money is to be saved or spent, and on what. They participate in decision making on the buying of nets, boats and other fishing equipment, as well as on the handling of domestic purchases. In larger villages where capital-intensive technology has expanded the scale of the activity and the financing comes from outside capitalists, women's economic role has diminished and they have lost their traditional right to the catch. There are various adverse effects that have been noted. For example, the introduction of the net-making machine in Tamil Nadu in the early 1980s meant that hundreds of women lost work. In addition, increased commercialization has been accompanied by the giving and taking of dowries, which in turn has an impact on women's role and status (Nayak 2005).

Community fisheries contribute to food security, as fish is a crucial source of cheap protein. Today, in the areas where SNEHA works, by convention approximately 25 per cent of the catch is given by fishermen to the women of their households to be used for family consumption and local sale. Some fish may be dried and salted and kept for later consumption. The other 75 per cent of the catch is taken by the men to the auction halls that have been constructed by the government. These halls provide a common space where fishermen bring their catch and buyers come to bid, and this enables fishermen to sell at the best price offered. The buyers include traders dealing in export markets and with other parts of the state and country.

A survey carried out by SNEHA to identify the potential members of the community for the formation of women's groups showed that with the commercialization of activities, women's roles have also changed in many ways. For example, while auctioning fish is mainly done by men, it is also an important activity for middle-aged and older women with fewer household responsibilities. Among women fish workers, single women were found to constitute nearly 30 per cent.

Caste panchayats and the fishing industry

The sale of fish, on the face of it, involves a buyer and a seller, but in practice there can be a long chain of intermediaries. There are profits to be made when the buyer represents an export market. Caste *panchayats* have developed various ways to maximize their earnings from the industry. Space in the market place where fish is sold is leased out by the government. *Panchayats* from the big fishing villages take turns at leasing this space through collusive bidding. Individual spots within the auction hall are then sub-leased so as to make some profit. The sub-lessee in turn collects a levy from the fish vendors.

A fraction of the catch is auctioned at the landing centre and both men and women who sell fish here are required to pay a levy to the caste *panchayat*. But auctions at the auction halls require a similar levy only from women auctioneers. Men do not have to pay this levy because it is said that, as members of the caste *panchayat* which has leased the space, and which receives a regular tax payment from them, they are exempted from the market levy. Revenues collected in this way go into the village common fund.

The auction trade is extremely male-dominated and women who work as auctioneers have a difficult time. There is intense competition for places in the auction hall. Women who want to work as auctioneers have to be extremely 'bold' and able to hold their own with men. This is a new type of work for women. Women have always sold fish in the market, but small-scale and local marketing is distinguished from the cut-throat competition of the auction halls. SNEHA's finding is that women who step into new roles are frequently subject to sexual harassment at work and are reportedly often forced by boat owners to have sex if they want to continue to work. Other problems include transport difficulties, since women rarely have their own means of transport and there is limited access to public transport. They do not have ice boxes to preserve fish. Fish markets do not have amenities like dormitories or crèches, good toilets or clean drinking water facilities, which are seen at other markets where women go to sell produce. Better-equipped markets include the agriculture producers' marketing centres and the cocoon markets, where women are allotted separate spaces to keep their produce and separate rooms for women are marked for overnight stay if they are not able to get back to their villages late in the evenings.

SNEHA's approach and strategies

Early issues and approaches

SNEHA started its work by focusing on women from the fishing community. It began by organizing women into groups (known as *sangams*) in the villages of Thanjavur and Karaikal districts of coastal Tamil Nadu. The size of the *sangams* varied according to the size of the village, with larger groups for the larger villages. SNEHA sought to draw in women from the poorest strata, who were engaged in small-scale and shallow sea fishing, and vendors' families. Households with fishing as the primary source of income face seasonality in earnings and are vulnerable to various factors. When the weather is rainy and stormy, the government issues a warning against going to sea for fishing. This may last from a few days to a few weeks. In addition, the government has banned the entry of fishing boats and trolleys for a period of 45 days during the breeding season. During these periods when fishing activities cannot be carried out, many people are short of money even for daily expenses. At such times, women are under pressure to withdraw any savings they may have been able to make from their earnings. Once *sangams* were formed, women were thus encouraged to begin saving on a regular basis in amounts that all could afford, and to engage in small-scale income-generating activities to supplement their income from fishing. They could also decide whether to lend to members and for what purposes.

Once the groups had become established, they were able to identify issues of concern. These were largely practical issues like roads, drinking water and electricity: these are basic concerns for both women and men in rural communities. As a result, they received the support of the men from their families as well as the caste *panchayats*, who considered these issues to be of benefit to the entire village. They were successful in pressurizing the government to respond to some of these concerns, and this gave the women's groups the strength to take up a wider range of issues. Some examples will illustrate the range of issues around which women mobilized.

For example, women vendors faced a major problem in getting space on the buses to transport their baskets of fish for sale in local towns and villages. The groups took this up with the administration as a basic livelihood issue, with the support of men within the community. As a result, space was allocated in two morning buses for women travelling with baskets of fish to nearby markets and residential areas within a range of 30–40 km, and again in the late afternoon for their return trips.

One incident related to the behaviour of the shopkeeper of a fair price shop[4] who was known to routinely ill-treat women who came to the shop. On one occasion, a member of one of the groups (the Nambiar Nagar *sangam*) was given less than her entitlement of sugar. Her protests were met with abusive language from the shopkeeper. She returned to her village and mobilized the other members of her group and together they went to the collector's office with a petition. This led to the suspension and transfer of the shopkeeper.

In another place, members of the *sangam* were concerned about the sale of home-made liquor (*arrack*) near a residential area. They decided to petition the collector and went to see him in person. They were successful in closing down the *arrack* shop.

One of the strongest groups is the Karaikalmedu *sangam*, which has 170 members. It has dealt with family disputes, and other such matters that would normally be taken to the caste *panchayat*. Its presence came to be regarded as a threat by the *panchayat*. In a recent incident, a conflict broke out during which one of the group members was alleged to have thrown chilli powder at her opponent. The *panchayat* wanted the group to expel this woman. The *sangam* took no action against her. This became a matter of prestige for the caste *panchayat* leaders. They summoned the group to the *panchayat* meeting, made other (false) allegations against them, and forced the president of the *sangam* to resign. But the members did not let matters rest there. A number of meetings were called to protest the *panchayat*'s action until finally it was forced to undertake in writing that it would never again interfere with the functioning of the *sangam*. This was the first time ever that a group of women had stood up to the caste *panchayat* and forced it to retract a decision.

In Kilinchalmedu, the growing profitability of the chilli/coriander powder supply unit run by the local women's group came to the attention of the caste *panchayat*, which decided to ask for the accounts of the *sangam* and to demand that a share of the profit be contributed to the village fund. The women discussed this demand and decided that if they were to contribute a share of their profits to the village funds, they would have to be given equal representation in the caste *panchayat* system. Faced with this demand, the *panchayat* decided to drop the matter.

In 1992, the groups mobilized around the rape and murder of a five-year-old girl from the fishing community by a man from her village, but not from the fishing community. SNEHA supported them in taking the case to court and the accused man was convicted. There was a second case – the rape and murder of a ten-year-old girl – but the perpetrator was not known. Women's groups across the state mobilized to demand action. Members of Tamil Nadu Women's Network and Tamil Nadu Women's Coordination Committee also participated in large numbers to show solidarity. Although legal intervention was not possible, the support they gained, the increased awareness, and joint action with men helped to strengthen the women's groups.

Sangams and self-help groups: challenges in organizing
In the early 1990s, the Indian government adopted a Self-Help Group (SHG)/Bank Linkage Programme which required rural banks, nationalized since 1969, to lend money to SHGs through

the intermediation of NGOs. Large numbers of SHGs came to be formed as NGOs, microfinance organizations, government officials and even bankers began setting up SHGs, increasingly seen as vehicles for the promotion of microcredit and various government development programmes. SNEHA also came under considerable pressure to form self-help groups in order to access government schemes and programmes but found that formation of SHGs led to a disintegration of the groups that had evolved organically. After debate and reflection within SNEHA, it was decided that it was necessary to keep the larger groups, which had evolved around a range of shared concerns in fishing and the community. For the narrower purpose of credit and savings and for accessing government schemes, women were organized into small groups (SHGs). Within a village, the SHGs were networked so that a bigger group at the village level existed to take on larger issues. The groups were also federated at the *taluk* (block/sub-district) and district levels. This helped to maintain linkages across groups and so allow common issues to be addressed collectively.

Engaging with men

Around 1994, SNEHA decided to tackle the fact that it was only women who came to the large rallies organized by the groups to draw attention to issues that affected the whole fishing sector, such as protecting the marine environment. It was not easy to work out how to draw more men in. At a purely practical level, men were out at sea from 3 a.m. till late evening, depending on the availability of fish. They were often out at sea for two or three days at a time until they got a catch. The caste *panchayats* had control over money in the village fund but were reluctant to use it to support protests, despite the collective nature of the issues. By contrast, the money that women collected as a group was being used to raise issues that affected the whole sector.

What this meant was that women had to earn a livelihood, manage care and domestic tasks – and take on community-wide issues as well. This imposed an enormous burden on them.

SNEHA tried to organize young men's groups and encourage their involvement in these sector-wide issues. In a few instances this was successful. However, when these young men started raising questions in the caste *panchayat* meetings, this was met with hostility by their elders. Young men are expected to follow the lead of their elders and their active stance was leading to a potential schism in the male community. The *panchayats* were able to tolerate women getting organized, but they forbade the organizing of youth, saying that youth cannot function as a separate group. This put an end to SNEHA's attempts to engage with men around common concerns.

SNEHA needs all the support it can get to carry out its strategies and cannot afford to alienate any section of the community if it can be helped. Despite the patriarchal structure of the traditional system, and its bias in favour of the rich and powerful within the community, SNEHA has tried to avoid viewing it in oppositional terms. It has regularly invited members of the *panchayat* to meetings on sector-wide issues and sought their support. This has helped to create some 'lobbying space' within the *panchayats*. But while livelihood matters might unite the men and women, gender relations are very sensitive and generally viewed as a private matter. The groups have taken up matters of women's rights but *panchayat* members have remained passive.

Building alliances

Small-scale fishing is under great threat from government policies such as the 'harbour-based fisheries policy' (a term coined by activists), which displaces and destroys the shoreline fisheries and marginalizes the women vendors.[5]

In 1987, SNEHA began interacting with the National Fish Workers Forum (NFF). NFF organized a national-level campaign and a march through the coast in 1989 under the slogan 'Protect Water Protect Life' to protect the rights of small-scale fishing, the future of their coastal communities and the marine ecosystems upon which they depend. Large numbers of men and women from the fishing community participated in this coastal march. In

1994, SNEHA allied with activist groups to address the issue of industrial aquaculture. It started a campaign and provided support to a public interest litigation that was taken to the Supreme Court: SNEHA collected field-level data for the Citizens Committee Report about the impact of aquaculture on fertile lands, mangroves, coastal ecology, lagoons and ocean resources. It also organized public hearings. The views of different groups were noted, including those of scientists and environmentalists. These views were presented to the Supreme Court and the Citizens Committee Report was heavily quoted in the verdict. The judgement says that 'the damage caused to ecology and economics by aquaculture farming is higher than the earnings from the sale of coastal aquaculture produce'. The judgement also prohibits any aquaculture farms within 1,000 metres of a lake, and forbids the use or conversion of agricultural lands, salt pans, mangroves, wet lands, forest lands, village common lands and land meant for public construction purposes. This decision gave a lot of strength to the women who were part of the campaign. For the first time, they had been able to voice their concerns regarding loss of livelihood from the reduced area available for shallow-sea fishing and the impact of commercialization and trade expansion on their livelihoods.

SNEHA is also an active member of the Coastal Action Network (CAN), a state-level network for the protection of coastal ecology and the livelihoods of coastal people, which was formed in 1996. It has been involved in various campaigns promoted by CAN to protect the coast from environmental degradation and disaster. The impact of these campaigns is evident at the policy level: for example, the government withdrew the draft Coastal Zone Management Act of 2008 because of sustained opposition, although the overall approach has not changed. The NFF led a 6,000 km coastal march in 2008 protesting against the draft Coastal Zone Management Notification of 2008, which, it was felt, did not protect the rights and livelihoods of traditional fishing communities. SNEHA's participation has ensured that, within the larger debate, issues of women find a place and that the whole community is sensitized to the fact that decisions and choices made in fishing technology and fisheries policy will influence the role played by women, their ability to provide household food security, and their traditional space in small-scale vending. A bias towards larger boats, for example, will reduce village-based employment for women.[6]

Networking has helped to strengthen the village-level groups and to raise their awareness on various issues – for example, the impact of shrimp culture, women's vulnerability and the incidence of rape and violence. It has also helped build solidarity and bring the issues faced by women to the notice of local government officials. It has exposed them to new issues and collective learning from experiences. SNEHA has been able to take the micro-level struggle to the national level through its participation in organized advocacy.

Gender issues in the post-tsunami period

The destruction wrought by the tsunami of 2004 in the coastal areas of Tamil Nadu brought a whole new set of challenges. After the tsunami, many more NGOs, including international NGOs, came into the area. These new entrants either directly or through the *gram panchayats*, were in charge of the distribution of large relief and rehabilitation packages. The traditional governance system was hence somewhat weakened, although it reasserted its supremacy within a short while. SNEHA became a voice of opposition to the creation of new channels, and wanted local capacities to be strengthened rather than have new and external groups involved in the management of rehabilitation.

The tsunami had some unexpected effects on family life and gender relations. One was the considerable rise in child marriage, which had been on the decline prior to the tsunami. One reason was that relief and rehabilitation packages needed a family identity to procure a ration card. Many child marriages took place to fulfil this identity: as newly married couples, young people could be given ration cards as independent families. Further reasons include the lack of security in temporary camps and the increased number of single parents with adolescent girls. SNEHA took up the child marriage issue with the state and in its own programme of awareness raising. One of the ways in which it tried to raise awareness among young people was by forming groups for children aged ten to fourteen years. These groups were known as '*Bal panchayats*' or 'children's governance bodies', where children could talk about their problems and any issues that concerned them, facilitated by SNEHA's representatives. A few children would be elected by the larger group, and encouraged to receive complaints from other children and seek a consensual resolution.

The federation also attempted to form similar groups with adolescents (fourteen to eighteen years) to help them address their own needs. It was not socially acceptable for adolescent girls and boys to be part of one group, so separate groups were formed for boys and girls. These groups were also encouraged to think about ways to address larger issues, including child marriages and the displacement that took place after tsunami. The boys' groups have not been successful, for reasons similar to those discussed earlier in relation to building alliances with men. Since boys are future members of the caste *panchayat*, and would have responsibility for maintaining social norms and traditions in that role, the caste *panchayats* strongly resisted the efforts of SNEHA to organize boys: this was seen as a threat to their supremacy and a potential dilution of their concerns and priorities. Adolescent boys were permitted, however, to form their own clubs around sporting activities.

Another important gender issue that surfaced post-tsunami was the re-canalization of women who had lost children in the tsunami and were under societal and familial pressure to give birth to another child. Many women had undergone surgical sterilization before the tsunami. In this area, as in Tamil Nadu as a whole, sterilization is the contraception method most strongly promoted by the government, with women as young as 24 being sterilized once they have two children. The government supported re-canalization surgery in government hospitals, or paid up to Rs25,000 (approximately US$550) for this treatment in private hospitals for women under 45 years old.[7] In some cases there were reports of domestic violence when women did not want to undergo re-canalization surgery. Given high levels of anaemia in Tamil Nadu, pregnant women even as young as 30 fell into the 'high risk' category. SNEHA encouraged women to get medical advice on the advisability of re-canalization surgery. Case studies are being documented by SNEHA and a report is being drafted, with findings and recommendations for influencing policies on this issue.

Relief and rehabilitation

Because the federation had established a presence at *taluk* and district levels, its members were able to intervene in relief and rehabilitation after the tsunami. One of the significant impacts of the women's groups was their ability to ensure that single women were included on equal terms with male-headed households in the list of beneficiaries. They were also able to see that benefits reached the excluded, including elderly people. Initially the focus of relief and rehabilitation was on the marine-fishing community, which incurred major losses in tsunami and was also well organized. Because Dalits and other communities not directly engaged in fishing were not organized, it was difficult for them to access relief efforts. SNEHA encouraged the organizing of these groups and subsequently promoted their access to relief efforts. However, compensation given by the state for tsunami losses was designed and implemented based on asset loss. This excluded those who did not have assets in their own names, such as labourers and women fish workers, especially single women, instead compensating only men with boats, engines and nets. The rehabilitation experience underlined the need to continue the work to visibilize women's labour.

Many income-generating programmes for women were implemented after the tsunami. Most of the NGOs tried to implement a number of innovative programmes with the idea of creating other livelihood options beyond fisheries. SNEHA lobbied with NGOs and funders to emphasize that when fishing became possible again, many women would go back to vending, so there was a strong need to investigate avenues for strengthening this area. The fisheries sector is not only the primary livelihood for this community, it is also a way of life, so SNEHA sought to use this opportunity to make some aspects of it easier for women – for example, by acquiring vehicles in some villages to take women to market. But the *panchayats* were eager to control the management of these vehicles and use them as village property, as they did for other assets created in the villages. This was prevented in various ways. In some cases, letters were needed from the *panchayat* promising not to interfere in how the women would use these assets. In others, vehicles were given to *taluk* and district level federations instead of village groups, so that women could retain control over them.

In addition, SNEHA's livelihood-recovery programme focused on coastal and Dalit women, who were neglected by the official rehabilitation programme. It provided vending accessories to women, seed money to groups to restart their traditional livelihoods, reconstruction of the drying yards at landing sites, and other interventions designed to support women in fishing, including the formation of a fish vendors' forum was another contribution.[8]

A lot of money was also pumped into the area by the state, donor or international organizations for rebuilding houses. Many NGOs and INGOs were formed to build houses without making any effort to find out what people actually wanted. SNEHA strongly contested this approach and developed a shelter recovery programme protecting the livelihoods of coastal communities by promoting *in situ* housing – that is, with people having access to their own land rather than being evicted to other places. This shelter programme is driven by the survivors, almost all women, and responds to their needs at a pace of recovery determined by them and not by donors' budget deadlines. SNEHA's input was in enabling people to rebuild or repair their own houses, with financial requirements being estimated by group members and engineers and given to individual beneficiaries through their bank accounts in instalments. The amount of financial support varied from Rs5,000 to Rs75,000 (approximately US$110–1,600), depending on the damage or need, and was not a fixed amount. SNEHA did not itself build houses.

Current concerns, broader challenges

Approaches to economic development: the harbour policy

Post-tsunami rehabilitation has been accompanied by a strong bias towards large-scale and export-oriented fishing, and investments by multinationals. Coastal development is increasingly linked to tourism. SNEHA is working with various forums such as the Coastal Action Network and the National Fish Workers Forum on this issue, protesting against over-exploitation of marine resources and the corresponding decline of traditional fishing methods and increased vulnerability of fishing communities, especially women, within them.

In the context of tsunami relief and rehabilitation, there was a suggestion that coastal communities should be shifted further away from the coast – but this would involve significant increases in travel time for trading and collecting fish for the women. The Indian government is rapidly promoting harbours all along the coast. The total number of ports in India was twelve before 2000, but increased to 185 by 2006 and to 200 by 2009. Twenty-eight new harbours are being planned and promoted in Tamil Nadu alone. These attempts to promote harbour fisheries instead of shoreline fisheries tends to reduce women's participation.

Social security

Both categories of women fish-workers, paid and unpaid, lacked access to welfare benefits under the Manual Workers Welfare Board as they were not classified as 'workers'.[9] Even the social benefit schemes implemented by the government discriminated against women: for example, in the off-season monsoon, men were given social benefits to compensate for lack of income, but women were not, even if they were contributing considerably to the fishing economy.

More recently, the Tamil Nadu Fisherman and Labourers Engaged in Fishing and Allied Activities (Social Security and Welfare) Act 2007 has been enacted. This provides for comprehensive social security for fish workers. The various welfare benefits are administered through the Fisheries Welfare Board. Continuous pressure from SNEHA and other groups has meant that women fish workers can now be enrolled as members of the Welfare Boards. The Act identifies several categories of eligible workers and ancillary activities – such as 'beach workers', 'boat building yard workers', 'fishermen', 'labourers', 'processing labourers' and 'small-scale fish distributors'.[10]

Research and continued struggle

Research has been an important tool in SNEHA's work, starting with simple surveys to find out the numbers of women engaged in fishing and their varying needs. The tsunami experience highlighted the need to continue with data collection and analysis to make women's contributions more visible to policy makers. It also generated the need for specific types of more technical work on reproductive health and the impacts of surgical interventions on women. More recently, SNEHA has undertaken research on value chain analysis with a gender perspective, to contribute to a better understanding of how to implement economic programmes for women and how to add value to the product in a manner such that women can gain more revenue at each step of the value chain from the post-harvesting stage (auctioning, vending, drying, processing) to marketing (from the local to the state level).

Strengthening women's role in the marketing of fish is a key concern for SNEHA. Traditionally women were responsible for marketing, but one of the unanticipated outcomes of tsunami rehabilitation processes was the formation of several men's cooperatives formed for the purpose of auctioning and marketing fish. These cooperatives were set up by male-headed NGOs that were new to the area and lacked knowledge of established marketing practices. The result has been that women auctioneers and vendors are now facing competition from organized men's cooperatives that did not exist earlier.

Conclusion

SNEHA's experience with women fish workers shows at one level the challenges faced by small-scale fishing communities within a development trajectory that emphasizes mechanized, large-scale and commercial exploitation. SNEHA's strategies include national and regional advocacy, especially with the government, in partnership with other organized fish workers' movements, seeking to maintain a space for small-scale fishing and in support of household food security. The specific contribution SNEHA has made in this struggle has been to ensure that the gender implications of new policies are made clear to the whole group of fish-workers as well as to the state.

Specific to the context in which SNEHA works is the struggle to develop more equitable gender roles and relations, in a context of persisting male-dominated and tradition-bound governance structures that oppose changing roles. At the local level, SNEHA's work with women extends from organizing around practical and everyday concerns to dealing with conflicts – especially with the traditional caste *panchayats*. While SNEHA does not set itself up in opposition to the caste *panchayats*, conflicts do come up and are constantly being negotiated by the village groups.

The tsunami and the subsequent inflow of relief and rehabilitation money led to new concerns – women's reproductive health and child marriage, for example – and the need to develop sustained advocacy around these. It also led to the creation of new groups and the stronger emergence of men in fish marketing. Creating and maintaining spaces for women to vend is a key objective of SNEHA's efforts. While specific strategies keep changing and developing in response to need, the overall approach of supporting women in their daily and practical needs as a path to strategic change and new relationships within the household, village and larger community is vindicated by the achievements so far.

Notes

1 This chapter is based on Jesu Rethinam's presentation at the conference on 'Organising Women in the Informal Economy: Lessons from Practice', New Delhi, 20–21 October 2008 (organized by the Institute of Social Studies Trust and Pathways of Women's Empowerment RPC, a programme of DfID). It also uses additional information contributed in follow-up interviews and drawn from available reports on the organization's work.

2 The fishing people here are known as 'Meenavars' or 'Pattinavars'; other caste groups include members of the Vanniyars.

3 *The Deccan Herald,* 14 April 2004, http://infochangeindia.org/ 200406143459/Human-Rights/News/Ban-village-courts-Madras-High-Court-tells-TN-govt.html (accessed 9 April 2010).

4 These were set up under the Public Distribution System to provide rations at fixed prices.

5 The 'harbour-based fisheries policy' refers to the policy emphasis on large-scale fishing. Shoreline fisheries have been reduced by construction of stone walls across the beach for tourism purposes. Only small gaps which have been left between the walls are now available to anchor fishing boats.

6 For more details, see National Fishworkers' Forum (2009).

7 See G.O. Ms. No. 30, Health and Family Welfare (F1) Dept., =dt.02.03.2005.

8 This programme was reported in Bhatt and Krishnamurthy (2007).

9 Welfare Boards are usually tripartite in nature, run by representatives of government, industry and workers.

10 For a discussion of the national and international thinking around fish worker rights, see Sankaran *et al.* (2008).

References

Bhatt, M. R. and R. Krishnamurthy (2007) 'Women lead tsunami recovery: SNEHA evaluation', mimeo, 15 December.

National Fishworkers Forum (2009) 'Let's protect fish and fishermen: towards revising the draft marine fisheries regulation and management act, 2009', www.trinet.in/?q=taxonomy/term/47 (accessed 23 September 2011).

Nayak, N. (2005) 'Sharpening the interlinkages: towards feminist perspectives of livelihoods in coastal communities', paper presented at seminar on 'Women's Livelihood in Coastal Communities: Management of the Environment and Natural Resources', Institute of Social Studies Trust (ISST), Bangalore, 6 June.

Sankaran, K., S. Sinha and R. Madhav (2008) 'WIEGO Law pilot project on the informal economy: fish workers background note', http://previous.wiego.org/informal_economy_law/india/content/iei_background_paper_oaw_and_law.pdf (accessed 23 September 2011).

Sharma, C. (2005) 'Women of coastal fishing communities in the Asian region: an agenda for research', paper presented at seminar on 'Women's Livelihood in Coastal Communities: Management of the Environment and Natural Resources', Institute of Social Studies Trust (ISST), Bangalore, 6 June.

5

'If You Don't See a Light in the Darkness, You Must Light a Fire'

Brazilian Domestic Workers' Struggle for Rights

••

Andrea Cornwall with Creuza Maria Oliveira
and Terezinha Gonçalves

Brazil's domestic workers constitute 17 per cent of the country's women workers; 93 per cent are women and the majority are black.[1] They are the largest professional category in the country at 7.23 million workers, and are amongst the most poorly paid, marginalized and exploited:[2] 27.7 per cent of them receive half of the minimum salary and 41.3 per cent receive between half (US$130) and the full minimum monthly salary (US$260). Nationally, almost three quarters of domestic workers do not have a Worker's Card, which would entitle them to labour rights and formalize their status as employees (IPEA 2011). Most work for monthly pay, many working more than 44 hours a week; a growing number, a fifth of all domestic workers in some municipal areas (PED 2011) are 'daily' cleaners, who experience precarious employment security and have no access to labour rights such as sickness or maternity pay. Almost half a million Brazilian girls are domestic workers, doing all types of housework and working long hours with little or no financial remuneration. Almost half are below the age of sixteen – a likely underestimate given the illegality of employing children under that age – the vast majority of whom have had disrupted or no access to schooling (Gonçalves 2010).

Shaped by the legacy of slavery, and associated with distinctive forms of gender, race and class exploitation (Ávila 2008, Santos

149

2008, Gonçalves 2010), the domestic workers' struggle for rights and recognition has been complex and difficult. Yet they have wrested a formal recognition of rights that were only a distant dream when domestic workers began mobilizing almost a century ago. Constitutional provision now guarantees the right to the minimum wage, advance notice (30 days), one day off a week, maternity leave (120 days), paternity leave (five days) and an extra third of a minimum salary before taking holidays. These rights were won in the making of the 1988 'Citizens' Constitution' that marked the rebirth of democracy in Brazil after twenty years of military dictatorship. In 2000, these rights were further extended to include the right to unemployment compensation.

The election as President in 2003 of the Workers' Party candidate, Lula da Silva, and his re-election in 2006, has yielded gains for workers of all kinds – amongst them domestic workers, who gained the right to twenty days' vacation and time off for civil and religious holidays, the guarantee of a return to work for pregnant women, and the recognition that employers may not deduct housing, food and personal hygiene products used at the place of work from their wages. In 2008, the government prohibited adolescents and children under eighteen years old from doing domestic work, in line with ILO Convention 182 on the elimination of the worst kinds of child labour. The ILO Convention 189 of June 2011, on the minimum conditions for domestic work, is still under debate in Brazil. Ratification would require the amendment of Article 7 of the Constitution, to extend to domestic workers benefits enjoyed by all other workers – and so fulfil the hard-fought struggle of the domestic workers' rights movement for their recognition as part of the Brazilian working class.[3]

The story of Brazil's national federation of domestic workers' union (FENATRAD) and their strategies of alliance building, mobilization and tactical engagement is one from which broader lessons can be learnt about mobilizing informal sector workers. This chapter tells this story as recounted in a series of life-history interviews carried out in the period 2006–9 with one of the key figures in the struggle for domestic workers' rights in Brazil, Creuza Oliveira, then leader of FENATRAD, as part of a participatory research project on domestic workers' rights.[4]

The struggle for domestic workers' rights in Brazil

The quest for domestic workers' rights in Brazil began in the 1920s. Black women organized themselves in the Brazilian Black Front, arguing for the recognition and status of paid domestic work, with rights and duties as in any other work. This movement resulted in the creation in 1936 of the first domestic workers' association in Campinas in the southern Brazilian state of São Paulo, by a black communist activist named Laudelina de Campos Mello. Born on 12 October 1904, Laudelina started working as a domestic worker at the age of seven, became a lifelong activist at sixteen, and went on to join the Brazilian Communist Party (PCB). Concerned by the lack of recreational activities for black women, Laudelina became actively involved in promoting leisure along with politics; as President of the Campinas Professional Domestic Workers' Association from 1936 to 1949, she initiated a process of organizing that was the forerunner of today's FENATRAD (Pinto 1993).

Domestic workers' organization at national level began with an informal network of associations from various Brazilian states. This resulted in the creation of a National Front of Domestic Workers in 1981. This Front achieved recognition as the Domestic Workers National Council in 1985. In the wake of twenty years of military dictatorship, from 1964 to 1984, the political freedom to organize as unions in the new democracy gave the movement new impetus. The result was the creation of 45 unions in different Brazilian regions and the formation of the Domestic Workers National Council and of FENATRAD. There were also union affiliations to national and international labour organizations, which constituted the last step in recognition and consolidation of domestic workers' organizations in Brazil. The National Federation of Domestic Workers' Associations

(FENATRAD) was founded in 1997. In 1998, this Federation was affiliated to the National Confederation of the Workers of the Commerce and Services (CONTRACS), the Central Workers' Union (CUT) and the Latin American and Caribbean Domestic Workers' Confederation (CONLACTRAHO).

Political freedom brought other opportunities for the domestic workers' rights movement. As Brazil returned to democratic rule, there was a tremendous opening of spaces for citizens from all walks of life to come together and frame demands for rights in the new Constitution. Social movements – of women, of indigenous people, of black Brazilians – came together in deliberative fora, forging new alliances (Sader 1988). For the domestic workers' movement activists, these constitutional debates created opportunities for engagement with the women's movement and the black movement, which in turn influenced and provided support for their struggle for rights. The result was what came to be called the 'Citizens' Constitution': one of the longest and, at that time – 1988 – the most progressive in the world. In the Constitution were inscribed rights that domestic workers had been fighting for since Laudelina's times.

To give greater visibility to their cause and to strengthen their struggle for rights and recognition, domestic workers' organizations have sought to participate actively in various spaces of power and to seek representation in the legislature as well as a presence in a number of organs established by the executive branch of government. FENATRAD is present in various government bodies such as the National Council for the Promotion of Racial Equality and the National Council for the Defence of Women's Rights. These alliances with others working for gender and racial equality have become an important part of the strategy of advancing domestic workers' rights as workers, as women and as citizens.

The alliances domestic workers' organizations have made range from advocacy groups in Parliament to partnerships with international organizations such as the International Labour Organization (ILO), the United Nations Development Fund for Women (UNIFEM), the United Nations Children's Fund (UNICEF) and feminist NGOs. Other partnerships have been built with domestic workers' unions in Latin America. International cooperation projects have been important in obtaining financial resources to develop actions for collective empowerment. Broader perspectives are exchanged in meetings with other social movements such as the National and Latin-American Feminist Meetings, the Women's National and International Conferences, the Racial Equality National Conferences and Human Rights Conferences. Domestic workers' standpoints are now included in institutions such as the Child and Adolescent Defence Forum, the National Council of Defence of Women's Rights and the National Council of Promotion of Racial Equality, and in many other state and city councils where public policies are discussed and monitored.

The government has established a permanent negotiating platform with FENATRAD to debate problems standing in the way of rights for domestic workers – an initiative expressed in the 'Rights Cannot Be Less, Only More' campaign. In recent years, the government has worked with FENATRAD to implement the Domestic Workers' Citizenship Programme.[5] Proposed by domestic workers and aimed at professionalizing domestic work and raising awareness of domestic workers' rights, the programme has been transformed into policy. FENATRAD and the affiliated unions in the states of Bahia, Pernambuco, Sergipe, São Luiz, Rio de Janeiro and São Paulo – and a series of public agencies, as well as the ILO – actively participate in this process. The validation and management of the Citizen Domestic Work Plan is carried out through meetings and workshops with the presence of grassroots leaders and workers, union representatives and FENATRAD.

Organizing for change

How did the domestic workers' union manage to gain these openings? How did they manage to enlist members in a situation where so many of their would-be constituency work long hours in isolated conditions, moving long distances between home and work or living in the cramped 'servants' quarters' in employers' homes? How did they address the effects of marginalization, such as lack of confidence, lack of knowledge of rights, lack even of a sense of the right to have rights and fear of reprisals from employers? In the sections that follow, we draw out insights from life-history interviews with one of the Brazilian domestic workers' movement's leading organizers, Creuza Maria de Oliveira, former president of FENATRAD. Speaking both as an organizer, and as a black domestic worker who began her working life without rights, respect or wages, Creuza's story reveals the interplay between the personal and the political in the struggle of domestic workers for rights, representation and recognition. Through an analysis of the strategies and tactics that she and other domestic workers used to organize for change, we seek to explore some of the answers to these questions.

Starting to organize

Creuza Maria de Oliveira began her life in a poor neighbourhood in Salvador, the capital of the state of Bahia, in the late 1950s. Her parents had eloped from the rural interior to the city, running away from disapproving parents. Of their eight children, only three survived. When her father died, her mother returned to the interior, and left Creuza first with an aunt in town and then with her grandmother. She'd see her mother from time to time, and as her grandmother's health deteriorated, her mother took her home with her. Her mother had met a new partner, who moved in with them. Soon he started complaining about having too many mouths to feed and not wanting to have to look after Creuza and the other children. He was employed as a farm worker, drinking a lot, beating up her mother – and they were living from hand to mouth, often going hungry. His sister arranged a job for Creuza in a nearby town, as a nanny. She was ten years old. By the time she was a teenager she had been through a series of abusive employment situations – from being physically beaten, humiliated and sexually harassed, to being teased by the children she cared for and being made to feel worthless and ugly. And she had worked for these years without any pay.

Creuza reflects:[6]

I was always asking myself about my situation – about not earning any money, not having time off, about having so much to do, about having nowhere to live and having to live in the house of my employer. I found all this frustrating. I wanted to have my own house [many domestic workers have to live in their employers' houses or in rooms in informal settlements], I wanted to go home after work and go out, not to have to live all the time in the employer's house. And I kept asking myself, how is it that my employer can have time off, a decent wage, a house – and I can't? Why can't we domestic workers have this? And then I began to question this and wonder why other workers organize themselves in unions, and domestic workers don't. But up to then I'd never heard anyone talking about there being a union of domestic workers or a movement or anything.

In those days, every domestic worker had a little battery-operated radio that they would carry everywhere with them, with the sound turned down low. Creuza recalls:

There was one of those programmes where they have music and then interviews and then music again. I liked the music. I wasn't much interested in the information, but that day there was an interview with a woman who was running for municipal office. The DJ asked her if she was elected, what she would do. And she said various things about education, health and women's rights and the rights of domestic workers. When she said *that* it was like something completely new for me, I'd never heard anyone say that they were going to defend the rights of domestic workers. I turned up the radio. I stopped what I was doing – I was washing plates at the time – and I listened. She said it again, that she was going to fight for the rights of domestic workers. And the DJ asked her, 'But do domestic workers have a union?' She said, 'No, no, but they meet in Colégio Antônio Vieira every month on the second and fourth Sundays.' I drummed 'Colégio Antônio Vieira' into my head.

This was it, for me, this was the light at the end of the tunnel. I'd never heard anyone talking like this about defending the rights of domestic workers. I'd been to various groups organized by the church for domestic workers. I'd gone to see if they were saying anything about struggle or about rights. But when I got to these groups, they'd say things like 'you need to be nice' – they were generally more concerned with preparing people to be baptized or confirmed. I talked with those church people, but they just told us that domestic workers should be glad to have a house and food, that they ought to be obedient to their bosses, because the boss is like their second mother and she shouldn't be disobeyed. It wasn't what I wanted to hear. I wanted to hear things about change, about struggle, about rights. I didn't say any of this, but it wasn't what I wanted to hear and I just went away again and didn't go there again.

During the two decades of dictatorship, domestic workers' struggles for rights had been mediated through the Catholic Church – and especially the youth movement, the Juventude Operária Católica (JOC). The 1970s was an era in which Brazilian liberation theological ideas and practices inspired others outside the country to associate their faith with the struggle for social justice. The church provided a relatively safe space for activism in an era of repression, although the regime murdered several radical pastors, particularly Dominicans, in its ruthless attempts to quash resistance. It also offered a site in which there was a politicized vision of the injustices that domestic workers experienced as a class, rather than simply an attempt to stem their consequences through acts of charity. The school where the domestic workers' meeting that Creuza heard about on the radio was held was associated with a Catholic church, run by Jesuits, and the meetings were held in the church itself.

Hearing about the meeting piqued Creuza's interest. But she had to find a way to get there. And she didn't even know where it was. She didn't want to risk her boss stopping her from going to the meeting, so she came up with a ruse:

> I waited until my boss was resting – she always took her rest after lunch – and when she woke, I asked her where Colégio Antônio Vieira was, and how I could find it. And then I asked her, 'Can you show me on a calendar which is the second and the fourth Sunday?'

She went to the calendar and showed it to me, and marked the days for me. Then she asked, 'Why are you interested in this?' I told her that I'd heard on the radio that there would be a mass there, at the sanctuary of Our Lady of Fatima, and I wanted to go. She said 'Oh' and turned away. It was then, when she'd gone out of the room, that I began to plan how I was going to be able to get there, who I was going to call to come with me to the meeting. And that's when I started to mobilize people. I called my cousin, my sister, colleagues at the school – I was doing a course at the school, and I arrived in the classroom and started talking to my colleagues in the break about the meeting – 'Look, there's a group at the Colégio Antônio Vieira who meets every second and fourth Sunday, they say it's for the struggle for domestic workers' rights, to found a union.' The girls just said, 'What's all that about, I'm not going to go.' One said she wasn't free, another said she was going out with her boyfriend, another said she was going to the beach and the last girl only said, 'Union? What's the point'?

As Creuza was later to recognize, with so little time off work and lives in which it is so difficult to form romantic relationships, attracting domestic workers to spend their precious leave days at meetings is far from easy. But for her, the meeting represented something else:

I was anxious to go to the meeting, and waited for the day to arrive. I exchanged my day off – I only had a day off every two weeks – and I wanted to be free to go there and stay for as long as I had to, I needed that. I knew it was in the afternoon, but we got there early – it was me and my sister – so we could find the place. We arrived at 11 a.m. At two, people started to arrive. I thought there were going to be lots of people, but only five or six arrived and that was it. It was a huge disappointment. It was like having a bucket of cold water thrown over you when you're really excited about something. I felt really deflated. But I went in. And when the women there started explaining that the objective of the group was to organize domestic workers to fight for their rights, to fight for dignity, because domestic work is a profession and that we aren't recognized as such and so on, it was then that I said, it is just this that I wanted to hear, just this! When the meeting finished, I took my leave and the people said, 'Are you coming back?' I thought for a bit, and then I said to myself: who knows, maybe this group needs me too to grow. And from then on, I stayed with the group. For me, the second and fourth Sundays of the month became sacred. So much so that I was criticized by my relatives who said I only think about the group, why don't I go to any other places? 'Creuza, you're wasting your time with that business of the group of domestic workers, it won't come to anything.'

For workers in such insecure employment, getting involved in activism to secure labour rights can put their jobs at risk. Many employers – even feminist employers, Creuza pointed out – are not keen on their employees making demands for more money, or better conditions. And, given the informality of domestic work, where so much depends on the capacity of the worker to negotiate their own working conditions, 'empowered' workers may make themselves unemployable. Creuza found herself in this situation, over time. She talks of how she first told her boss at the time that she was involved in the movement.

I participated in the group without saying anything to my boss. One day, I came to her and told her. She said, 'Look Creuza, you're wasting your time because domestic workers have got rights, they've got the right to a Worker's Card, they've got rights to pay national insurance, what more do you want?' 'We want salaries, holidays...' She retorted, 'Ha, you're dreaming! Maybe in 30, 40 years you might get this, but not now, you'll never get this now.' And I said to her, 'But we'll continue to struggle, because without struggle we'll never succeed.' Well, after that I was resolute. I knew what I wanted. I'd tell her I was going to a meeting, and she'd tell me, 'You should be in the square with a lover, this business of these meetings, it won't get you anywhere.' But I didn't give up. Although she tried to talk me out of it – and not just her, relatives of mine too – I didn't stop going to the meetings.

For domestic workers – the majority of whom are black, poor and uneducated – alliances with other movements have been critical in their struggles for rights and recognition. At the time that Creuza was getting more involved in activism, other social movements were on the rise in Brazil (Álvarez 1990). These were heady days. Brazil's dictatorship was coming to an end, and its death throes were unleashing a tremendous wave of social and political energy amongst Brazilians. Getting involved gave Creuza more than connections. She began to recognize other dimensions of political subjectivity; she began to articulate an identity as a woman, as a black woman, and as a black woman worker (Collins 1990, Lorde 1984, Castro 1992).

> I started to get to know other movements, to participate in the women's movement, the black movement. Every movement I heard of, I wanted to know about it. I had a great thirst for knowledge. One time, I saw a black woman speak and looked at her hair – she wore it natural and I always straightened mine, or hid it behind a scarf, I hated my hair so much, it was so hard, so ugly – and I saw her looking so good, so beautiful, so black. And I wanted to know more about her, 'Who is this woman, this woman who is so different?'[7] I was curious to know about the group she was part of, the black movement [Movimento Negro Unificado, MNU]. So one day, I went to get to know her, I went to a meeting and participated in the discussion. I resolved that I'd also join the black movement – even if at that time it was a movement of people from the university. It was in about 1984, 1985. These university people, I used to go to the meetings and found their language very difficult to understand, very academic, I had problems understanding what they were talking about. But I did understand, and I saw that what they were saying had something to do with me. They talked about questions of race, of violence, of discriminatory laws, of police violence, of the young men assassinated by the police, of black women who suffered violence. After that I got to know the women's movement.

Building the movement

Creuza continued to try to enlist domestic workers in the meetings, despite all odds. Her persistence slowly began to pay off. But even when she got women to come to the Sunday meetings, getting them to continue coming was another challenge:

> By that time, we'd created an association of domestic workers and

the group continued to grow, with meetings every second and fourth Sunday of the month. More and more domestic workers joined. There were those who came who wanted instant results, and because they didn't get them, they left. There were those who came to two, three meetings, and found it all boring, monotonous, and they disappeared and didn't come again. There were some who persisted, like me, Lucia, Josefina, my cousin and my sister, we all continued together along with a few others. Sometimes we'd only have five or six people at our meetings, like that first meeting I went to. Some would come to one meeting, and skip the next one. For me it had become like an obsession, I had to be at the meeting. I remember there was a time that I went to the meeting and sat under the tree in front of the college waiting for people to come. I sat there for two hours and no one came. I carried on waiting. Two, three, four, five… no one came. Eventually, I went, but I stayed for the whole time we would have had that meeting. Sometimes only one or two people would appear, and I'd say, 'We don't need to open the room, let's sit here under the tree and chat.' And if others came, we'd go into the room and have the meeting there.

The group had begun when those working at the Colégio Antônio Vieira had become aware of how many of the women coming to study at night were domestic workers. Creuza's recollections evoke the shame and stigma associated with domestic work, and serve as a reminder that the struggle for rights is also a struggle for recognition (Fraser 1995), and for society to treat domestic workers as human beings rather than as the invisible hands that keep houses clean:

> Most of those coming to study at night were domestic workers. When they were asked about themselves they'd say they lived in their aunts' houses. But when they said where they lived, it was in the middle-class areas of the city, not where poor, black people live, and so it was evident that they were domestic workers. So then discussion started about why they were ashamed to say that they were domestic workers. And it was from there that the group began to meet on Sundays.

In the early days, people from the school led the group. Creuza's recollections touch on themes of considerable significance for mobilizing informal sector workers: leadership – and in particular the creation of new leaders – and continuity:

> When I joined the group, the person leading the group was called Claudia. When she left, we had great difficulty continuing the group, that thing of you have a leader and you're there, and then when that leader goes you start questioning: will the group continue? I had a teacher at that time, and her name was Conceição. Conceição was really important to me at that time. I remember how, when Claudia left the group, Conceição motivated me to think about what could be done to ensure that the group didn't die. I didn't think I was capable of helping the group to continue, I didn't think I had what it took to take the group forward, because when I arrived, Claudia was the one who was mobilizing people and it was because of her support that I'd got involved in the first place. When Claudia left, I felt like an orphan. An orphan in the struggle. But at the same time when Conceição said, 'You shouldn't let this group die', I thought I'm not worse or better than anyone else, I am capable, I can motivate the other women not to leave the group, not to let it die. And I began. I continued to mobilize others. I didn't drop the meetings. And when I went to the meeting and no-one turned up, I'd stay there until the end, and only then I'd go home. The next week two people would come, and say 'Claudia's gone.' And I'd say, 'Yes, but we need to carry on.'

From organizing to organization

Creuza's persistence paid off. Brazil's re-democratization process was under way, but at this stage the law did not permit the creation of unions, only groups or associations. By that time, it had become evident that the Church had extended its protective wing a little too paternalistically to enable the domestic workers to organize themselves effectively. They needed their own association. And so the Professional Association of Domestic Workers was born.[8]

> In 1986, we founded our association, and we haven't looked back from that day onwards. I was its first president. From there, we

began to struggle to get our own headquarters. We'd experienced some problems. Our mail had been opened. There were topics – like abortion – that we were not allowed to discuss, because we were meeting there in the Sanctuary of Our Lady of Fátima [in the Colégio Antônio Vieira]. If we wanted to bring a politician to talk about anything with us, we weren't allowed: we had to ask the permission of the priest. We all began to see the importance of getting our own headquarters.

Gradually, the association was beginning to shape its own agenda. Creuza's reflections touch on another important theme – the significance of a wider movement within which fledgling associations can feel a sense of belonging, and the inspiration that can come from collective expressions of solidarity:

Something that helped us to grow, and which helped me in particular, was in 1985, when I went to the fifth National Congress of Domestic Workers in Recife. It was the first time Bahia had participated. And it made us realize we weren't alone. I got there and saw domestic workers from various parts of Brazil, from the south to the north, each with their own reality. Each talking about their own situation, but when you came to it, their situations were the same. We didn't have guaranteed rights, and the few rights we did have were not respected. At that time, we didn't have the right to a minimum salary. It was a big debate at that time, and Benedita da Silva – a former domestic worker – who was a state representative in the National Congress was there, participating in our congress. Dona Laudelina was there too, our matriarch in the struggle. She was 82 years old by then. It was she who started the first movement of domestic workers in Brazil. Well, when I got back from Recife, I came back certain that nothing would tear me away from this movement. Neither husband, nor religion, nor boss, nothing, nothing would tear me away. Because when I got there I saw the experience of others, the struggle of others, who had been struggling to build a movement since the 1970s. I came back from there full of energy.

It was at this point that Creuza started experiencing more difficulties holding down a job as a domestic worker. Something had to give:

I always used the strategy of not telling my new boss that I was involved with the movement, because if I told them, they wouldn't want to employ me. And what I'd do is work for a while, and then when I'd got the trust of my boss, I'd tell them I was in a group. Some of them, when they knew about this, they'd send me away saying, 'Someone from the movement won't do.' I had a lot of that. That thing of hiding that I was in the movement, so as to be able to get work. There came a time when I felt I had to tell them, like a kind of challenge, to show them that we were organizing ourselves. To say, we're not like we used to be, now we have a movement. There were moments when I felt I had to deny being involved, to stay silent so that I could get work, and then the moment would come when I would tell them. Even if I lost the job, I had to tell them. My boss used to complain and sometimes I had to go out secretly without saying to her where I was going. But no matter where I went, she'd associate my going out with the movement. Even if I was visiting a relative, she thought I was going to a meeting of the domestic workers and she'd say, 'I am not paying you to do activism.'

Creuza recalls her own growth as a person, and as a leader, during this time, and how she began to change the way she perceived herself and her own agency. Solidarity and a sense of the collective – 'power with' – loom large in her narrative, as does the influence of the movements that she came into contact with, which shaped her own sense of political consciousness and agency. With this came a sense of identity and identification, which in turn shaped her emerging self-recognition – and her sense of 'power to':

No-one took me to the movement. I went because I couldn't understand why there was this difference, why domestic workers didn't have rights. And from there I began to participate and began to discover things. I began to recuperate my self-esteem. I didn't use to look at myself in the mirror, I couldn't manage to do this, I thought I was ugly, I thought I was horrible, so I couldn't look. Then after I started participating in the domestic workers' group, after I started participating in the black movement, I started to participate in various movements and from that I got a sense of the stories of other women, in other situations and I began to realize that I wasn't the only one, that there were others in the same situation as me. I began to identify myself with these other women, whether they were friends or people I had never met before. And I began participating in workshops.

Creuza remembered one of these courses – the kind of feminist consciousness raising and advocacy training that was being run by organizations in this part of the country as they mobilized women in the struggle for rights – as having been a turning point for her.

I remember that there was a time that there was a training course that was run by a feminist organization in Pernambuco, and I went every two weeks, sometimes once a month, to Recife. The project paid for the journey to Recife.[9] I didn't say anything to my boss. I left here on Friday night, came back on Sunday night and arrived in the morning on Monday. I put together my days off so I could have all these days off together, and didn't say anything to my boss about where I was going. I learnt so much there with the others. There were moments there where I wasn't able to speak – there were things it felt shameful to speak about, that I didn't have the courage to speak about. Things like that issue of my hair. Harassment by the boss, the experience I had as a child of an old man of 60 who masturbated in front of me, looking at me, calling me to take his organ in my hand. It took me many years before I was able to speak about this. Even in the movement I couldn't bring myself to speak about this. I didn't have the courage to talk about it, this situation of sexual violence in my workplace. It was after that I began to have the courage to speak, and to motivate others to speak.

So much of the brutality experienced by domestic workers remains hidden. By gaining the courage to speak openly about her experience, Creuza not only empowered herself, but also acquired the power to move and motivate others to name those experiences as violence and make them matters of public concern.

It was at that time that Creuza's activism brought her into contact with people in positions of power. These encounters served to strengthen her sense of herself at the same time as giving her a feeling of efficacy. They brought her not only contacts and connections that would prove important for the movement, but also knowledge about how the system works – knowledge that was new, and powerful.

> In the movement, I learnt a lot of things that strengthened me and continue to strengthen me. We had an audience with Ulysses Guimarães in the time that he was the president of the House of Representatives; with Minister Almir Paes, all of this was a process of growing to know about things. And that's how we created a union, in May 1990.

Finding a voice: the creation of FENATRAD

The process of collectivization had progressed from the domestic workers convening their own meetings within the space offered by the college, to founding their own association, to finding a place of their own where they could pursue their own agenda. Now, with this new-found knowledge, it was time to create a union. Creuza tells of the subterfuge she had to engage in to deal with mail sent to her as leader of the association at her employer's house where she lived, and then of how the conflicts with her employer escalated to the point where she decided to quit monthly-paid domestic work and take up a job as a daily cleaner.

> Once the association became better known, and during the struggle for the Federal Constitution, I began to be sought after more and started to travel more: that's when the conflicts at work got worse. My boss wouldn't release me so that I could travel, and used to answer the phone and say I wasn't in or that I wasn't there at all. Because at times people would call and ask, 'Is this the association of domestic workers?' And he'd say, 'No' and hang up, knowing it was for me. And afterwards people would say to me, 'I phoned that number you gave me but he said you weren't there'. I knew then that until we had our own headquarters, only then would this problem be resolved.

The need for the association to have its own space had become paramount. 'We'd had enough of having our post opened and not being free to do what we wanted – what we wanted to talk about, what days we wanted to meet and so on.'

As Creuza talked about the little house that they had been able to secure with support they got from the Nucleus of Interdisciplinary Women's Studies at the University of Bahia – who had established an advisory wing to work with local women's groups and whom she knew from the women's movement – it became clear that the significance of having a space of their own was something that worked on many levels. Sunday had, by then, been established as a day off for domestic workers, so she and her colleagues would go to the house after work on a Saturday, and spend the evening chatting, laughing and enjoying each others' company. This kind of support and solidarity made a world of difference; having their own space, rather than to have to be in someone else's space, was important in giving Creuza and her colleagues the emotional sustenance that is so important for those engaged in activism on issues so intractable and difficult.

> That headquarters was small, a little house, but it was a space, which for us was like a dream. We had our own headquarters, we could say, 'Here is the headquarters of the domestic workers.' Usually on days off, people would usually go to their relatives' house or to the beach. Now we had our own space to go to. We managed to get an oven, a fridge. There were times when we got off work Saturday night and went straight there, slept there and spent our Sundays together there. And it became a hub of activity, of meetings, of friendship, of us the people who had our own space. After that came the union and we continued in this headquarters, attending to people there.

As time went on, the union expanded:

> Then we got another project, which allowed us to employ someone to attend to people, and do the accounts. And we began seeing that we couldn't provide these services for free, we had to charge some kind of dues so that we could maintain the union, because that project wouldn't last forever and the project wasn't enough to sort everything out. We began to grow and grow and we began to realize that our HQ was too small. We needed a bigger place in a more visible location. That's when we got some money from an international prize given by the women's movement, and that allowed us to buy a bigger HQ, which is where we are now. We

bought it, renovated everything and were able to run it for quite a while on that money that we got.

Creuza's own horizons were also expanding. She was travelling a lot, not just within Brazil, but also elsewhere in Latin America. She was chosen to represent Brazil at the conference on racism in Durban, South Africa, and attended meetings in Geneva. When Brazil came to put forward their candidates for the 1,000 women who were suggested for the Nobel Peace Prize in June 2005,[10] Creuza was among them. By then, Creuza had begun to reflect on the significance of visibility for domestic workers through representation in the legislative arena, and on how this was the next logical step to advance the struggle. She began a campaign for public office that was to take her to defeat in four elections – and into the full glare of the racism and discrimination against women that pervades the arena of formal politics.[11]

From organizing to influence

The domestic workers' rights movement has successfully articulated its efforts to influence policy, through representation on high-level national committees on women's issues and racial equality, and internationally, but with a continued presence at the grassroots. This connection with the grassroots is fundamental to the strength and survival of the movement. How do activists manage to reach the many domestic workers whose days are spent in isolated private homes, in inaccessible apartment blocks with security guards at their gates, and in situations of employment where their working hours are so long that they leave little if any time for leisure of any kind, let alone for meetings?

A key strategy has been to use any available opportunities to meet with domestic workers as a group, and for this reason the night schools where domestic workers go to take courses after work are a vital entry point for activists to make contact with them. Arrangements are made with those who run the courses for a domestic worker rights activist to come and give a talk, and this enables the initial connection to be made – participants are invited to attend other events, especially social events, on their days off and it is from here that they get involved in the movement. Some get involved when they have a dispute or problems with their employers and need to seek out the union; sometimes they continue to be involved after that has been resolved, as they've become aware of what the union does, and become more motivated to support the union's work for other domestic workers and the struggle for rights and recognition. The domestic workers' union sometimes puts on its own courses. Other entry points include popular associations in poor neighbourhoods in the city, with which domestic workers may be affiliated, and churches. The movement also produces pamphlets and other material that give domestic workers information about their rights and entitlements, and about upcoming events. There are regular celebrations to mark important landmarks in the struggle and commemorate inspiring leaders from the past like Laudelina de Campos Mello.

But it's not easy: Creuza estimates that out of every hundred domestic workers, perhaps two or three might get involved with the movement:[12]

> Obviously, one knows that it's not immediate [that people would get involved], at times, you get the impression that you're banging your head against a brick wall, you are there for years preparing people to come together, and you're there in the midst of it all recognizing that this person won't do for this, or isn't interested, until they find something in the struggle that grabs them. They will enjoy some of the benefits that the struggle has brought them, the advances, but they won't want to put themselves out, or dedicate themselves to the struggle, they prefer to find themselves a lover and spend their time with them. They prefer not to commit themselves, or to sit at home watching TV. There are people who get involved and then they realize it's not what they thought it was, it's not their thing, that being an activist is not comfortable for them. And there are those who stay.

A constant preoccupation for the movement is with finding new leaders. As Creuza comments, everyone has a different leadership style and it's about spotting who has the potential and then working with them, in whatever way suits their way of working, to enable them to lead.

It could be that someone is very outgoing, and has the capacity to mobilize people that way, it could be that someone is very timid but is someone with the kind of persistence that everyone admires, and can be a leader who attracts followers for that. Without new leaders, they will end up with the same people staying forever in the leadership. When that starts happening, it affects the movement, especially where those who are in leadership positions are unable to cede power to others and want to be the gatekeepers for everything.

The domestic workers' movement has sought visibility as a strategy in the struggle for recognition. They've sought to make themselves present in union and government forums, even when they weren't invited; and now the invitations come, and efforts are made to include them. They've invested in publicity, working closely with the government to broadcast the rights that they have succeeded in securing and to urge domestic workers to claim those rights. Posters advertising the importance of getting a Worker's Card and getting it signed by employers feature in public facilities in poorer areas. The national state-sponsored professionalization programme 'Citizen Domestic Work' has gained access to widespread media coverage, with announcements on the radio and TV. One tactic has been to promote public recognition of the iconic figure of Dona Laudelina de Campos Mello, as the founder of the domestic workers' struggle in Brazil. This works both to give the movement a sense of antiquity, and urgency; Dona Laudelina comes to represent the quest of black Brazilian women for dignity and a life free of discrimination.

The election of President Luiz Inácio Lula da Silva in 2003 was a major boost. Here, at last, was a President who was himself from a union background, a former metal worker, elected on a ticket that was all about putting right the wrongs of discrimination and inequity in Brazil. In July 2006, the movement celebrated a series of gains in labour rights, as a new law was passed that gave them the right to paid holiday and maternity leave. For all of these gains – including a professionalization programme that began in Bahia and has been taken up in other states after successful lobbying at the Federal level – survival of the union is a constant struggle, due to the lack of continuity of resources and the kind of resource base other unions can call upon:

> We don't have the finance of other unions for our own union activities, and it's usually we who pay for things, or survive through involvement in other projects – and when there's no project, we lose our jobs and we have to go back to domestic work again. Because of this, the union is very precarious – because to have a strong union, you need to have that kind of support, and you need infrastructure. You need things like a car to use for broadcasting your cause, to carry people from one place to another. We do our activism travelling by bus. And it's not everyone who is cut out for doing this, doing activism without money, at times going for three months without having a salary. People can end up staying home because they don't have money for transport. It's very hard. Those who do their union activities with a vehicle with sound, a car to fetch and carry, a cellphone whenever they need it, a salary every month, are those who are in unions who can pay or subsidize their organizers, and they can do activism in the union movement. In our case, no.

For domestic workers there is an additional issue: societal discrimination extends into the labour movement, where, as a category that consists largely of black women earning very low wages, they have little clout. Brazil's union movement is powerful, but it is dominated by men and by categories with economic leverage that the domestic workers' union lacks. Not only this, some of the most influential unions are categories who themselves employ domestic workers, and would feel the effects of improvements in workers' pay and rights.

Sacrifice, solidarity and struggle

Creuza's story is of one individual, but it tells of a life so closely entwined with the movement that it offers rich insights into some of the challenges of organizing in the informal sector. In this last section, we pick up on a theme that is vital to understanding many dimensions of the domestic workers' struggle: relationships. Spending such large parts of their lives in intimate proximity to other families makes for complex affective relationships (Brites 2008). For many a domestic worker, talk of being 'part of the family' opens up the possibility for exploitation: longer hours, taking liberties with what employees are expected to do, and a failure to respect basic rights (Motta 1986). Domestic workers, especially those who live in the houses of their employers, can find it hard to make and sustain their own families. Being involved in the struggle, Creuza reflected, made it hard for her to form relationships with men – not only because she was so busy organizing domestic workers, travelling and going to meetings, but also because she was not willing to compromise on the kind of relationship she believed ought to be possible: an equal partnership.

> Activist women pay the price. The price of loneliness, of the incomprehension of men, and it is not a coincidence that many of them are separated. Because when they get to know the movement, they discover that women need to change and fight, and then they end up alone.

In a society where women are still expected to be subordinate to the men in their lives, a path that takes women out of the house and job and into the public arena, to meet, and to protest, can be frowned upon by male partners. Some actively seek to restrict women's engagement with the movement. Creuza comments:

> Some men accept their partners being involved in the movement. A cousin of mine, when she first got to know the man who is now her husband, he knew she was involved in the movement, and he still got involved with her. After they married, he started trying to restrict her. And she said to him, 'You got to know me in the movement. If you want to leave my life, you can go, but I am not going to leave the movement.' And she carried on fighting and going to meetings; they fought over it, but she carried on

going. Then finally they separated. She never left the movement. I had a colleague who had such a lot of potential, but her husband pulled her out of the movement and she opted for him. I had to respect her. It was really up to her. It's better for her to do what she thinks than to stay in the movement and be unhappy. And so she's with him, and they have children. And there are those who men won't go near, because they know that they are in the movement – and if he goes near them, he will be afraid that the woman won't be the one for him, because she will be more intelligent, more knowledgeable, and won't obey him, that kind of thing. So they don't come anywhere near.

The struggle can be a lonely place to be, for all that it brings activists into contact with the women whom they seek to organize and mobilize. Sustaining their energy, their optimism and their courage is something that becomes vital for the movement to sustain itself. For Creuza, her source of sustenance is spiritual; her faith and her church are a vital support. She draws inspiration from ancestral black Brazilian activists who struggled against slavery and won their freedom. These ancestors come to represent the journey that Brazil still needs to make towards greater justice and equality for all. The domestic workers' struggle is largely the struggle of black, working-class women, and is at the centre of this larger struggle for a Brazil where everyone has the right to decent work, leisure and a life free of discrimination.

Conclusion

Looking back over almost a century of domestic workers' activism in Brazil, a trajectory can be traced from the first actions developed by the domestic workers' leadership, which were centralized into a workers' mobilization around labour rights and social welfare. Domestic workers started gathering in neighbourhoods, schools and churches. These meetings were strategies to build the organizations in each town and in different states. These groups have been extended and the struggles consolidated. In subsequent years, and in the years following Brazil's return to democratic rule and the flowering of movements in search of rights and citizenship, this was followed by other meetings, seminars and workshops at the local, regional and national levels, for professional and political formation. The creation of unions by the domestic workers' rights movement enabled the movement to gain a space – albeit one of continued marginality – within the central workers' union, the CUT. Under PT (Workers' Party) administrations, the unions have gained greater strength and have been able to secure important advances in workers' rights. For the domestic workers' movement, alliances with other players in the field of activism and action have been hugely significant. Alliances with social movements – significantly the feminist and black movements – were pivotal in securing the gains that the Constitutional process brought domestic workers, as workers, as women and as black women. Alliances with the state have become increasingly significant, giving rise to important collaborations and to the possibilities of influence and voice in key policy arenas. And alliances with international organizations such as ILO, UNIFEM and UNICEF have proved critically important in generating sufficient visibility to drive changes in legislation and policy.

Retracing the steps taken by the domestic workers' movement in Brazil, a number of lessons emerge for organizing some of the most hard-to-reach, disempowered and exploited workers. Undoubtedly many of the gains that the movement has made have been due to a conjunction of factors that may be scarce on the ground elsewhere in the world – strong labour unions, leftist political parties in government, populous and vocal social movements, committed and visionary leaders in pivotal political positions, and political opportunities such as the constitutional deliberations that first brought the domestic workers' movement into alliance with the feminist and black movements, or the election of a government led by the former leader of the metalworkers' union, and in which organizers from other unions came to hold powerful positions. But the story of Brazil's domestic workers does lend us insights into strategies that are used the world over to organize informal sector workers, and into tactics that travel.

Domestic workers are notoriously difficult to reach. They are largely invisible, often isolated, and can be completely out of reach of organizing efforts that depend on literacy. Most work long and anti-social hours for pay so low that the time and transport fares to attend meetings may be an unaffordable luxury. The tactics used by Creuza and her colleagues create capillaries of contact – communications via the radio, via evening courses attended by domestic workers, and via networking within condominiums and neighbourhoods, and through friends and relatives. Contact leads to invitations, which lead to further contact: meetings on days off that combine the work of organizing with leisure, celebrations and fun – such as 'clinics' to advise workers on rights issues and through this bring them into the movement to help advise other workers, and similar activities that raise the visibility of the movement and the cause.

Then comes the hard work of maintaining the movement, raising funds to keep basic infrastructure in place and keeping people going through hard times. A challenge that all movements grapple with is that of leadership, and there are insights from the Brazilian experience into the significance given to the task of finding and supporting new leaders. Recognition of the many different qualities that leaders can bring has been one way in which the movement has fostered new leadership; mentoring, support and the creation of opportunities is another part of this. What has been vital to the Brazilian domestic workers' movement is the connection that leaders have maintained with the grassroots, even where leaders have been unable to sustain their jobs as domestic workers, caught between the demands of the movement and the opposition of their employers.

Friends and allies become all the more important as the movement grows. Solidarity is such a vital nurturing and sustaining form of power, and one that underpins all dimensions of the struggle. Two specific aspects are, however, worth noting. The first is the power of situating the struggle of a particular group within a broader struggle for rights and freedoms – the domestic workers' struggle became emblematic of the struggle of black, working-class women, and drew solidarity and alliance from other movements seeking to address inequality and discrimination in Brazil. The second is the opportunities that cross-movement solidarity and connection can bring. Through alliances forged in political spaces that brought other social movements together, Creuza and her colleagues became acquainted with middle-class feminists who knew about proposal writing, sources of funding, avenues for support, and with the black movement activists who were such a source of political sustenance.

Formalizing the movement – the move from group to association to union – brought other opportunities for alliance building and for contacts that were later to yield important gains, as union and social movement colleagues from Bahia took positions in government in Brasilia. External organizations played a role in this, but, as Creuza's story shows, domestic workers themselves led the struggle. The part played by the church reveals paradoxes of external assistance. On the one hand, the more radical arm of the Catholic church brought practices of consciousness raising that liberated domestic workers' sense of themselves and enabled them to recognize the injustice they were experiencing. On the other, the disciplining effects of a more conservative Catholicism were evident in the early days of the movement in Bahia – constraining voices, limiting the issues around which domestic workers could mobilize and reducing domestic workers to objects of charity rather than subjects of struggle.

Operating from a position of extreme marginalization, domestic workers recognized that they needed to engage people in positions of power in their struggle, and sought to make themselves visible to them. The tactics that the domestic workers used to make connections included inviting themselves to meetings, using every opportunity to put their demands on the table in public events, and mounting a campaign that could win longer-term gains as well as meeting the shorter-term political priority of greater visibility in the demand for a professionalization programme. The challenges they faced within a union movement dominated by men, and by categories of workers who themselves employ domestic workers and who would themselves be affected if domestic workers won greater rights, should not be underestimated.

Ultimately, the election of a government that put labour rights, racial equality and gender equality high on the agenda helped the domestic workers break through and achieve the formalization of many of the labour rights that they spent so many years struggling to gain. But this also needs to be seen as the outcome of a strategy of building connections: the successful articulation of the domestic workers' movement with other more visible and powerful movements and institutions nationally and internationally, and of grassroots mobilization of thousands of domestic workers around the country.

The Brazilian domestic workers' rights movement has secured gains that two decades ago would have seemed completely impossible to achieve. These conquests owe much to the persistence of key figures in the movement, from Laudelina de Campos Mello to Creuza Maria Oliveira, who never gave up the hope that things could change for the better. There is still a very long way to go, but the victories that have been achieved are a reminder of what is possible when women come together to demand their rights, against all odds.

Acknowledgement

We owe a great debt to Cecilia Sardenberg for all her help. The research on which this chapter is based was partially funded by the UK Government's Department for International Development as part of financial assistance to the Pathways of Women's Empowerment Research Programme Consortium.

Notes

1 See PED (2011: 1), citing PNAD (2010). Nationally, 59.3 per cent of domestic workers are black, rising to 96.7 per cent in the metropolitan area of Salvador, where Creuza Oliveira lives and where her activism began.

2 See Saffioti (1978), Nobre (2004), Ávila (2008), Sanches (2006, 2009) and Gonçalves (2010).

3 It is beyond the scope of this chapter to discuss the issues at stake here, but it is worth noting that part of this debate is about the risk of further informalization as a result of changes in the status of domestic work as a result of ratification of Convention 189.

4 This project was conceived of and led by Terezinha Gonçalves, working closely with Creuza Oliveira and her fellow domestic workers.

5 The programme has three parts. The first is a course that serves as a professional qualification for domestic workers, with a status equivalent to courses taken in formal education. The second is leadership training. The third is support for public policies for domestic workers, such as the struggle to enable domestic workers to have their own homes so that they no longer need to live in the houses of their employers.

6 Translated by Andrea Cornwall from life-history narratives gathered in 2006, 2007 and 2009.

7 The woman who inspired Creuza was none other than Luiza Bairros, who was appointed Minister for Racial Equality in Dilma Rousseff's administration.

8 See also Motta (1992, 1987) for discussions of these developments. For discussions of domestic workers in other Latin American countries, see also Chaney and Castro (1989).

9 The advocacy course in Recife was organized by SOS Corpo, one of Brazil's leading feminist organizations and one that has played an important part in supporting the mobilization of domestic workers. Betânia Ávila, SOS Corpo's coordinator, is a distinguished sociologist and has written a number of important works on domestic work in Brazil (Ávila et al. 2005, Ávila et al. 2008).

10 The '1000 Women for the Nobel Peace Prize Association' from Switzerland.

11 A short film, *Creuza*, documents her campaign for election and the

challenges faced by a black domestic worker in getting elected to political office, www.pathways-of-empowerment.org, accessed 20 October 2012.

12 Domestic workers have low levels of unionization in general, compared to other Brazilian workers, with under 2 per cent of all domestic workers belonging to a union. The highest levels of union membership are found in the centres for union activism in Salvador, Recife and São Paulo (PED 2011).

References

Álvarez, Sonia (1990) *Engendering Democracy in Brazil*, Palo Alto, CA: Princeton University Press.

Ávila, Maria Betânia (2008) 'Algumas questões teóricas e políticas sobre emprego doméstico' ['Some theoretical and political questions on domestic work'] in Maria Betânia Ávila, Milena Prado, Tereza Souza, Vera Soares and Verônica Ferreira (eds), *Reflexões Feministas sobre Informalidade e Trabalho Domestico* ['Feminist Reflections on Informality and Domestic Work'], Recife : SOS Corpo.

Ávila, Maria Betânia, Carmen Silva and Verônica Ferreira (eds) (2005) *Mulher e Trabalho* ['Women and Work'], Recife : SOS Corpo.

Ávila, Maria Betânia, Milena Prado, Tereza Souza, Vera Soares and Verônica Ferreira (eds) (2008) *Reflexões Feministas sobre Informalidade e Trabalho Domestico*, ['Feminist Reflections on Informality and Domestic Work'], Recife : SOS Corpo.

Brites, Jurema (2008) 'Trabalho domestico: políticas da vida privada' in Maria Betânia Ávila, Milena Prado, Tereza Souza, Vera Soares and Verônica Ferreira (eds), *Reflexões Feministas sobre Informalidade e Trabalho Domestico* ['Feminist Reflections on Informality and Domestic Work'], Recife: SOS Corpo.

Castro, Mary (1992) 'Alquimia de categorias sociais na produção de sujeitos políticos: gênero, raça e geração entre lideres do Sindicato de Trabalhadores Domésticos em Salvador' ['Alchemy of social categories in the production of political subjects: gender, race, and generation amongst leaders of the Domestic Workers' Union in Salvador'], *Estudos Feministas*, 92: 57–74.

Chaney, Elsa and Mary G. Castro (1989) *Muchachas No More: Household Workers in Latin America and the Caribbean*. Philadelphia, PA: Temple University Press.

Collins, Patricia Hill (1990) *Black Feminist Thought*, London: Routledge.

Fraser, Nancy (1995) 'From redistribution to recognition? Dilemmas of justice in a "postsocialist" age', *New Left Review*, 212: 11–13.

Gonçalves, Terezinha (2010) 'Crossroads of empowerment: the organisation of women domestic workers in Brazil', *IDS Bulletin*, 41, 2: 62–9.

IPEA (Instituto de Pesquisa Economica Aplicada) (2011) 'Situação atual das trabalhadoras domésticas no país', *Communicados do IPEA*, 90.

Lorde, Audre (1984) 'Age, race, class and sex: women redefining difference' in Audre Lorde, *Sister Outsider*, Trumansburg, NY: The Crossing Press, pp. 14–23.

Motta, Alda Britto da (1986) 'A relação impossível' ['An impossible relationship'] in F. Hardman *et al.*, *Relações de Trabalho e relações de poder: mudanças e permanências*. Fortaleza: Imprensa Universitária da UFCe, pp. 229–38.

⸻ (1987) 'Association of domestic servants: the case of Bahia, Brasil' in *Book of Abstracts: International Interdisciplinary Congress on Women*, Dublin: Trinity College.

⸻ (1992) 'Emprego doméstico: revendo o novo' ['Domestic work: reviewing what's new'], *Caderno CRH*, 16: 31–49.

Nobre, Miriam (2004) 'Trabalho doméstico e emprego doméstico' ['Domestic work and domestic employment'] in Ana Alice Costa, Eleonora Menicucci de Oliveira, Maria Ednalva Bezerra de Lima and Vera Soares (eds), *Reconfiguração das Relações de Gênero no Trabalho* ['The Reconfiguration of Gender Relations in Work'], São Paulo: CUT.

PED (2011) 'As caracteristicas do trabalho domestico remunerado nos mercados de trabalho metropolitanas' ['The characteristics of paid domestic work in metropolitan labour markets'], Sistema Pesquisa de Emprego e Desemprego (PED).

Pinto, Elisabete Aparecida (1993) 'Etnicidade, Gênero e Educação: a Trajetória de Vida de Laudelina de Campos Mello (1904–1991)' ['Ethnicity, Gender and Education: The Life Trajectory of Laudelina de Campos Mello (1904–1991)'], MA dissertation, FE-Unicamp, Campinas, 1993.

PNAD (2010) *Pesquisa Nacional por Amostra de Domicilios 2009* ['National Household Survey'], Rio de Janeiro: Instituto Brasileiro de Geografia e Estatística.

Sader, Emir (1988) *Quando Novos Personagens Entraram em Cena* ['When New People Enter the Scene'], São Paulo: Ed. Paz e Terra.

Safiotti, Heleieth (1978) *Emprego Doméstico e Capitalismo* ['Domestic Work and Capitalism'], Petropolis: Vozes.

Sanches, Solange (2006) *O Trabalho Doméstico no Brazil* ['Domestic Work in Brazil'] Brasilia: International Labour Organization.

—— (2009) 'Trabaho domestico: desafios para o trabalho decente' ['Domestic work: challenges for decent work'], *Estudos Feministas*, 17, 3: 879–88.

Santos, Gilmara Silva (2008) 'Emprego doméstico: uma herança escravista na cidade de Salvador 1914 -1920' ['Domestic work: the legacy of slavery in the city of Salvador, 1914-1920'], unpublished paper given at the IV Encontro Estadual de História [4th State History Congress], Vitória Da Conquista, Bahia.

6
The Challenge of Organizing Domestic Workers in Bangalore
Caste, Gender and Employer—Employee Relations in the Informal Economy

• •

Geeta Menon[1]

Organizing domestic workers has been tried in many ways by many groups – in different contexts, and even in relatively similar ones, there have been movements, unions, small associations and committees. One of the reasons for the variety in ways of organizing is that there is so much heterogeneity within the sector. It is a sector where employer–employee relationships are very dynamic, flexible and arbitrary; domestic workers are often hard to reach, spending most of their time in the 'private' sphere of the home; and in some contexts, the non-monetary aspects of agreements between employers and workers may have particular significance. These are some of the many challenges to organizing.

This chapter discusses the situation of domestic workers in Bangalore and the experience of Stree Jagruti Samiti, a women's organization inspired by the women's movement of the 1970s, in initiating and building the Karnataka Domestic Workers' Union (KDWU), including the many challenges it has faced. Stree Jagruti Samiti had been mobilizing women in slums in Bangalore, raising their awareness of their rights, and organizing them around various issues including domestic violence. In the course of this work, we observed that the majority of slum women worked as domestic workers, and that the slums were not just a place where poor people live, but were in fact labour colonies: places from where various employers sourced their workers.

The KDWU was set up in 2004 in order to concentrate efforts with this group of women. The goals of the union were to achieve basic rights for domestic workers; to change the widespread perception of domestic workers from being 'servants' to being 'workers'; and to ensure that employers and governments recognize them as workers with entitlements to social security.

The context: domestic work and gradual commercialization

Domestic work and feudal roots

Domestic work is one of the most unorganized and invisible categories of work. Paid domestic labour, because of the personal, intimate and continuous nature of the work, involves a unique relationship between workers, employers and the workplace. Domestic workers form an invisible backbone of the economy, and their numbers in this area of South India have increased sharply in the last two decades. This increase is linked to the shift from agriculture to an economy based on services and manufacturing, with greater in-migration into urban areas bringing a supply of domestic workers. In the agrarian economy from which many of these workers come, landowners employed workers to carry out tasks related to agriculture as well as household chores, and in return gave shelter and food, not only or always a money wage. This kind of economic relationship has been transformed in the urbanized space into paid domestic worker–employer relationships. Bonded slavery on farms has also been replaced by a paid work relationship, with stipulated wages and specified tasks, but often the mentality of employers and state officials towards domestic work and workers is still tinged with semi-feudalism.

A result of lingering semi-feudal perceptions on the part of employers as well as workers is an undervaluation of the work of domestic workers and failure to accord them dignity as workers. They are commonly referred to as 'servants', a term that has associations with bondage and serfdom, rather than as 'workers'. *Kelasadauru* means simply 'one who does work' and this is the term that employers generally use for domestic workers in Bangalore.

We wanted to change the commonly used term to *karmikaru,* which connotes a more political sense of the worker with rights.

Ambivalence to formalization

To achieve changes in the perception of domestic workers in this context, we realized that workers would also have to change their attitudes. In the KDWU, we found that women initially were enthusiastic about joining a union, and were proud of their identity cards, but it was difficult to sustain their participation or get them to engage actively with issues around wages and conditions of work. The workers needed to 'unlearn' many things and this took time: for example, they were used to a relationship between employers and domestic workers that was very flexible. This was presented as an advantage on both sides – it allowed women workers to deal with unexpected demands on their time in their own homes; or it allowed them to ask for a loan or an advance on pay when needed. One worker said, for example, that she was paid only Rs300 (approximately US$6) a month, but was reluctant to ask for even a slight increase because her employer had given an advance of Rs50,000 (approximately US$1,100).[2] Workers feared that insisting on a higher salary would mean losing the right to ask for a loan or advance from employers – a right which they valued because they knew of no other sources of such occasional and interest-free loans. Many feared losing their jobs if they started insisting on higher wages or other rights, as there is strong competition for jobs. Taking occasional holidays or changing the timing of their work were also priorities for many domestic workers and, in order to retain this flexibility, workers were reluctant to agree to a fixed weekly day off. The perception that there was some flexibility if the relationship remains loosely defined was rooted in the reciprocal bonds which exist between employers and domestic workers. The KDWU encouraged workers to think differently, and has focused on explaining the value of an agreement/contract with employers as well as a regularized weekly day off.

Persuading the state and society to accept a contractual agreement and wholly monetary arrangement as the basis for domestic work was thus difficult. The KDWU made demands for payments to be made by cheque, which would give workers proof that they were 'workers' with an 'employer', such proof being necessary to invoke any labour laws. However, this suggestion was not fully operationalized, as domestic workers' relationships with their employers involved gratitude and loyalty, and in that situation the institutionalization of purely contractual ties was problematic. Nevertheless, many women came to understand that unless there was some disciplined approach they had no protection. Also, as news about the union and members' victories slowly spread, we expected to gain strength as a collective.

Profile of the workers

In terms of earnings, domestic workers were at the lowest end of the hierarchy of work. In addition, even within a household, members of the household themselves tended to give a low value to housework. In the absence of state-provided institutional facilities for the care of children or the elderly, working or non-working women who are unable or do not wish to do all the tasks of housework employ other women – domestic workers – to carry out these tasks. But such work is not accorded much respect within either the home of the employer or that of the worker. While men were also providing domestic services when KDWU began, there were far more women working within homes; moreover there is a gendered pattern to domestic work, with men working as cooks/gardeners/security guards, and rarely in the tasks of cleaning floors, washing clothes and child care. The gendered notion of housework means that young girls are encouraged and trained to take on these roles. Women domestic workers were perpetuating this situation by taking their young daughters (and less often their sons) with them to work.

In Bangalore, at the time KDWU began, domestic workers included 'old' migrants who had been in the city for thirty to forty years as well as new migrants. New migrants often saw domestic work as a temporary occupation until they found something that was better paid and of higher status, and therefore were reluctant to describe themselves as 'domestic workers'. For this reason they were less interested in being members of a union. This was also true of younger women. The average age of domestic workers in the KDWU was between 30 and 35, but we also had some women members who were older, up to about 55–60 years old.

The caste composition was not, as one might have thought, dominated by the most excluded social groups; in fact we found women from many caste groups engaged in domestic work. In certain slums, some members were from the Lingayat and Vokkaliga communities, which are dominant castes. The majority of women came from the middle castes, those that are slightly higher than the Dalits, although there are also many Dalit women. Levels of education were generally low, but we found that migrants from Tamil Nadu were better educated on average than domestic workers from within Karnataka. A small number of migrant women had completed schooling up to Class 10, but many had dropped out of school after completing Class 4 or 5.

Distinctions within the sector

There were several different categories of domestic workers to try to mobilize. Live-in full-time or residential workers live with their employers and are on call for the entire day. Of all domestic workers, we found these the most likely to be in bonded labour situations, possibly subject to trafficking and vulnerable to sexual abuse. As a union, it was very difficult to protect them as we got to know very little about what happens inside households. It was difficult to make contact with these workers, or for them to get the time to leave the household to attend meetings. The little we knew about residential workers, we heard from other women in the organization. Live-in domestic workers are often provided to their employers by placement agencies, which were also difficult to get information about, as they do not easily share details of the arrangements they make. We knew of about 23 placement agencies in Bangalore, which mostly place live-in young women from West Bengal, Coimbatore, estates in Tamil Nadu and Karnataka.

Part-time workers are sometimes employed to perform only one kind of task, such as cooking, cleaning or child care. Often the task allocation had a caste basis. At other times, the work to be done was not clearly defined. Part-time workers often worked in two to four houses every day to make a minimal living. Their wages were low, they had no assured holidays or sick leave, and were dependent on the goodwill of the employer. If they fell ill, they often faced a wage deduction for taking holidays, or alternatively the work would be piled up for them to do the next day.

A further category of workers consisted of full-time workers who did not live in their employers' homes but worked there all day, commonly from 7 a.m. to 5 or 6 p.m. There were also some piece-rate workers who did a particular task and were paid on a task completion basis, such as *dhobis* (clothes washers).

For the KDWU, one crucial difference between a part-time and a full-time worker was the time available to each for union activity. As a result, most of our members are part-timers and day full-timers. We made attempts to trace live-in workers, but without much success, and there are some other categories of domestic workers we did not reach, such as domestic workers in the Army and government quarters. These workers are not paid in cash. Instead, they are given a room and a ration from canteens, and electricity and water are paid for. On the positive side, these workers have secure shelter, access to people in powerful positions, and relatively high status. On the negative side, they are always on call, and the absence of cash income makes dealing with emergencies or travel requirements a real challenge. Some workers come to an agreement with the employer so that they are permitted to take on part-time work for cash in other homes for a certain number of hours.

Initiating the Karnataka Domestic Workers' Union

Initial motivation and structure

Stree Jagruti Samiti had, in the course of their work, heard daily stories of harassment and grievances from domestic workers, such as having to work extra hours without additional payment, and unfounded accusations of theft. There was no law or redressal mechanism to protect domestic workers. This situation prompted the idea of an umbrella committee to address the question of domestic workers' rights. Several NGOs which we saw as our support groups came together to form the KDWU. Coincidentally, the Karnataka government had issued a minimum wage notification for domestic workers that very year. We felt this wage had been arbitrarily fixed and the KDWU would be a platform to initiate protest and struggle.

The KDWU was built on a two-tier structure: the executive committee, which included the president, secretary and treasurer; and the general body, which included all the groups of women. While it started in Bangalore, members today also hail from adjacent districts of Bidar, Bijapur and Gulbarga, and the KDWU plans to extend its work to the city of Mangalore. It was proposed that two representatives from Mangalore should become members of the executive committee. KDWU's general body decides who forms the executive committee, and there are usually seven to eleven members. We currently employ one full-time person, who is responsible for holding the partner NGOs/support groups together and consolidating the union.

The KDWU primarily works in the Jayanagar and J. P. Nagar areas of Bangalore. The union was built up by tapping into the member base of other non-profit organizations working in adjacent areas, and bringing them together around work-related issues. From the outset, the KDWU charged a nominal membership fee of Rs25 (US$0.40) for lifetime membership, or Rs2 a month. It has therefore had very limited resources, given the low level of these subscriptions. Women made this payment willingly, once they understood the idea of the organization and its functioning.

Over the last five years the KDWU has become more stream-lined. Dates of meetings, programmes and general body meetings became more frequent and better established. The KDWU also gained immensely in its outreach and strength over this period. There are currently two other domestic workers' unions in Bangalore; for the time being, each functions independently, although we have been willing to come together, for example around discussions on the proposed national Domestic Workers' Bill.

Early strategies

One of the first things the KDWU did was to try and get an idea of how much domestic workers actually earn, and what would constitute a 'living wage'. The Karnataka Minimum Wage Act of 2004 stipulated that eight hours of work per day should receive Rs2,080 (US$46) per month for work including child care and cleaning, but excluding cooking. Part time work should receive Rs247 (US$5.50) per month for an hour's work a day. This pay level included cleaning vessels and washing clothes.

These rates were very low, and as a union we did not accept them. However, we felt we could contest the decision better if we could provide an alternative formulation. To arrive at this formulation, in 2005 we undertook a study that involved collect-ing information through public meetings on the number of hours worked, in how many houses, and what workers were earning. This information was collected from about 250 workers. Women were also asked about their consumption patterns – loans, education, health, et cetera. We found that in a family without children, essential consumption expenditure was around Rs5,000 (US$110) a month, rising to Rs6,000 (US$130) a month in a family with two children. Even if both parents worked full-time, they would not earn enough to make ends meet, and often a child was sent out to work to fill the gap. Using this information, we worked out a desirable minimum 'living wage' of Rs20/day/hour (US$0.45) – this was roughly twice what was being recommended by the government for part-time workers.

The process of collecting the information was itself empowering for the women, who came from poor homes in the slums and now were being invited to come forward and talk around a table at which the union leaders were seated, and be treated as equals.[3]

Building up the KDWU

Increasing the numbers

The main focus of the KDWU was on building up collectives. For our voices to be heard, increasing membership strength was essential. For recruitment to our organization, women themselves were expected to spread the word and we also conducted public sittings. The KDWU was built up by encouraging women associated with NGOs or self-help groups (SHGs) to join, but our experience has been that women in SHGs were not very interested – they had come together around savings and credit and did not usually have a stronger political awareness. We held cluster meetings that focused on local issues like the difficulties in obtaining subsidized rations or work-related problems. Meeting locally as a group helped to bring women together, gradually strengthen a collective voice, and inculcate a sense of dignity. We held these meetings in the afternoon if possible, or in the evenings, after the day's work was over.

An early priority in these meetings was to instil a sense of how each member is important to the organization. Upon joining, an identity card was issued to each person with photo and address; and a database was maintained on the workers, their workplace and other details. The card was valued for its symbolism – becoming a member of a trade union – and for its practical uses: female domestic workers have been able to confront the police, the employer and local political heavyweights (such as the Public Distribution System ration depot owners, as described later) with great confidence, because they were able to show a card and have an identity, and could call on the KDWU office bearers if needed.

The brief given to a domestic worker on joining the KDWU

was candid: all members are expected to bring in other members; the emphasis was on increasing membership, because only then could we help each other and speak effectively to the authorities. Women were made to understand that while the card is a source of great empowerment, it could only be so if they as members were willing to exercise their power to make the government listen.

The placement agency

Early on in the KDWU's work, we tried approaching domestic worker placement agencies, posing as prospective employers in order to get a better picture of how they worked and more information on the situations of domestic workers. At one of them, after a lot of talking, we were told that they had agents who bring the women from villages, and that they currently had 25 women; women came every week, each 'batch' included around fifteen women, and none were below the age of eighteen.

Later, we started our own placement agency as a strategy. The idea of 'unionization' worked very well at one level, because it started to gain some recognition for these women as workers, including by themselves. But we found this was not enough to sustain their membership, because working on their rights was a very slow process. Increasingly there was a feeling that unionization and struggling for rights could not be the only activity of any union. Distributing economic benefits to members was not possible, but some services were needed in the form of skills training, stability, regulation of work and contractual placement. Some members said that they could stand up for their rights, but were not getting anything concrete out of being in a union. The KDWU was not offering them any kind of welfare support. In response, we began developing the idea of of trying to help our members find work against clear contracts, and so we started a placement agency.

The placement cell was operated by the members themselves. The cell drew up an agreement of responsibilities on both sides, thus introducing some accountability amongst workers and employers, and a clearer identification of tasks. The agency began by distributing flyers and pamphlets to newer residential buildings. The response from the city was overwhelming. Calls started pouring into the office, but progress was slow and only one or two women were placed. Matchmaking between employer and employee turned out to be no mean task. Timings, task particulars, caste/community requirements, working conditions, wages and holidays – all had to be negotiated. We ran into several problems. We could not 'control' women, who would sometimes leave after a week, even though there was a contract and there were no particular problems. We operated in Jayanagar and J. P. Nagar where we knew people, but calls started coming from all over the city, where our outreach was less strong. Caste issues were also significant, particularly when it came to cooking. It was difficult to place women without reference to caste. Moreover, operating an agency required business acumen and we lacked the necessary skills. We gave women their full salary, not withholding anything, whereas other agencies take money for registration, one month's salary from women, and so on; so we were not building up our own resources through this strategy.

The KDWU also collaborated with Microsoft Social Research in their project 'Interface Technology for Emerging Markets' to explore whether technology can make recruitment for domestic workers easier. A kiosk was designed, where employees could enter their specifics into a database and employers could come and choose a domestic worker (part-time or full-time) according to their requirements. In India, recruitment generally takes place through social networking – it is usually the *dhobi*, the night-watchman or the neighbour's domestic help who finds domestic workers for new employers. However, the advantages of a database and registration were tremendous from a union's point of view.

Setting up a placement cell was a strategy, a way to get women used to the idea of bargaining, developing new processes and norms and conditions for domestic workers. By running it, we also acquired insights into what kind of placements were available, and some information on residential workers, trafficking, and other agencies working legally and illegally. It was also a foothold into tracing where migrant live-in workers were coming from and what sort of commissions were being paid. However, our insights still offered only a very incomplete picture.

The agency is now still in its pilot stage. We want it to continue, but staff and resource shortages have been very challenging. KDWU members have not been able to run the agency by themselves. A dilemma emerged: while the KDWU was not interested in the agency as a business, it needed to be run professionally if it was going to be run at all. After a feature article in the newspaper about the agency, the number of calls shot up. In spite of sourcing only in the Jayanagar and J. P. Nagar areas, demand was still extensive. Employers were mostly interested in hiring live-in workers and we found it difficult to source full-time workers. The KDWU requested organizations working in the suburbs to see if poor households were interested in this employment option in the city, but this did not meet with any success. Networking with other placement agencies has also not helped, and in this interaction KDWU struggled with the awareness that other agencies' ways of operating might not be equally ethical.

Starting a placement agency did not really help the KDWU in terms of an increase in membership. New women came to the KDWU for jobs, and not to join the union. The net effect was hazy. The placement that has taken place was mostly of full-time workers; part-timers did not need a placement agency because, for part-time work, other domestic workers often played the role of a placement agency in apartment complexes – and charged a commission for this service.

Training

KDWU also experimented with a partnership with UNITUS, a company that was willing to fund a skills upgradation programme for domestic workers. Training would be imparted in three departments – cooking, child care and housekeeping. A feedback form was designed for employers, who were asked if they wanted their domestic worker to be trained in any of the above skills. The employer, of course, would have to pay for the training. However the programme ended before it could really commence. UNITUS ran out of money and the KDWU is still trying to restart the programme. From the little experience we gained, we found that employers had unrealistic expectations from 'training' – North Indian homes wanted their domestic worker to be adept at making North Indian food; another client wanted her domestic help to come ready with new recipes every day. The challenge was a massive one: to build up a market for trained domestic workers on the one hand and to organize training and placements on the other.

Responding to accusations of theft

The KDWU often had to deal with overt forms of harassment faced by workers. Thefts were the most common issue brought to the union's notice. Because domestic workers come and go from the house every day, employers were quick to suspect that domestic workers could use this access to help themselves to what they needed, such as stores and supplies. If there was a theft in the house or something went missing, most often it was the part-time domestic worker who was accused of the crime. However, since these accusations were frequently made without any proof, employers often kept quiet after the initial accusation – particularly if they had to face the union. In one case, for example, a group of twenty women went to the house, where the employers then denied the charge they had initially made.

The local KDWU groups spent a lot of time addressing these issues, which was often time-consuming and difficult. If domestic workers were accused of theft, the police often treated them extremely badly – there have been cases where the police have strip-searched women accused of theft. While there were occasionally cases where the worker had stolen something, far more often she had not, and often the 'stolen' property turned up somewhere else, for example in one case it materialized that a family member had borrowed the contentious pieces of jewellery.

The police solution to crimes has frequently been to further harass domestic workers. Two years ago, the police commissioner stated that all slum dwellers should be registered at the police station. We protested against this. We felt that issuing identity cards was the purview of the Labour Department, not police authorities. In two recent murder cases in the city, the domestic worker was detained illegally at the police station for eight hours without any enquiry or the required filing of a 'first information report'. The case was subsequently taken up by the State Human Rights Council. The police department has recently again urged employers to take fingerprints and check the antecedents of their domestic workers. However, if the intention was indeed harmless record keeping, our position was that the state Labour Department should register both workers and employers. This demand has not elicited any response.

Other types of action

The KDWU's presence made a difference in the negotiations that workers engage in. If wages were pending, six members would go and negotiate the salary, or sometimes we went to the police station. On one occasion, the employer's family called the police because they suspected the domestic worker had stolen something, and so a group from KDWU went along with the domestic worker in solidarity. When there were cases of sexual harassment, the matter was taken to the police station if the woman wanted to take it forward. We were also able to put women in touch with organizations offering counselling and support.

Actions have also been used with some success to change common practices by employers. Domestic workers are usually given a bonus at the time of the Diwali festival, most often a sari, and employers can get away with giving them a cheap sari. The KDWU members wanted to receive one month's salary as bonus instead. Some women went on a *padayatra* (rally) with this demand, and succeeded in getting this bonus. In another instance, they wore black bands which said 'No sari but one month's wages' in Kannada. Since many employers could not read Kannada, they asked about the band, and the women talked to them about the KDWU and their bonus preferences. In 2009, ten members of the KDWU received cash bonuses using this new strategy.

Addressing divisions amongst the workers

Many domestic worker members faced social discrimination at work, usually stemming from caste-based attitudes. Many KDWU members were Scheduled Caste or Dalit women. Often they faced not being allowed to drink water at their employers' homes. Others were allocated separate glasses to drink from, were not allowed to use the toilet facilities, and were not given food in many cases. Some had the experience of having the dishes and clothes that they had washed symbolically splashed with water by employers in order to 'purify' them. These acts were plainly dehumanizing. Sometimes workers also played into this caste hierarchy, with women from higher castes stating that they would not do certain tasks such as cleaning, or cooking, or cleaning toilets. Citing her own sense of caste identity, for example, one woman refused to use the toilet she cleaned – even though she had been told she could. She preferred to use the common latrine elsewhere.

The KDWU found that more than just *roti-kapda-makaan*[4] slogans were needed to engage the attention of domestic workers, and that incorporating cultural symbols and festivities into its activities helped to increase solidarity amongst members. Thus, in the KDWU, women were brought together during festival times and made aware of certain axes of discrimination like caste and religion, but in an indirect way. During Sankranti, the harvest festival, for example, it is the tradition for women to gather together and to exchange *til* (sesame seeds) and *gur* (jaggery). The Kannada tradition is also to say something sweet during this exchange – there is a saying '*gur gur kha aur gur gur bol*' (eat the sweet, and speak with sweetness). This is an opportunity for social mingling and gossip. We used occasions like these to raise larger questions and initiate discussion through such questions as 'What does "marriage" mean?', 'Are we happy to be married?' Women spoke and shared their views with each other. Although this Sankranti custom is largely Hindu and upper caste, Muslim women also came and participated. By transcending religious and caste boundaries, we were trying to build up solidarity among women that rests on their common identity as women and as workers.

Gradually we started discussion on issues of culture, social control and violence – everything that makes women vulnerable. We also tried to change certain attitudes by working through symbols familiar to all. For example, during Dussehra, another festival, there is a particular day when workers worship the instruments of work. Generally, the implements worshipped are buses and rickshaws and carpenters' tools. Women come eagerly to participate, particularly in the religious ceremony. We used this opportunity to conduct a worship of the broom, with the worship conducted by a Dalit lady. This was important both because the broom is considered deeply 'dirty' and women's objections to this worship gave opportunities to discuss the dignity of work normally not considered of value, and because having a Dalit conduct the rituals broke the custom of ritual performance exclusively by higher castes.

We chose these actions to prompt discussion on how women perceived their own work, and there were mixed reactions. Some women questioned the practices, especially women from dominant castes like the Lingayat and Vokkaliga castes. We had to explain that their own instruments of work should also be worshipped and that there should be no discrimination on the basis of religion and caste.

The issue we were trying to address was the low status ascribed to women's paid domestic work. Dignity is important to everyone, and especially dignity in work. We are socialized into believing that certain kinds of work are less virtuous or respectable than others. In our discussions, we questioned these beliefs. By worshipping a broom, the contradiction between the fact that domestic workers from lower castes are deemed 'unclean' and yet they make homes clean, was brought to light. Our intention was not to start a new religious practice, but to find ways of getting women to respect the tools of their work, which is integral to the earning of their livelihood. We discussed how bus drivers or factory owners conduct small daily rituals before commencing a day's work, as well as the annual Vishwakarma Puja, because they respect their tools. By worshipping the broom, women were challenged to fight against stereotypes and think of their own work as valuable. By asking Muslims, widows or Dalits to conduct the ceremony, the status quo was challenged.

Involving the community

The PDS protest

Working with women has been much easier when their families support them in their union activities, and this in turn was more likely if the activities of the union benefited the whole family. So involving the community at large was also a continuous strategy in our organizing efforts. An active union can make a difference to the whole family. A major achievement of the KDWU was its success in getting accountability from the Public Distribution System (PDS) network in one of our areas of work.[5] Complaints surrounding the PDS ranged from long queues, delays, poor quality goods and irregular service. KDWU members had expressed these grievances time and again in meetings.

KDWU began to take up this issue. At a public sitting one day, KDWU members demanded that they get the legitimate quotas of food rations at the prices fixed by the government. In a queue on another day, when a woman spoke up and complained against the poor quality of grains on offer, the depot owner kicked her kerosene can and launched a stream of abuse. Events then proceeded at a quick pace. Overnight, fifteen women were taken off the 'Below Poverty Line' (BPL) list and put in the 'Above Poverty Line' (APL) category. This was an important act of aggression, because BPL card holders are eligible to obtain all items as well as kerosene at a reduced rate, whereas APL members are not entitled to any food grains. The KDWU members decided to oppose this arbitrary decision and approached the deputy commissioner. The APL category is supposed to include people who own LPG (cooking gas) cylinders, a black-and-white television, a cycle and a minimum income of Rs17,000 a year. The KDWU argued that almost all slum dwellers met these criteria, but it was impossible to survive with that alone in a city like Bangalore. In that case, should all slum dwellers be taken off the BPL list?

Women were encouraged to lead a protest themselves. A signature campaign protesting the local PDS depot's oversights was simultaneously submitted to the food range office, which monitors the PDS. This protest was no small matter. The struggle became extremely difficult as the depot owner asked the husbands of domestic workers to keep their wives 'under control', and he had the support of the Food and Civil Supplies Commissioner. In effect, the women were running the gauntlet of the nexus of slum lords, local mafia and politicians. Later, the women's husbands were threatened, and told that they might be evicted from their slum housing.

The protest did not end there. An inspection of the Citizens' Charter on the Targeted Public Distribution System (2005) revealed that people could form vigilance committees for each depot in the area to supervise its activities. Soon after, a public meeting with the commissioner and food inspectors was called to question the prevalent anomalies in the distribution system. Women brought the rice they were being given – it was not edible. The demand was simply to implement what is in the Charter. The vigilance committee was officially formed and included domestic workers. The commissioner himself put badges on the women. This was a tremendous victory for the women – they felt they were one step inside the bureaucracy. Pressure was stepped up on the food inspectors, who could not get away with food adulteration or hoarding for the black market as before. From the very next day, inspectors from adjacent areas came and admitted to small mistakes they now promised to fix. Through monthly meetings, women started inspecting the goods, overseeing timings of operations, and so on. Unfortunately, since most of them are illiterate, they were not able to inspect the depot owner's accounts.

Altogether the experience was a potentially transformative one. For domestic workers, a group barely on the fringes of the national economy, the symbolic value of being a part of a government-appointed vigilance committee was tremendous. To be accountable and responsible to the government and to one's neighbours, to be able to call meetings and oversee inspectors greatly empowered the women and gave them voice.

Two licences have so far been cancelled. Other women (relatives of the depot owner whose licence has been cancelled) in the locality did not always back these radical changes, but with the better quality of grains now available at the depot, they also began to come round. Currently, rations are still being given systematically. A food helpline was started by the food commissioner, who was very supportive. One more area of the city has set up its own vigilance committee. The challenge now is to follow up and sustain these initiatives. Confrontation cannot be a continuous affair. A small number of women cannot sustain the struggle – the demand for change must come from many.

Working with construction workers

Another example of the KDWU taking on problems, not just of the women themselves, but of the family, was in its work with male construction workers. The labour officer informed the KDWU that construction workers, many of whom were husbands of the domestic women in the KDWU, were not aware that there was a Welfare Fund for construction workers and that this was largely unutilized. The KDWU decided to get involved in raising awareness about the Welfare Board, eligibility for membership, benefits and so on among male construction workers. The intention was to create an awareness that having a women's organization in the area could be useful not only for the women members themselves, but also for the wider community.

Children of domestic workers

A further crucial link that was nurtured with the community was through the workers' children. Amongst domestic workers, the socialization of children into work generally begins early. Most women were taking their daughters to work as soon as they were able to lend a helping hand, and soon they too stood to become domestic workers. The KDWU emphasized that children have the right to an education, and women should see that both boys and girls are able to become educated. KDWU also formed a young girls' group, which was a forum for skill development, finding better placements as well as support for further education through scholarships. Girls were free to voice their aspirations and have a secure space of their own. For this generation, the combined experience of some education and a space for discussion generated different aspirations, and many began to seek more rewarding careers than their mothers'.

Looking to the future

Addressing employers

Union meetings with domestic workers were held in the afternoon so that they did not encroach upon work time, and this was an important factor in bringing the women in the union together. On the other hand, it was also important to find ways of holding discussions with employers, and in this the KDWU has been less successful. Employers, many of whom worked in the new sectors such as IT, generally earned well and were generally prepared to pay more – they were often desperate for good domestic help. Domestic workers, in turn, appreciated the better wages and also felt more answerable to employers who paid them better. On the other hand, they were uncomfortable with comments from employers such as 'What a big political leader you are becoming!' when it became known that they were members of a union.

There would be greater comfort all round if employers were aware of the intentions and objectives of the KDWU, and supported the union's efforts to get better working conditions and greater dignity for domestic workers. In one apartment complex, the Residents' Welfare Association actually approached the KDWU, wanting to establish a forum for both employers and employees, including both redressal and recruitment mechanisms. But nothing concrete emerged, and the proposed forum has not as yet progressed beyond discussion.

Negotiating with husbands

We observed that while the husbands of domestic workers could see the benefit of being in a union when they saw their wives earning higher salaries, they were less supportive when the women took on larger issues such as the PDS struggle, where there could be conflict with the authorities and there was a risk of being penalized. We wanted to ensure that the money earned by women remains in their hands. In some ways, our work with male construction workers was a strategy or entry point to the families of domestic workers, and a way to increase the men's support for the women's union activities. While usually husbands did not interfere with their wives' union-related activities, we experienced some occasions when men stopped their wives from attending meetings.

Addressing policy and the law

Until 2004, we paid considerable attention to the government. As employers and employees were so varied, we at first thought addressing them would be a more difficult strategy than confronting the government. But it became apparent that we needed a much bigger force to have influence at the level of the government – we would need a larger geographical spread and much greater numbers to be an effective voice. For the time being, therefore, we decided to focus our energies on the community.

At the same time, building these numbers set huge challenges. Given that domestic workers were so variable regarding the terms and conditions of their work, it was a struggle to organize the whole range, and our resources were very limited. By addressing the community, we were attempting to build the domestic workers' involvement in the structure and organization. Then eventually, as their confidence developed, we hoped to be able to make the government work in their interests.

Meanwhile, the biggest macro challenge remained the question of legal and policy recognition of domestic work at both state and national levels. A draft version of the Domestic Workers' Bill had been prepared by the National Commission for Women, and there was a campaign for domestic workers under way. But a strong national network was still to be built. KDWU came together with the other domestic workers' organizations in Bangalore to work with the National Domestic Workers' Movement, and became a member of the core committee of the Domestic Workers' Rights Commission that was pushing for legislation in Delhi. But progress in gaining legal provisions for domestic workers has been slow.[6]

At the state level, we lobbied for separate legislation for domestic workers and the creation of a Welfare Board and fund for domestic workers. Karnataka was in the process of setting up a board for unorganized workers, with representation being provided for civil society members, as well as seven government employees, seven employers, and domestic workers. KDWU negotiated a presence on this board.

Gaining this presence was not straightforward. Initially, domestic workers were not included, although *dhobis*, artisans and some sections of hotel workers had a voice. It was said that it was difficult to identify employers, and therefore domestic workers could not be represented. We argued that this was not a legitimate problem, because if domestic workers came for registration they could be identified, for example, by the Resident Welfare Associations or the Chamber of Commerce. Strategies like these had been used in Tamil Nadu and Kerala to include domestic workers in Welfare Boards. We therefore made the KDWU office a registration centre, and aimed to register part-time and full-time workers. In an added advantage, this process of registering workers and building a database made it more likely that workers in distress would reach out to the KDWU, manage a change of jobs if they wished to do so, and gain awareness about their rights.

Supporting domestic workers to make change

As the middle class expands and both partners in a household take on regular full-time employment, an increasing necessity has emerged amongst this class to have reliable domestic help. This has been a factor pushing wages up. But the pool of labour is large, so competition is fierce. Conditions of work generally continue to be arbitrary and to be based on personal relationships. Work relationships are still often ones of gratitude and helplessness on the part of the worker. We believe it is especially important that the workers understand their own power, their own ability to make the strategies of the KDWU effective. This seemed to be the first step. So currently our main focus has remained on those actions that have helped women workers to change their own perceptions. We have encouraged actions such as demanding salary vouchers, to create a record of wage payments (and how low they were). We request workers to note down in a book how many days they have worked, and make an account of the conditions of their work. We have encouraged them to assert themselves so that they are not treated as untouchables, for example, by refusing to drink tea in the plastic cup allocated.[7] Women have to be able to assert their equality themselves. Ultimately, if they are able to find the voice with which to refuse degrading conditions of work, this may be the most important achievement.

Notes

1 This chapter is based on Geeta Menon's presentation at the conference on 'Organising Women in the Informal Economy: Lessons from Practice' (20–21 October 2008, New Delhi) called by the

Institute of Social Studies Trust and Pathways of Women's Empowerment RPC, a programme of DfID. It also draws on follow-up interviews during 2009.

2 Although employers described such large sums as an 'advance', they do not necessarily expect return of the amount; what they do expect is abiding loyalty. Such 'advances' are commonly made to help with marriage or death rituals, or property-related needs.

3 The 'table' is also a symbol associated with affluence, offices and Western eating habits – it is not a part of the daily lives of domestic workers.

4 Literally bread-cloth-house, a reference to basic needs and minimum income.

5 The Public Distribution System provides grain and other goods at subsidized prices against household ration cards and these goods are available at Fair Price Shops.

6 By mid-2012, both the National Commission on Women and the Ministry of Labour had drafted separate laws on domestic workers, but neither had been passed, or even introduced in Parliament. So, currently, there is no national law on domestic workers, although Maharashtra has state-level legislation. At the same time, the Ministry of Labour, in consultation with many stakeholders, has drafted a policy on domestic workers. This policy is yet to be approved, but is very much in process.

7 In Bangalore, it is the custom to drink tea or coffee from stainless steel tumblers; separate plastic mugs may be kept for workers, thus emphasizing their lower status.

7
Power at the Bottom of the Heap
Organizing Waste Pickers in Pune
● ●
Lakshmi Narayan and Poornima Chikarmane

> *Until now we were counted among the animals. Baba Adhav has brought us to sit here as humans.*
>
> Hirabai Shinde, waste picker, at the first Convention of Waste Pickers in Pune, May 1993.

In 1990, while implementing an adult education programme, we and some others from SNDT Women's University in Pune met child waste pickers at one of the education centres. This encounter prompted the start of non-formal education work with these children. Inspired by the methods of Paulo Freire, we went with the children on waste collection forays and were struck by the idea that if waste was segregated at source, not only would the work conditions of the children improve dramatically, but they would also gain significant amounts of time which they could use for education. In the weeks that followed, we initiated a campaign for source segregation of scrap in the neighbourhood. The children's mothers, relieved that their work intensity had been dramatically reduced, also saw that the value of the scrap increased through source segregation. They became enthusiastic about sending the children to school and doing the segregated scrap collection on their own. About 30 women were issued identity cards by SNDT to collect scrap door to door in the neighbourhood.

---

* The narrative is separated into two 'voices' in this chapter in an attempt to surface the methods through which the chapter was developed, to make more explicit the voices of the author-activists in KKPKP, and to add a dialogue-like dimension. The chapter draws on the presentation made by Lakshmi Narayan

This was the genesis of Kagad Kach Patra Kashtakari Panchayat (KKPKP), a waste pickers' trade union formally established in 1993 that now has over 6,000 members drawn from the waste picker community across Pune and its suburbs. In the twenty years since that first project, the organization has grown and evolved; part of it has morphed into a refuse collection cooperative built on a business model and eventually named SWaCH (Solid Waste Collection and Handling). It has won important resources and recognition for waste pickers from the municipal government, and made significant contributions to the gradual repositioning of waste pickers as participants in a critical urban service with environmental sustainability credentials. Since 2005, it has been the secretariat of the Alliance of Indian Waste Pickers, a non-institutionalized network of 35 member organizations working with waste pickers and on solid waste management at different locations in India. It has also made alliances across international and national movements engaged in the larger struggle against injustice and exploitation, and working on environmental issues.

Flexibility and adaptability has been a necessity for an organization like this. Informal sector workers have no employers to stabilize or regulate the conditions of their livelihoods. Instead, they rely on a resource, and as the external environment changes the conditions, systems and terms of access to that resource, so too the work of those dependent on it must change. This is an important reason why KKPKP has developed in the ways it has.

(* *cont.*) at the conference on 'Organising Women in the Informal Economy: Lessons from Practice' (New Delhi, 20–21 October 2008, called by the Institute of Social Studies Trust and Pathways of Women's Empowerment RPC, a programme of DfID) and on available literature by and about the organization. A draft was prepared on this basis by Kirsty Milward, one of the editors of this volume. Kirsty subsequently conducted interviews with KKPKP, particularly Poornima Chikarmane and Lakshmi Narayan, in March 2011 in Pune. The italicized sections are intended to represent the more conversational nature of these later inputs, while roman sections reflect the more formal description and analysis of presentation and documentation.

When KKPKP began in Pune, waste pickers sorted through garbage for reuseable and saleable items – mainly paper, glass, some types of plastic, and metal – as has been the tradition in many parts of India. Some waste pickers worked at landfill sites on the outskirts of cities; some at garbage vats and designated areas within the city; and some at informal dumping grounds on the cities' vacant lots. They have been stigmatized and marginalized in ways that partly reflect caste-based marginalization: they are mainly drawn from former 'untouchable' castes, and their work is strongly associated with dirt. They occupied one of the lowest rungs of the occupational hierarchy, and, like the people they serviced, often attached little value to their work.

Within the waste-picking and scrap-reprocessing industry, there was a clear hierarchy of tasks, with graduations in income, work conditions and social status/acceptability distinguishing sub-sectors in the hierarchy. Women made up the large majority of those at the bottom of the pile, those picking waste at municipal bins and landfill sites. In Pune in 2004, women made up 92 per cent of this category. Of these, 30 per cent were widowed or deserted and 50 per cent contributed more than 50 per cent of the household income with their average daily earnings of about Rs60 (about US$1.25 at current exchange rates) (Chikarmane and Narayan 2004). Nearly all are from Dalit castes of Mahar and Matang, traditionally associated with animal carcass and leather processes, considered 'unclean' occupations. Itinerant buyers, on the other hand, who buy small quantities of scrap from households, offices and small shops for resale to scrap traders, are marginally better off. According to a study commissioned by the International Labour Organization (Chikarmane, Deshpande and Narayan 2001), at that time their average earnings were Rs75 a day (about US$1.60 at current rates) and 81 per cent of them were men.

One thing we learned quickly was that the journey of the scrap materials from the point of no further use in a household or business to the point where it is another reusable product is long and complex, and mostly invisible to the uninitiated. It involves many stakeholders: housewives, business people, the municipal government, itinerant buyers, owners of scrap shops where good scrap can be sorted again, stored as like with like, agents who sell reusable material to factories, and of course waste pickers. We began to see that for waste pickers, the map of the city is dotted with formal and informal dumps, collection routes, spaces where it is safe to sort and temporarily store collected 'good' scrap, and scrap shops.

In several respects, waste pickers pose challenges to organizing: they are physically dispersed, have no employer, many work long hours, and they are socially shunned. Yet for nearly twenty years KKPKP has sustained a vibrant organization that has made tangible material and social gains on behalf of its membership. Its offspring, SWaCH, is growing in strength as a model for the new face of solid waste management in India – one which has made the interests of a very marginalized constituency of waste pickers in retaining access to waste its top priority. This chapter highlights some aspects of the approach and strategies that have contributed to this progress.

Strategies and approach

Building 'worker' identity amongst waste pickers and the administration

The decision to organize as a trade union, rather than another type of organization such as a cooperative, had much to do with the fact that, even amongst waste pickers themselves, their occupation was widely seen not as 'work' but as *kachra chivadne* (rummaging through garbage) (Chikarmane and Narayan 2004: 2). In legal terms, a trade union is a 'workers' organization', so this step was important in establishing waste pickers' identity as *workers*. It was also clear from early interactions during the original project at SNDT University that waste pickers were less engaged by the prospect of transferring occupations through 'rehabilitation' than by the possibility of regulating and upgrading the conditions and livelihoods potential of the occupation they were in. Organizing as a union placed the waste picker as 'worker' and the issue of working conditions firmly at the top of the agenda.

Much of the business of establishing worker identity took place at the level of the workers themselves: issuing identity cards and taking registration details of all members, including family profile and work details, was an important part of the process, as was participation in the union's mass programmes of rallies, protests and demonstrations. At the same time, it was important to articulate to government bodies and the general public that waste picking constituted work.

This involved constantly making visible the ways in which waste picking is economically productive and environmentally beneficial work. We argued that waste pickers are essentially recyclers, collecting and trading recyclable commodities, and are therefore key service providers in the waste economy, not 'scavengers' freeloading on the surplus of the relatively wealthy. Going a step further, we also argued that the recycling service waste pickers provide is a far more efficient and sustainable recycling method than that offered by alternatives such as generating electricity from waste incineration. This was our position at the Copenhagen Climate Change Conference in 2009, because Refuse Derived Fuel – or electricity from incinerators – is now eligible for carbon credits from the UN-backed Clean Development Mechanism (CDM) funds.[1] So it is likely to become more widely established, but this system is inefficient in burning recyclable material, and not only bypasses waste pickers but also threatens their livelihoods.

The argument that waste pickers provide a key service was directed strongly at the municipal government in a process of claiming resources from them as workers. At first, quantification of waste pickers' economic contribution was made by simple extrapolations on the basis of turnover at the scrap shop run by the union. Later, formal research was commissioned by the ILO in 2000. This research calculated that waste pickers save the Municipal Corporation nearly Rs16 million (US$330,000 at current exchange rates) a year in transportation costs alone, and that each waste picker contributes Rs246 (US$5) of unpaid labour a month to the municipality. It was also calculated that the scrap trade contributes Rs185 million (US$3,850,000) a year to the local economy.

A later study established that waste pickers and itinerant waste buyers subsidize the waste generators and the formal system by an estimated Rs348 million (US$7,733,333) – a figure which includes the purchases made by itinerant waste buyers and a sum representing the reduced transport costs incurred by the formal system. In addition, they contribute to environmental preservation by avoiding the production of Carbon Dioxide Equivalents worth Rs169,819,980 (US$3,773,777) annually.[2] Simulations of a situation where the entire waste collection is handled by a waste pickers' cooperative showed that this would allow for avoiding even greater amounts of greenhouse gases, amounting to 308,713 metric tons Carbon Dioxide Equivalents, a saving of Rs178,127,220 (US$3,958,382) (KKPKP 2006).

On the basis of initial arguments, the municipal government granted certain concessions, such as endorsing the waste pickers' union identity card, thus effectively authorizing them to pick waste. This endorsement had a profound effect on the waste pickers' self-image as well as on their identity in the eyes of the public. Later, KKPKP used this recognition to further argue that the health costs of this work – such as musculoskeletal problems, respiratory and gastro-intestinal ailments – were borne by the waste pickers, who should therefore be eligible for medical insurance schemes, the costs of which should be borne by the municipality. This demand was eventually granted in 2002–3.

Keeping control of the scrap by diversification

KKPKP recognizes that since waste pickers have no employer, the struggle is not only about negotiating directly for better wage/earnings and conditions, but about keeping control over the resources on which their livelihoods are built – the scrap. Because most waste pickers are women, this is a particularly difficult task. Each time the technology of waste picking changes – from sacks to handcarts to trucks, for example – there is a real danger waste picker women will lose out to new entrants – mainly men entrepreneurs – attracted by new opportunities as the process changes. This happened clearly, in an incident in the early 1990s, to the first group of waste picker women we were involved with – an entrepreneur *tried to take over the waste collection in their area. We responded by organizing direct action to prevent the newcomers from taking the original bins away. So KKPKP's strategy has been focused here: on maintaining waste picker women's access to the resource, and where possible, increasing the value that accrues to them from it.*

The first venture in diversification was Kashtachi Kamai, a cooperative scrap shop started in 1998 using working capital provided by donors to SNDT University for KKPKP. This set out to explore under what conditions the scrap retail trade could be profitable without being exploitative of the pickers – that is, seeking to offer prices for buying and selling scrap that ensured the survival of the initiative without generating unwarranted profit. A second scrap shop in a different area was added a few years later. Both shops run as profit-making enterprises, and profits are shared with waste picker members on an annual basis as a bonus. At one of the shops, this bonus amounts to 13 per cent of annual earnings. Since the bonus is a feature attracting waste pickers to sell at the shop, several other scrap shops have begun offering their regular sellers a bonus, too.

On the basis that waste pickers are already workers located in the waste-processing chain, KKPKP has consistently argued for the integration of waste pickers into new arrangements for the doorstep collection of source-segregated waste (see Narayan and Chikarmane 2006). Until 2000, municipal governments were officially responsible for waste collection from community bins. How the waste got to the bins was not their responsibility. New government recommendations in 2000 pressed municipal governments to extend their responsibilities from these bins to doorstep collections. The most popular method of fulfilling this new task was to contract out to local or multinational enterprises, thus displacing waste pickers from the recycling chain.

In order to demonstrate how waste pickers could be integrated into these new processes, KKPKP initiated Pune's only eco-friendly doorstep collection service, with 400 members collecting segregated waste from 40,000 households for a monthly service charge paid by the apartment block according to the number of apartments covered. These collectors put organic waste in a composting pit and sold scrap through existing channels. This programme, which formally became the Solid Waste Collection and Handling (SWaCH) cooperative in 2007, by 2008 had a presence in 127 of 144 sub-units in all fourteen administrative wards of the Pune Municipal Council, and involved 1,500 waste pickers servicing 200,000 households (Chikarmane, Narayan and Chaturvedi 2008).

SWaCH works with authorization from the Pune Municipal Corporation to provide door-to-door waste collection and other services. Waste pickers are provided with a handcart and uniform, and are responsible for particular routes. In 2010, SWaCH began a second unit in Pimpri Chinchwad Municipality, just outside Pune. This is a motorized door-to-door collection service, involving 115 small trucks and 250 waste pickers who service set routes on a daily basis, with householders bringing waste – as yet usually unsegregated – out to the truck as it passes.

In Pune SWaCH, we have also experimented with ways of retaining the value of waste in waste pickers' hands by offering a combination of skills and services. Some of these services aim at adding value to the scrap. Along with the drive for source segregation in Pune city, we offer a composting service for the organic waste, so that housing associations can have good compost for their gardens. In some areas, the waste pickers also offer housekeeping services to businesses: this way, they have good control of the best scrap generated by shops and offices – which is often of high value. We have also experimented with the final stage of the recycling process: making products from scrap for sale, such as by making paper and paper bags. And in Pimpri Chinchwad, where SWaCH uses trucks, we are training young women – the daughters of waste pickers – to drive the trucks.

Bringing waste pickers into door-to-door collection services has perhaps been the most challenging of KKPKP's activities to waste picker identity, as this brings waste pickers face to face with householders. On the one hand, the waste picker becomes accountable to the householder for a paid service, and is no longer so free-roaming, flexible or independent. Many had to change their dress and their mannerisms, in addition to the actual nature of their daily work. SWaCH actively trains waste pickers involved in door-to-door collection to take on this new kind of relationship. On the other hand, householders are less able to put waste pickers beyond their frame of reference, and must begin to address them as people, and indeed as people for whom servile roles are not the norm.

In some ways the changes in this relationship are complex. Whereas, earlier, waste pickers could elicit a certain amount of sympathy from at least a section of the middle class for their terrible conditions and thankless work, they are now brought into a service relationship with the middle class, where expectations of service can generate criticism and resentment. Sometimes householders complain about occasions when waste pickers didn't take all the garbage, just picking off what they could sell; sometimes they complain that they didn't show up at the right time so the garbage is stacking up. On the other hand, waste pickers working in the Pune SWaCH regularly service about 200 households each, and their relationships with households are therefore often quite personalized, which sometimes brings opportunities. Waste pickers sometimes earn extra income from other tasks that come up, such as domestic work duties while someone is on holiday or sick.

In the interests of diversifying further in scrap collection, while also aligning with environmental groups and discourses, since 2006 SWaCH has also been involved in collecting and recycling waste generated during religious festivals such as the Ganesh Visarjan (when images of Ganesh are immersed in water bodies at the end of the festival period). Offerings and other materials that would previously have been immersed in the river are now placed in waste bins, and collected and processed by SWaCH.

Using and moderating trade union approaches

ACKNOWLEDGING THE POWER OF NUMBERS. The original decision to organize as a trade union owed much to an awareness that in the history of organizing the poor, who are generally expected to keep a low profile, establishing a 'critical mass' has often been an essential factor. Dr Baba Adhav, President of the Hamal Panchayat (a 50-year-old trade union of coolies/headloaders) and veteran labour leader of informal sector workers in Maharashtra, was very supportive of the waste pickers' initiatives in the early days, and he particularly emphasized this approach. Under his leadership, the first waste pickers' convention was organized by the SNDT activists and Mohan Nanavre, the son of a waste picker, leader of the Dalit Swayamsevak Sangh (a Dalit rights organization) and a long-time associate of Dr Adhav. The convention in 1993 was attended by over 800 waste pickers from across the city and set the parameters for the new unions' approach.

As the organization has grown, it has also been clear that numbers were one – although not the only – important factor in gaining resources from the municipal government. Over the course of three years several public demonstrations, in which thousands participated, eventually resulted in municipal endorsement of the photo-identity cards that the union had issued to member waste pickers. This endorsement amounted to recognizing waste pickers as service providers having certain rights to access and sort waste in municipal bins.

Numerical strength has also been important in changing local relationships within the scrap trade. Although, as discussed below, KKPKP avoided threatening the waste pickers' central business relationships even when these were in some respects exploitative, it was clear from the reaction to the union of retail traders in scrap that they were more wary of KKPKP than, for example, of individuals attempting to move into the trade, who were sometimes greeted with arson and physical intimidation.

USING THIS POWER WITH DISCRETION. Over its years of work, KKPKP has promoted and exploited many conventional trade union tools, such as rallies, struggle, mobilization, and a widespread profile. Nevertheless, it has also been careful to distance itself from the more aggressive aspects of union politics and to emphasize peaceful, disciplined, agitational methods and an orderly approach. It has been careful, for example, to avoid a reputation for using its strength in numbers indiscriminately to threaten other actors. KKPKP's members, particularly in the initial stages of organizing, were among the most vulnerable of workers, with virtually nothing to fall back on in the event that crucial work relationships should fail.

We have had to be fully aware of the risks of struggle, and recognize that in this sector it is the waste pickers themselves who pay the heaviest price in the short term. We couldn't antagonize relationships too much, especially those on which the waste pickers are very dependent. We realized that although scrap traders and scrap shop owners often have an exploitative relationship with waste pickers, these are often close and long-term relationships, established sometimes over generations. They often have aspects of mutual interdependence: scrap traders also help waste pickers in various ways as well as buying their scrap.

In fact, the group that reacted most strongly to the establishment of the trade union was the scrap traders, who tried to resurrect a defunct Association of Scrap Traders within months of the KKPKP being formed. However, this attempt was short-lived because of the intense competition within the retail segment of the trade. Rather than waging war on this group, KKPKP has picked its battles, focusing on specific behaviours such as usurious money lending, which was practised by some individuals within this group as well as many beyond it.

MITIGATING RISK WITH SOCIAL DEVELOPMENT AND ALTERNATIVES. KKPKP has combined social mobilization with a series of social development activities designed to expand livelihood options and increase the security of the material base from which waste pickers can take their struggles forward. These include credit provision, education, and eliminating the practice of child labour, in addition to work-related economic issues.

Two important initiatives set out to build alternatives to exploitative situations, in the form of a credit cooperative and Kashtachi Kamai, the cooperative scrap store. The credit co-operative, KKPKP-NPS, collected members' savings, deposited these in the cooperative's office, and approved loans to members. With this service in place, waste pickers were able to substantially reduce their reliance on money lenders, who charged very high interest rates. Related to this, the union also ran a 'gold loan scheme', which allowed members to pawn their gold and silver to the union at the same interest rates used by the credit cooperative, and a campaign to reduce interest rates on waste pickers' small amounts of gold held by money lenders and pawn brokers all over Pune. This campaign successfully saw the redemption of Rs250,000 (US$5,200) worth of gold belonging to a few hundred waste pickers. In addition to these initiatives, a group life insurance scheme was introduced in 1998 in collaboration with the Life Insurance Corporation of India. Enrolment is optional and members pay their own premiums, which insure them against natural and accidental death and disability.

These activities have been put in place in the belief that while they cannot by themselves challenge or transform entrenched power structures, they can sustain the involvement of members, for whom the costs of struggle can be very high in the process of pursuing that transformation.

Responding to issues as prioritized by the women workers

An important departure from conventional models of worker organization has been KKPKP's explicit efforts to represent and follow through on the perspectives of its members as they perceive and articulate issues. KKPKP has taken a very process-oriented, organic approach, prioritizing participation of the waste pickers who constitute the organization. Within KKPKP, empowerment is understood to be a process in which the poor critically reflect upon their life situation, analyse it and experience a sense of confidence and self-worth through the building of a collective identity. With this confidence, it is then possible to exercise the power to make, influence or control decisions that affect their lives (Chikarmane and Narayan 2004).

One early aspect of this was acknowledging that alternative occupations were not the agenda of the waste picker women. Other occupations realistically accessible to them they saw as demeaning in important ways – 'Who wants to work as a construction labourer? The supervisors treat you like their wives' (Chikarmane and Narayan 2004: 2) – and they recognized that lacking an employer has the advantage of freedom from the servile feudal relationships common in wage labour in Indian villages. They were also not interested in income generation programmes that involved long training courses and a risky process of learning to survive in the market.

JUSTICE STRUGGLES. This organic approach has meant that the organization is constantly evolving in response to changing perceptions of what needs to change, and that a substantial part of its work has been around issue-based justice struggles, arising from incidents and problems as they are encountered.

In the early days, these struggles included several instances of speaking out against the police, or specific police officers, against harassment of various kinds, and against extortion. Agitations along these lines started with a sit-in protest outside a police station in 1993, in response to three complaints by members against police officers located there – who eventually had to make a public apology for harassment and return a bribe taken from an itinerant buyer. In another event, a woman waste picker supported by other KKPKP members directly confronted the police officer who had been extorting money from her in return for 'allowing' her to collect from certain bins. Members were encouraged to accompany extortion victims to confront the police, and within a few years 'it [had] been perfected to an art form when a telephone call to the police station [resulted] in the money being returned to the waste picker' (Chikarmane and Narayan 2004: 23). Extortion by the police is now very rare.

These justice struggles have also involved confronting a trader who was severely in debt to a number of waste picker clients, and following through in the courts a case in which two waste pickers were accused of stealing a gold chain that they had found in a bin. This latter case involved successfully challenging a generalized public perception of waste pickers as dishonest thieves.

NEGOTIATING CHANGE IN CULTURAL PRACTICES. The approach has not necessarily implied that KKPKP's 'position' on different issues emerges directly from majority opinion or waste pickers' customary cultural practices. KKPKP has also addressed social issues, including child marriage, child labour, domestic violence and other violence such as rape as and when they reach pivotal moments. These are issues in which values are clearly at play. Interventions have sometimes included confrontations between the union and particular groups of members, including over an incident in which a member attempted to go ahead with the marriage of her under-age daughter, despite promising to the union that she would not. The union successfully prevented the wedding, but bitterness over this event took some time to subside. Following this incident, KKPKP organized group weddings for a few years in joint ceremonies, which considerably reduced costs. These events took the unusual step of calling on Mahars and Matangs to share the wedding platform – a step which challenged both to confront their caste-based biases. Part of building KKPKP's identity has been around identifying the spaces where internal change amongst waste pickers is both necessary and possible, and in coming through internal confrontation intact as an organization.

Building relations with the government

In the absence of direct employers, it has been crucial to address the government as the responsible party in relation to recognition of waste pickers' rights, along with the rights of other informal sector workers. Since 2005, this has meant addressing the national government as the Alliance of Waste Pickers in India: amongst other issues, the Alliance has campaigned for inclusion in the social security benefits offered by the Unorganized Sector Workers' Social Security Bill of 2008. But, prior to that, it meant addressing the Pune Municipal Corporation to gain tangible improvements in waste pickers' lives.

This strategy was facilitated by the fact that municipal governments are constitutionally bound to accept responsibility for waste management. Through various methods, KKPKP argued that waste pickers make a significant contribution to waste management and should therefore be recognized and in some ways treated as partners of the municipality.

Gradually KKPKP gained a series of resources from the Pune Municipality: the medical insurance scheme, which covers over 5,000 waste pickers for hospitalization costs of up to Rs5000; the right to use space in by-lanes where traffic is not obstructed for scrap sorting; the right to constructed space for conducting this activity where earlier these activities had often generated harassment – to date, the municipality has provided over 30 such constructed spaces; and, with the help of a sympathetic press, the inclusion of waste pickers' children in a scholarship scheme for those in 'Unclean Occupations', a scheme originally targeting only at the children of 'carriers of night soil' (who clean out pit latrines on a daily basis).

These concessions were not won easily – they have involved continual struggle in the form of protests, demonstrations and collective action displaying both unity and numbers. Arguments are often evidence-based and substantiated by data and research. The existence of key supporters within the administration has been very important in gaining concessions, and we value relations with these supporters highly. At the same time, we know it is important to look beyond these key allies so that issues and initiatives don't get lost when they move on or are transferred out of their current posts.

Struggles as workers, struggles as citizens

Many of the specific struggles undertaken by KKPKP on the face of it demand better conditions as workers, but are underpinned by a more generalized struggle for recognition as citizens and people, and for acknowledgement of the dignity of their work. Waste pickers in the public eye have for many years been deeply associated with the 'dirt' that the waste generated by others represents, and this is compounded by caste ideologies that pair 'unclean' tasks with (ritually) 'unclean' people. Before the municipality granted rights to by-lane space to sort waste, waste pickers were frequently harassed on the basis of the 'mess' they apparently generated. An important area of struggle has been to emphasize that waste pickers do not make the mess, but rather clean up and organize other people's dirt. The eco-friendly doorstep collection service promoted by KKPKP in the early days of SWaCH was thus named 'Swachateche Varkari', or 'Harbingers of Cleanliness' (Chikarmane, Deshpande and Narayan 2001). Rebuilding the link between waste and those who generate it – households and businesses – is one aspect of this struggle.

Waste pickers were also strongly associated with theft and dishonesty, in general part of a semi-criminal underclass who thus deserved no protection from the police unless it was paid for through extortion. Waste pickers complained, for example, that the police rounded them up *en masse* whenever there was a theft in the neighbourhood. The court case that acquitted two waste pickers of the theft of a gold chain found in the bin was therefore a very significant moral victory – an endorsement of their right to fair treatment as equal citizens in a court of law.

We also did an informal study in 1998, reviewing police cases to see how many cases there had been against waste pickers for theft, and how many of them were conclusive. With these figures in hand, we were able to argue that the association between waste picking and theft was a sustained prejudice and myth, and that the police had a duty not to act on unsubstantiated assumptions. Later, when there were incidents of waste pickers finding valuable items in trash and handing them in or returning them, we started using the media to make sure the myths in many people's minds were challenged. In a focus group discussion for older waste pickers we held a few months ago, it became clear that their relationship with the police has changed enormously: they said the police don't dare touch them now, and that their children, who now have the trappings of 'real' workers in the form of uniforms and handcarts, are hardly even aware how much of a problem police harassment used to be.

Reinventing cultural symbols to claim rights

Waste pickers are street-wise and street-smart, often argumentative and willing to challenge or question. They are also willing to take risks, and are creative and entrepreneurial. Some of these qualities may be born of a perception on their part that, in terms of social status *vis-à-vis* society in general, they have little to lose – a perception which perhaps lies at the root of KKPKP's ability to come up with and then follow through several innovative protests that have appropriated recognized cultural symbols, recycling them to produce specific messages around rights and duties. In one event, KKPKP organized a bin *chipko andolan* – a reference to the iconic environmental Chipko movement, in which women hugged trees to stop them from being cut down. In this case, women hugged the bins in one neighbourhood to stop a waste entrepreneur from removing them in the interests of his new, motorized waste collection service. Thus the waste picker women claimed prior rights to the waste while also associating their work with the environmental sustainability issues that Chipko highlighted.

In a similar appropriation, waste pickers decided to tie a giant *rakhi* all around the municipal building. Raksha Bandhan is a widely practised ritual in which sisters tie thread bracelets on their brothers' wrists to symbolize their bonds, including the brothers' duties of protection and support. This action at the municipal building therefore served to emphasize that waste pickers make a large contribution to municipal work to take care of the environment, but this contribution has not been met with equal recognition or protection of waste pickers on the part of the municipality.

Waste pickers have also used street theatre to educate generators of waste about source segregation. This in itself is a reversal of a more common purpose of street theatre, which is to educate the poor about various issues. One of the dramas depicted the lives of waste pickers as women and as workers, but had no formal script and much was improvised by the different groups who enacted it. They have also composed songs set to the tunes of traditional folk songs and performed at ceremonial all-night folk events ritually performed following auspicious occasions such as weddings.

KKPKP have also reinterpreted cultural symbols to facilitate social analysis amongst members. For example, the *dahi handi* is an annual Janmashtami ritual in which a human pyramid is formed to reach a pot of curd and currency notes tied high up on a rope. The man at the top who reaches the curd gets the largest share. This image is used to analyse gender, caste and class, and the recycling sector – and to challenge the trickle-down theory of development (Chikarmane and Narayan 2004).

The role of national and international networks and alliances

Network building has become gradually more important as the organization has gained strength both in terms of real gains in the lives of waste pickers, and in terms of the ability to draw on several years of experience to take initiative and leadership in networks.

We need national networks especially in the informal sector because in the absence of an employer to negotiate with over work conditions, it is the duty of governments to take the role of regulating the sector and providing protection and security. Networks can raise the profile of informal workers in relation to government and create pressure for recognition and response in terms of policy. On the other hand, if there is no worker-level organization, it is too easy for policies to remain as elegantly written pieces of paper. What counts in the end is the ways in which conditions change for waste pickers, and if no one is there to demand rights, then policies do not actually change working conditions.

Nevertheless, KKPKP has played a significant role in building the strength of the Alliance of Waste Pickers in India, and in researching alliances of waste pickers across Asia (KKPKP 2008). Apart from direct networks with other waste picker organizations, it also seeks interfaces with informal sector labour organizations, environmental organizations and women's organizations. Issues-based alliances have sometimes been drawn on an international canvas – since 2008, for example, KKPKP has been interacting closely with Global Action for Incinerator Alternatives (GAIA), as the inclusion of incinerators for fuel generation in the Clean

Development Mechanism (CDM) represents a real threat to waste pickers, who compete for the same resources as incinerator owners. The technical and knowledge resource base of GAIA, and the reach and perspectives of its members, are supportive of the entire recycling economy and waste pickers in particular.

Pune waste pickers have also been a presence at the international climate change conferences, and attracted discussion and debate at the Copenhagen Climate Change conference in 2009 where they represented themselves as important links in recycling processes.

International networks, such as the Global Alliance of Waste Pickers, have also been important to KKPKP for solidarity and support, and sometimes for getting to know about different models and processes in waste picking elsewhere. But perhaps the most important purpose is in raising the visibility of KKPKP and Indian waste pickers in general. Raising the profile internationally can have the effect of raising the profile locally too, and creates some pressure on the national and municipal governments to recognize the role of waste pickers and respond. Unless this local effect takes place, the contribution of international networks can be quite limited.

Several aspects of waste picking in Pune are specific to India. The sector works in a context of relative poverty and a complex array of traditional recycling routes. This means that experiences from other countries can be very difficult to apply. For example, India has a much bigger proportion of wet waste to dry waste than most countries. Relative poverty means that waste from food and consumer durable packaging exists in quite small proportions. In addition, there are several systems for recycling and re-use that operate independently of new solid waste management systems.

The culture of recycling is by tradition very strong. No one, for example, puts newspapers out as waste. Very few put glass bottles out. These are collected and sold by householders direct to people in the scrap trade. Ultimately, the quality of waste that ends up at landfills in India is much lower, for example, than in Thailand because fewer recyclables are thrown out in the first place.

Addressing inequalities within and beyond KKPKP

Gender

The organization of the waste-processing industry is strongly and clearly mediated by caste and clas, and there is also strong gender segmentation of tasks and sites: nearly all landfill and bin waste pickers are women, almost all scrap traders are men. Most itinerant buyers are men, and those women that do itinerant buying use head baskets to carry scrap rather than the hand carts that men use, which are often hired and therefore require some minimal capital. This segmentation also produces income differentials, as by the time waste reaches dumps and landfill sites, most of the valuable waste has already been picked off.

As a result, work-related tensions within the sector have also sometimes had a 'gender flavour'. Often these are conflicts over waste resource rights: before SWaCH gave many waste picker women access to waste at source, sometimes women complained that men waste pickers use cycles at night to go round the bins and get the good scrap before the women. This work option was not readily available to women who don't get to use cycles easily and who risk harassment if they work at night. Women waste pickers also strongly resisted the entry of new, mainly male, itinerant buyers who had migrated to Pune from other states, claiming that a decline in the quality of scrap arriving in their hands was due to the increased presence of these buyers. KKPKP responded by insisting that these new entrants could not be pushed out on the basis that they were migrants, but began following up on their earlier intervention of promoting women as doorstep collectors of segregated waste.

There were also gendered conflicts over the KKPKP logo. This depicts a woman waste picker, and was rejected by several men who refused to take KKPKP identity cards in the early membership building processes. KKPKP responded by initiating discussion and explanation of the logo, and reminding members that the majority of waste pickers and KKPKP members are women. After some debate, the matter was resolved and the logo remained, but one group of men still refused to take identity cards for several years.

There is recognition amongst KKPKP and its members that men in the waste-picking sector are also poor and powerless, or enjoy a small degree of advantage over women. Nevertheless, within households men do exercise power, and women remain responsible for household work when not waste picking. On the whole this situation is not challenged by the union. However, KKPKP has supported women in domestic violence incidents, for example by helping them to talk over the situation with their partners or to file police cases when the woman wanted to press charges or needed police intervention.

Gender ideologies around sexuality remain powerful, and many women worry about sexual harassment at work partly, or mostly, because their husbands will suspect their fidelity if they know about the harassment. This is also a reason for not speaking up about it. Many women also are very anxious for their daughters. But the changes in the sector brought about by SWaCH have also reduced some of these anxieties.

Before we did door-to-door collection on a large scale, many women used to pick waste from municipal garbage vats. These vats were also used by men as public urinals, so the risk of young women waste pickers being exposed to lewd jokes and sexually threatening situations was very real. With the removal of vats and the emphasis on door-to-door collection, which mostly brings waste pickers into contact with housewives and domestic workers, much of this risk has been removed.

Caste

As discussed, in Pune scrap collectors are almost exclusively Dalits, previously known as 'untouchable' castes. Within this, they mostly belong to the Mahar caste (including Mahars who have converted to Buddhism after Ambedkar's intervention in 1956, and are now called Neo-Buddhists) and the Matang/ Mang castes. Mahars by tradition were village watchmen, as well as being responsible for the disposal of dead animals. Matang/ Mangs were leather workers. Despite much anti-caste activity in Maharashtra, waste pickers still usually live in caste-segregated ghettos within slums. Some early critics of KKPKP were sceptical of an organization that they believed had the potential to reinforce the relation between caste and occupation. KKPKP at the time argued that once the conditions and profile of waste picking improved, its association with specific castes would weaken, and this position has to some extent been vindicated recently.

There hasn't been much change in terms of caste make-up of the waste pickers, and inter-caste rivalries between the Matangs and the Mahars still exist. Some OBCs ('other backward castes' – of higher status than Matangs and Mahars) have newly arrived on the scene as it begins to be more profitable – in SWaCH, for example – and there has been some resistance to this, although KKPKP's formal position is that it is fine as long as new entrants do not displace the older communities of workers.

Relative homogeneity in caste terms means that intra-sector task segmentation is stronger by gender than by sub-caste and within the sector there is little caste-based friction. But on social issues there is some tension, each sub-caste believing the other is inferior. Marriage remains within each caste. KKPKP has confronted these divisions explicitly by organizing mixed community weddings, but more generally, the organization draws on the history of Dalit struggle and anti-caste movement in the area and seeks unity through this broader struggle.

What does appear to have changed is how the waste pickers are treated, despite their caste – meaning that there has been a reduction of 'untouchability' status and routine bad treatment, which is of course more significant than the caste label by itself. This seems particularly evident to us in the new household/waste picker interface brought about by SWaCH, where the relationship has changed from mistrust and denial to recognition and a fair scattering of appreciation for the waste pickers' services.

Migrant and newcomer status

Scrap collectors in Pune are most likely to be illiterate, landless, Dalit women aged between 36 and 50 years, migrants from the Marathwada region of Maharashtra State who have been resident in the slums of Pune for at least two decades. However, as mentioned, some waste pickers have migrated to Pune from other states, and there are a small number of seasonal migrant pickers. There has been significant resistance to opening KKPKP membership to these new entrants, mainly on the basis that the newcomers were not present to invest in the early struggles, and therefore should not be entitled to the hard-won benefits (Chikarmane, Deshpande and Narayan 2001).

Perhaps this resistance should be seen from the perspective that early KKPKP members not only had to take something of a leap of faith to participate in an untested process, but also were required to invest money and considerable time in the community meetings and wider demonstrations that allowed the organization to take off. The cost of producing the first ID cards, for instance, was covered entirely by the waste picker members and amounted to almost a day's wage each. Members were also required to pay dues, and about 20–30 per cent of members did so immediately, rising to 60–70 per cent within six months. Some voices argued against the union, and some members did not pay and remained on the fringes. Defaulting members who, with growing confidence in the benefits collective action offered, wished to remain in the union were required to pay arrears.

KKPKP has been firm that since migration across states is an important citizenship right, the union cannot exclude migrants. Ultimately a compromise was reached whereby KKPKP regulates membership, for instance by visiting the homes of new members to establish that they are indeed waste pickers and need to work. It was also agreed that, whether migrants or not, new members were required to pay arrears since the unions' founding, which now amounts to around Rs650. While this is a large sum to find, arrangements are made for payment in instalments, and this has proved an important and effective strategy for levelling the ground between old and new members in terms of rights within the organization. There is agreement amongst membership that having paid the entire amount, new members have become equal members, and after a few months of participation there is little difference in status. Relatively new members have, for instance, become members of the executive body, as in the leadership of SWaCH.

Activists, paid staff and waste pickers

KKPKP has been careful to keep activist participation in waste picker leadership to low levels, as well as to 'surface' or openly address the reality that the activist members do not share the same social and economic class background as the waste pickers. Similarly members are clear that although the activists are not paid members of the organization, they do take part in governance processes. While effort has been made by the activists to understand the life worlds of the waste pickers, they also acknowledge that their role has a normative aspect to it, and that they are there in part to contribute to social change, including amongst the waste pickers.

Some tensions and differences of opinion have arisen between the activists and waste pickers, for instance over child marriage and to some extent over child labour and education. But the organization has nurtured an open, discursive and deliberative culture in which all are free to thrash out issues, discuss, and disagree, and this has been an asset to the organization's sustainability.

This discursive culture has been part of building an internal democratic process. The governing board consists of three activists and eight scrap collectors (two men and six women), but decision making is largely the responsibility of the representatives council, which now consists of 75 female and five male elected representatives. Together these members are also responsible for communicating with other KKPKP members in their communities. For some years fieldworkers were employed to work in the slums and keep contact with waste pickers in their homes and at their convenience. But this strategy was gradually replaced by elected representatives, partly because members were aware that their membership fees partly paid these workers and considered a system of representatives to be more efficient.

We have consciously tried to keep the leadership dispersed. We know that political processes need icons, and that the existence of leadership depends both on how the group perceives leaders as well as who the general public identify as leaders. But by keeping the leadership dispersed we have tried to avoid concentrations of power. The emphasis is always on consultation and negotiation, and we think styles of consultation are very significant in building a democratic process. For instance, we go the 'building consensus' route, rather than voting on issues to settle disputes by majority verdict. If there is a disagreement that can't be settled, we flag it for future discussion and bring it up again later. The child marriage issue has worked something like this – many waste pickers strongly thought it necessary to marry daughters early, but slowly, though a long deliberation process, many now wait some time longer.

Conclusion – and future challenges

In the context of climate change and attention to preserving global natural resources, solid waste management systems which promote environmental sustainability are increasingly in the spotlight. Yet it remains a constant struggle to include waste pickers in that focus – as workers who have been integral to the waste recycling system for generations, and who are entirely dependent on their role in that system for their livelihoods. New actors in waste management, attracted by increasing recognition of waste as a resource with monetary value, also continually threaten to hijack the benefits of better recognition of this service.

KKPKP has won rights and recognition for its largely female membership. Working conditions and levels of respect for many of the waste pickers in Pune have improved over the years. These improvements have been carefully negotiated through a mixture of strategies accommodating the realities of the women waste pickers as well as the exigencies of the Pune Municipal Corporation and the emerging marketizing of waste management. But the task is not yet over, either in Pune or for other waste pickers in India.

The task of convincing KKPKP members that the terms of their work will have to change if they are to remain in the sector is not yet complete.

Some members do not want to change the ways they work, and are resistant to upgrading skills even in terms which apparently unequivocally improve the conditions of their work, such as using handcarts instead of sacks to collect waste. KKPKP has managed to bring about a range of choices regarding the ways that the work can change – for example by conjuring roles in compost or biogas production, or in making saleable products direct from waste. But KKPKP is unable to prevent – and in some ways would not want to prevent – the wider changes in solid waste management that are developing partly in response to the garbage challenges of our times. Waste picking and waste pickers must find a secure location within these new systems before their livelihoods are swept away from under their feet.

Notes

1 'KKPKP puts forth the merits of recycling at Copenhagen', Laxmi Birajdar, TNN, 9 December 2009.
2 Based on the average price of carbon credits earned from the Clean Development Mechanism under the Kyoto Protocol during the first quarter of 2006.

References

Chikarmane, P. and L. Narayan (2004) 'Organising the unorganised: a case study of the Kagad Kach Patra Kashtakari Panchayat (Trade Union of Waste Pickers)', available online at www.inclusivecities. org/pdfs/case-kkpkp.pdf (accessed 20 September 2010).

Chikarmane, P., L. Narayan and B. Chaturvedi (2008) 'Recycling livelihoods: integration of the informal recycling sector in solid waste management in India', study prepared for the sector project 'Promotion of Concepts for Pro-Poor and Environmentally Friendly Closed-Loop Approaches in Solid Waste Management', SNDT Women's University and Chintan Environmental Research and Action Group.

Chikarmane, P., M. Deshpande and L. Narayan (2001) 'Report of scrap traders and recycling enterprises in Pune City', International Labour Organisation, Geneva.

Kagad Kach Patra Kashtakari Panchayat (KKPKP) (2006) 'Economic aspects of informal sector activities in solid waste management', draft city report on Pune, India, for WASTE, Advisers on Urban Environment and Development, German Technical Cooperation Agency (GTZ), and the Collaborative Working Group on Solid Waste Management in Low and Middle Income Countries (CWG).

—— (2008) 'Visibility and voice for decent work for waste pickers', report to Women in Informal Employment: Globalizing and Organizing (WIEGO).

Narayan, L. and P. Chikarmane (2006) 'Solid waste generation and collection in Pune: a situational analysis', Pune Municipal Corporation Study, Kagad Kach Patra Kashtakari Panchayat.

8

Sex, Work and Citizenship

The VAMP Sex Workers' Collective
in Maharashtra

• •

Meenu Seshu[1]

The Veshya Anyay Mukti Parishad (VAMP) collective was born in 1996 in the context of a growing HIV/AIDS movement that has taken a mainly instrumental approach to sex workers. In contrast to many sex worker organizations emerging around that time, VAMP took an explicitly rights-based approach from the outset. It aimed to forge and consolidate a common identity among women in sex work that would empower them to articulate and assert their full range of rights as well as protecting themselves from HIV infection.

Formally, VAMP was initiated by Sampada Grameen Mahila Sanstha (SANGRAM), a health and rights NGO in India working with a peer educator model for health risk reduction in the context of HIV/AIDS. But SANGRAM's explicit objective had been self-determination on the part of VAMP, and it maintained sufficient flexibility and vision to allow this to happen. VAMP grew rapidly, and now covers six districts in Western Maharashtra and two in North Karnataka bringing together more than 5,000 women who engage in several different forms of sex work. Its membership includes a few male and transgender sex workers.

For VAMP, as for many organizations working on HIV, the peer educator model is an important component of its approach, but the focus is on education for rights and collective awareness as much as for HIV information and condom distribution. As a result, the organization has evolved different spaces alongside peer educators in order to confront justice and rights issues that seemed too broad for the relatively narrow scope of project-based formats. For many sex workers, the collective has forged radical changes in their lives and livelihoods, in their self-perception and in how they are perceived by others, and in their ability to claim their place as women with rights, as citizens. This chapter explores the challenging context in which they have made this journey, as well as some of the strategies that have wrought those changes.

Sex and sex workers

Sexuality has, so to speak, come 'out of the closet' during the era of AIDS in India, and been put under tremendous public scrutiny. The epidemic has forced society to confront innumerable types of sexual relationships both within and outside marriage, heterosexual and homosexual – and, of course, the world of multiple partnerships in a commercial context. Though openness around sexuality has its obvious advantages, it has come at a price – particularly for the sexually marginalized. Society has, by and large, always frowned upon prostitution, but the 'depravity' associated with it has sharpened with the advent of AIDS. Sex workers, particularly those living with HIV, are now condemned not only for their immoral practice, but also for risking the lives of 'innocent' people: the 'innocent' are clients and their families. Social, emotional and economic marginalization of sex workers is at its highest. Effectively, being a sex worker means all of one's human rights are suspended – most critically, the right to life without discrimination and violence.

An extremely vulnerable population, sex workers are routinely exposed to policing and coercion by family, state and other non-state players. They frequently have their homes raided in the name of being 'rescued' and are subjected to varying kinds of rehabilitation. At times, the motivation underlying these actions is regulating sex work for a notional 'good' of society, or reforming 'lifestyle', presuming that sex workers need a 'better' life, while the impulse is to abolish sex work altogether. Such standards are set by patriarchal norms, and social stigma provides the fodder for upholding them. Not only are women in prostitution constructed as a bad influence upon others, especially 'good' women, they are also considered the 'vectors' of disease.

Sex workers experience stigma as a major barrier to accessing their rights and sustaining a livelihood. Interestingly, stigma manifests, in different circumstances, both as exclusion and as unwarranted attention. On the one hand, it reveals itself as social exclusion. Not only are sex workers refused service in shops and hospitals, but school authorities routinely discriminate against their children. Based on a fear that sex workers might corrupt, infect, or offend other 'upright' citizens, or trigger moral panic in communities, in the last few years there has been an increase in evictions from well-established red light areas. In 2004, for example, Maharashtra's neighbouring state government in Goa flattened an entire locality known as a sex worker area and economically supporting both sex workers and non-sex workers. Hundreds of sex workers were 'deported' back to their 'own' states, as if they were not citizens of India.

Stigma also manifests in the undue amount of attention paid to sex workers by governments and international bodies. Sex workers find themselves at the receiving end of continual interventions aimed at preventing HIV or seeking to curb trafficking. Rather than being of assistance, most of these interventions result in adding to the stigma associated with sex work and also to the marginalization of sex workers. Denied the usual course of justice, even when bodily integrity or property has obviously been violated, for sex workers the constant need is as much about the arduous struggle for rights to be recognized and to be treated as human, as it is about organizing around their rights as workers. Indeed, in VAMP, the struggle to be treated with dignity in general terms has been far more significant.

Strategies of resistance: collectivization

VAMP eventually developed a variety of strategies and methods to confront the hostility embedded in this context, but key among them was building collective identity across what had been a separated and isolated group of people. The backbone of the sex work business in Maharashtra was and remains its brothels. These were previously all 'closed' brothels – meaning that there was little, if any, communication between sex workers from different brothels, and sex workers faced the daily trials of stigma and exclusion as individuals.

SANGRAM began working with sex workers in Sangli, Maharashtra, in 1991. The closed brothel tradition started to open up in response to peer educators, and this began to bring sex workers together around a common rights-based agenda. In 1995, 150 sex workers from seven districts in North Karnataka and South Maharashtra at a meeting in Ganapatipule voiced the idea of an independent collective with a separate identity from SANGRAM. In 1996, this group registered themselves as the VAMP collective, Veshya AIDS Muqabla Parishad (Prostitutes Fight AIDS), with a clear agenda of promoting condom use not simply to protect others but for their own benefit and as a right, but also aiming to explore ways of broadening initiatives to assert their rights.

Within two months, VAMP had changed their original name, tied to the HIV agenda, to Veshya Anyay Mukti Parishad, which means 'Prostitutes' Freedom from Injustice'. This was a political and strategic move by the women not only to dissociate from their group from the narrower confines of HIV-related work, but also to reclaim the usually pejorative term 'Veshya' (which translates as 'whore'). Generally the women refer to themselves as 'women in business' or '*dhandewali*'.[2]

Beyond the peer educator model

At the start of the epidemic, a typical Government of India AIDS intervention viewed women in sex work merely as vectors of

HIV. This position, combined with top-down planning, resulted in interventions designed to protect clients, or the 'bridge population' as they were called. Sex workers were expected to cooperate in government programmes, but were never consulted. Later in the epidemic, sex workers were mobilized as 'partners' in AIDS prevention activities, the peer education approach becoming the most popular strategy. Generally, strategies of this type aim at 'empowering' women with ways to access health services but rarely take into consideration sex workers' overall socio-economic situation – either to facilitate the realization of their rights or serve as a tactic for better prevention. Instead, the complexity of vulnerability to HIV – fuelled by a range of factors including poverty and power in the sex trade, knowledge and risk perception, sexual risk, access to health services, and the violence of stigma, discrimination and abuse – is often overlooked. Simplistic solutions such as increasing condom distribution are chosen. In other words, most interventionists regard sex workers as a necessary means to end HIV transmission to the 'bridge population' of male clients, but as an otherwise unimportant, group in AIDS prevention. The gender and social inequities that marginalize female sex workers, both as women and workers, are inconsequential to programme implementation. Hence 'empowerment' remains a token phrase, in effect concealing a whole host of problems that sex workers encounter in everyday life, including exploitation, oppression and human rights abuses.

VAMP is one of the few organizations that have been able to subvert and go beyond this agenda. VAMP emphasizes that a peer educator's portfolio spans the entire continuum of HIV: before, during and after infection, and with an emphasis on the person in sex work. Their preventive work on HIV/AIDS is mainly through peer education, condom distribution and assisting sex worker colleagues who have sexually transmitted infections and other health problems to access medical help. But VAMP women also play a crucial supportive role when community members become HIV-infected, and often peer educators become the *de facto* families and care givers of ill colleagues. They ferry these women back and forth from hospitals, organize food for them, look after the women's children or even lovers who could be sick as well, and offer unconditional support. When a colleague succumbs to AIDS-related health complications they have to grapple with funeral arrangements and also deal with questions about their own vulnerability to HIV infection.

In this way, VAMP has drawn successfully on an extension of the peer educator model and uses this widely in its work. At the same time, however, it is the idea and process of collectivization that has given the organization the ability to negotiate steps towards claiming rights and treatment as citizens and as human beings.

By functioning as a loose collective, VAMP has been able to attract a variety of members in the sex worker community. Early discussions brought into focus that a more formal structure or membership-based organization, such as a trade union, would be likely to discourage a number of sex workers from joining – those, for example, who work part time as sex workers, and/or who have families from whom they keep their sex work secret. In short, many were unwilling to formally identify as sex workers. A 'collective' model allows for membership to remain not formalized so that any woman in sex work who utilizes VAMP's services or gets involved in the activities can become a member.

Secondly, it is the collective identity which has helped thousands of women in sex work combat stigma, address the social and health pressures in their lives and organize on several fronts – politically, economically and as a powerful force to be reckoned with. Changing the image of sex workers, they are flying in the face of those who call them immoral, setting stringent standards for condom use and curbing trafficking, generating respect as HIV workers, sex workers, breadwinners, and upwardly mobile women.

The VAMP women believe in collectivization as a vital weapon for resisting stigma, and gaining rights. SANGRAM's mission statement declares 'People should believe that they can change things. It is not about a few activists fighting for other people's rights. Anybody who has imbibed this understanding should be able to go and fight for their rights.'[3]

The collective interest began with enforcing condom use, the logic being that if every woman could convince her customers to use condoms, the whole community would stay healthy, continue to work, and contribute to stemming the epidemic. This collective strategy enabled the women to be the strongest and best advocates of condom usage and effective educators of their clients. Placing less emphasis on the numbers of condoms distributed, the VAMP programme conceived condom negotiation not only in terms of tackling AIDS, but dealing with safety and control in a wider sense. This included the health and well being of their children, family members and community, exercising control over rates, preventing exploitation of women both within and outside the community, and making choices around how they do sex work. Thus, the collective strengthened sex workers from within as a central goal, rather than as a by-product or goal of AIDS prevention.

Earlier, the women had competed for clients and resources. Through VAMP they find resonance in each other's experience of multiple discrimination, and share personal resources to improve business and tackle social prejudice. A common identity is fostered as an end in itself, rather than a means to prevent HIV. Consequently, VAMP has gained recognition as a collective that prevents HIV *and* ensures women in sex work are treated as human beings, with the same rights and dignity as others. Indeed, collective action of VAMP goes much beyond preventing AIDS. It is about getting those in sex work, and non-sex workers, to comprehend the larger picture. The collective understands HIV as inextricably linked to issues of gender, sexuality and rights. It links HIV vulnerability to other vulnerabilities, such as violence, discrimination, gender and human rights violations. Fighting to be treated as human beings was the most important reason why the women came together.

The formal organization structure

While the collective model has been carefully nurtured and was widely inspiring, it was apparent that a formal structure would also be necessary. This was mainly due to the need to become eligible for receiving funds, for which registration as a society/ non-government organization is necessary. Registration rules require a governance structure, the terms of which were then put in place. Since the collective identity has remained a priority, however, this governance structure has little relation to the actual functioning of the group or the location of its functional leadership. Rather, VAMP has a changing hierarchical structure depending on responsibilities and roles accorded to members. Collective meetings decide changes in this structure and the roles of members elected to various posts, and actual leadership is hence negotiated in these meetings.

The language of rights

Generally, it has been easier to organize sex workers around the clear denial of their rights, simply because most of them are marginalized by the state and society. For many years, sex workers did not use public transport for travel, each time fearing humiliation and even physical violence. The women took up using public buses as an organizing principle, and as a political statement of their right as citizens to use public transport.

Condom use was another organizing principle for sex work communities: the women viewed condoms as life-saving equipment to which they must have access, in accordance with the right to life and health. In the early days, VAMP had to fight to make condoms freely available to sex workers. Then, frequently finding holes in the government-issued condoms, they fought for better-quality equipment.

Gaining entry to government health facilities was another major barrier to accessing the right to health. The women faced routine discrimination from medical staff, exacerbated if they were HIV-positive. Hours of access to outpatient departments were awkward. The women worked nights and often slept in late. VAMP lobbied with the hospital administration for an onsite VAMP staff member to ease access. They further convinced the authority to create access times to accommodate their unorthodox working hours. This advocacy effort resulted in a policy change across the district, enforcing a new mechanism in all the hospitals. This not only supported sex workers, but also had the wider impact of including other vulnerable and at risk populations. However, fighting for better condom quality and access to hospitals as sex workers has reaped better results than fighting for facilities on an equal footing with others as citizens with rights. At one point, VAMP members tried organizing a demand for information about general drug availability in the hospital, but this was considered very threatening.

There are many examples of how, through articulating their knowledge of rights, VAMP women have found respect in places where otherwise there had been utter contempt. Before the VAMP collective was formed, for example, women sex workers could not do much about routine police harassment. Now, they demand more respect when they approach police officers for help. The road to this has been tough, given how the police and general public had previously viewed them. Some VAMP members remember, for example, that when they used to go to cinema halls to speak to sex workers there, they were often treated with hostility by the theatre owner. In one incident, they had buckets of water thrown at them. Theatre owners could also contact the police to have them removed from the site. As a result of the collective identity nurtured through VAMP, however, sex workers have been able to assert their rights of access to the cinema halls, and have been able to negotiate with the police not to harass them.

The language of justice

These struggles for equal recognition and treatment as citizens took the VAMP women far beyond peer education. But it was the ritual of condom distribution that provided the energy and the space for the evolution of a different way of working. Condom distribution was carried out in different ways by different peer educators responsible for certain communities. Some carried out distributions in the format of regular meetings – and it was these that by 2004 had evolved into the *mohalla* (neighbourhood) grievance committees. These are now local justice forums: regular Saturday meetings in various sex worker communities, where any local issues can be raised, mediated and eventually resolved in a collective format. They address disputes amongst sex workers, between sex workers and brothel owners, between sex workers and clients or families, and between brothels. They deal with issues of debt bondage, child sexual abuse, force, deception, violence, abuse, and harassment both within and outside the community of sex workers. They also address anti-trafficking measures and issues of conflict with the wider community. They are forums for news of specific difficulties or rights violations, and spaces in which support can be garnered and responses planned.

Through the *mohalla* committees, VAMP has negotiated a number of justice issues successfully. For example, the women achieved an end to police hostility during brothel raids that are conducted with evangelical zeal. They have negotiated that the police do not terrorize the community or treat the women in a violent manner during the raid. Raids now are conducted without police *lathis* (truncheons) and no one is beaten or pulled by their hair. VAMP also has demanded that only female officers can touch a sex worker during the raid. Improvements in this relationship with the police have also meant that sex workers are more willing to help the police, as in the case of the murder of a *kothi* (male sex worker) that some members recall.

Such gains do not mean that all VAMP members are always able to confront and challenge police harassment. What has happened is that more women have become aware of their rights and recognize that they have the capacity to negotiate with others, including those in authority, to diffuse threatening situations. No longer are they in a position where they are simply told by others how to act; they are now empowered to know what they want to do about problems, and to frame methods of conflict resolution through the *mohalla* committees.

Some struggles for rights have not yet been won. When a sex worker attempted to enter mainstream politics and stand for elections, for example, there was public outrage. The constituency was an area where many sex workers lived, yet she was refused candidacy on technical grounds because her caste certificate was not from Maharashtra – she was from Karnataka – and hence further identity proof was required, in the knowledge that this was too complex to arrange in time. In another incident, a sex worker wanted to stand for election on a Scheduled Caste ticket,[4] but was refused because she didn't possess proof of her father's caste papers. This was a sophisticated technical de-railing. The woman was Devadasi, as are a large proportion of sex workers in the Maharashtra–Karnataka area. Devadasis (literally, servants of god), by an outlawed but still fairly vibrant tradition, are ritually dedicated to the Goddess Yellamma. The custom equips dedicated girls and women with considerable skills in poetry, music and dance, as well as providing for their livelihood, security, community identity and support. They are never married, being figuratively married to god, and hence their children have no identifiable father. This Devadasi woman, daughter of a Devadasi, therefore had no identifiable father whose caste papers she might produce, but the administration was incapable of taking this into account. In response to the refusal of her candidacy, VAMP decided to boycott the election, and as a result the sitting municipal councillor was ousted.

The glue of communication

Regular meetings, and the open communication that happens at them, have been an important feature of the glue holding the collective – and its diverse activities across a large area – together. The VAMP leaders from each district meet regularly in Sangli every Monday; some have to travel long distances to do this. For some time, the location of Monday meetings was rotated, to share the travel time more equitably. But eventually it was decided that it was more efficient to hold the meetings in a regular – and central – place. Meetings are both flexible and purposeful: each leader reports news from their area and strategies are discussed to resolve difficulties. This is also a space for solidarity and for solidifying common ground: the leaders are from different types of sex work, including brothel-based, part-time housewives, streetwalkers and brothel owners. Usually they emerge into leadership by taking initiative in their local areas. Both the Monday meetings and the Saturday meetings of the *mohalla* committees are spaces that allow members to work across the differences of position and specifics of location to foreground their common experience within each issue that they encounter.

Work and dhanda (business)

VAMP women, as discussed, decided against organizing as a trade union. For several reasons, though VAMP believes that sex work is work, women at VAMP have not taken up organizing themselves as 'workers'. First, the term 'worker' suggests cohesion amongst the category 'sex worker', which does not fit the reality. Second, the term denotes certain parameters of employment, such as being open about one's job. Considering the attendant stigma, being open about sex work requires careful negotiation.

Sex workers in VAMP organize their lives in relation to sex work in different ways and with varying degrees of openness. Some have multiple sex partners, others are in long-term monogamous sexual relationships, but these relationships are of a commercial nature. There are housewives who are doing sex work part-time, and brothel workers who do business full time. Others work for shorter periods in lodges or maybe have a regular arrangement with a lodge. Unionization implies a level of formalization that does not encapsulate the multiplicity of experience.

Trade unions require all members to have an ID card naming the person's nature of work. There were long discussions on the impact this might have, and most felt it would add to their problems. Some sex workers might identify as a sex worker in Sangli, but not in Mumbai. Others are reticent to identify as sex workers altogether; identification would have excluded many of these members.

Part of the decision to reject the union category was also rooted in the fact that many identify sex work first as business. 'Business' encompasses the independence and the experience of own-account work and relations with clients which are at the core of their livelihoods. For a good number of VAMP women, it has enabled financial independence, management, and decision making over money as key features of empowerment, allowing women to take charge of their lives on a personal level.

At a political level, this association defies the negative stereotyping that permeates social consciousness of sex workers as victims, irresponsible, uncaring, bad mothers, et cetera. In their financial practice, the VAMP women completely overturn the notion that sex workers are victims of patriarchal systems. Indeed, sex workers prove that they are relatively freer of patriarchal shackles, as Kamala Bai explains,

> We have bank accounts in our names and our nominees are our children. We have no accounts either in the partners' name or in joint name with the partner. We have cars, property, land. All this is from our earning as sex workers. It is all in our names. We encourage other sex workers to open accounts, invest, and buy land, TV, fridge and things like that. We are sex workers, earning our living; we are under no one's control. If the *malik*[5] wants to buy a TV or fridge or car, he can do so. We can do the same. We make our decisions.[6]

The members of VAMP have had to strategize to alter their self-image. They have developed the ability to challenge powerful people and deep-seated social norms, evolving from changes in self-perception as the starting point. Many women had to address not only social stigma in this process, but also a powerful sense of shame about their work derived from pervasive social messages. Re-imagining their work not as 'wrong' or sinful, but as business enterprise has been very restorative. Indeed, developing an image as prosperous businesswomen and breadwinners for the family, overturns the stereotype of sex workers as victims and challenges the all-pervasive 'morality' that surrounds sex work. Other people, be it neighbours, taxi drivers, even local MLAs, begin looking up to the women, because they are building houses for themselves, driving new vehicles, and taking care of their families.

In one initiative, VAMP women bought a plot of land and a brothel for their own welfare work. The local community had lived with this brothel for more than 80 years but took objection when VAMP wanted to open it up and use it as an office and meeting space. The brothel made women in sex work invisible, and that was fine, but the office made them visible and vocal, which was not acceptable. They had a long struggle to confront and reverse community hostility to this visibility and work, but the building now runs as a hostel for about 30 children of sex workers in the most difficult circumstances. According to the VAMP women, money is very effective in helping them transcend an otherwise stigmatized position. As Durga points out, 'The stress is on business. We are businesswomen. Since I came to VAMP, I believe I am good. I am earning and that is good. I like doing sex work, I decide. Who are they to decide?'[7]

Sex workers are clear about the commercial nature of their transactions. Some feminist scholars have argued that in marriage, sex, if not commercial is 'paid for' in other ways. Whereas, in marriage, sex might be couched in the notion of love or silently accepted as 'duty', the transaction in sex work is apparent. Sex work is a service for money and, for the women, the more the better. But this is not to say that money is always involved in sexual interactions. Sometimes, sex workers themselves ostracize their friends in sex work for offering free sex to lovers. However, if sex is viewed as on a continuum between romance, love and commercial transaction, then sex with love can happen in a commercial context and sex for money can happen in a love context.

Asymmetries of power

The question of morality

There remains much confusion around sex work from a perspective of morality. From feminists to politicians and NGOs, the lobbies against organizing sex workers are usually fought on moral grounds. Moral concerns often stem from the question of whether sex workers have choice and agency, but these debates fail to reach any conclusions because the binary of choice and force does not reflect human experience. Questions need to be broadened beyond that of whether women have alternative choices to sex work. In other words, different questions need to be asked.

Choice is a kind of illusion. By giving consent, most of us believe we are making 'free' or unfettered choices. This can be said of marriage. People consent to getting married but the 'choice' to get married is usually made within a fairly rigid set of social parameters. If we don't get married, doubts begin circulating around one's 'character' or family reputation. Marriage therefore can hardly be considered freely chosen, and yet it is most often consensual.

Most sex workers say they do not do sex work by choice or by force. The key issue is not whether choice is involved or not, but that they consent to what they are doing.

This is a different world view. From their perspective, they fail to comprehend why they should be blamed for consenting to have sex with different men, just because other women do not. Moving beyond the question of how they began to do sex work, sex workers have a clear agenda of improving work conditions, and demand that control must be in the hands of those who conduct the business. Sadly, their viewpoints are largely unheard. Because of the asymmetry of power between governments, anti-trafficking and other organizations and those actually doing sex work, the constructions of the 'truth' by the former are generally those that get carried into policy and the practice of enforcing social 'order'.

According to this more powerful viewpoint, efforts should be directed towards ending sex work. Perhaps one of the most damaging lobbies advocating this view recently was the international attempt to prevent the organizing of sex workers, particularly in developing nations. The US President's Emergency Plan for AIDS Relief (PEPFAR), an anti-prostitution clause adopted during the Bush administration, made funding for HIV/

AIDS contingent upon not legitmizing sex work as a livelihood option. This clause affected the very existence of many sex worker collectives in India. VAMP, for example, had to withdraw from USAID funding almost immediately after the pledge came in. They were fortunate to have had other avenues for funding. However, many other CBOs, who had previously organized sex worker collectives, either became dysfunctional or decided to adhere to the pledge by running abstinence programmes.

Today, few groups remain to fight for the right to sex work. This position is most often seen as improper compared with a health rights stand, which speaks of the rights of sex workers. As a consequence, there are considerable tensions within the broader movement working with sex workers. There are those who, even while working on sex workers' rights, believe the end result should be a society free of sex work, where sex work is no longer necessary. Most sex workers argue that this is another example of how society controls and directs sexual exchanges – limited to the heterosexual, monogamous ideal only within the circle of love. The onus of this ideal rests solely on 'good women'.

Anti-trafficking groups also want to stop the organization of sex workers on moral grounds. A basic tenet of anti-trafficking rhetoric is that bodies are unwillingly 'sold' and transported across borders, and, where women are concerned, this is uncritically conflated with prostitution. A particular strand of feminism joins hands with the extreme right wing that informs the anti-trafficking discourse, in which prostitution is viewed as a form of violence against women. Such discourses stem often from privileged positions of class, race or caste, and they analyse the trading of sex through a narrow framework. This in effect limits an understanding of sex work, epitomizing sex work as oppression, victimization and exploitation of women and constructing the women only as victims of unequal gender relations. The necessity to stop prostitution has therefore become pivotal to the movement to stop trafficking.

This conflation has presented major obstacles to initiatives working for the rights of sex workers, including VAMP. For example, in 2005, an American evangelist working for the anti-trafficking NGO Restore International arrived in Sangli and, with assistance from local police, conducted several brothel raids. A series of assumptions had been made: that all the young women living in the area were doing sex work; had been trafficked; and needed 'rescuing'. Thirty-five women were picked up and sent for medical examinations to determine their age. They were detained for several days at the behest of Restore International, which was determined to malign the name of VAMP as an organization supporting trafficking. It was found that only four women detained were under age, out of which two were not doing sex work but living with relatives in the area. The women received no apology or compensation for loss of income, and the organization has continued to conduct raids periodically.

VAMP therefore faces an ongoing struggle with a powerful set of players who misconstrue their work, interpret the business and empowerment successes of the women as necessarily involving illegal practices, and take on an aggressive policing role under the mantle of moral authority.

Contesting viewpoints of state and law

In order to address the spread of HIV, the government has given considerable support for collectivization of sex workers into community-based organizations. However, there has been some inconsistency to this support. There have been major contradictions between the Health Ministry and the Home Ministry over amendments to Section 377, the law that criminalizes anal sex. Whilst in the last two decades the Health Ministry has encouraged (and funded) the mobilization of male sex workers and MSM (men who have sex with men) for AIDS prevention, the consequent increase in visibility gave free reign to law enforcers to persecute these populations, by wielding the archaic law. While the law was in place, HIV interventions faced constant difficulties in carrying out their work with MSM. Repealing the law became a mobilizing point for male sex workers. In 2009, the Delhi High court ruled that this law was unconstitutional.

However, it still remains unclear as to how this affects MSM in the rest of the country.

The proposed amendment to the Immoral Trafficking Prevention Act has created contradictions between different sets of women demanding their rights. In most settings, including India, prostitution is neither legal nor illegal; it has no status. The amendment in India seeks to penalize the client. For a group of 'positive women' in Chennai, the amendments represent some kind of justice: they have been infected by husbands who, they believe, contracted the virus from sex workers. Thus two sets of HIV rights activists are placed in opposition to each other. Sex workers have opposed the amendment, arguing it will affect their livelihood and will entail the greater risks of doing sex work under clandestine conditions.

The challenge of identity

The question of identification as (sex) workers remains on the backburner in VAMP, but is unresolved. Discussions were held, for example, around whether sex worker organizations should be getting involved in the struggles of bar girls in Mumbai, who were protesting against the 2005 ban on bar dancing by the state government. These discussions were cut short when it was realized that most of the bar girls did not identify as sex workers. In fact, not being sex workers was an important part of their argument against the government repression they were experiencing. The issue of identity prevented an alliance from being formed between the two movements.

For many sex workers, the identity of worker does not capture what they do. There remains an important distinction between being a 'worker' and being a person doing whatever it takes to make a livelihood for themselves and their families. Many locate their commercial activity in the realm of family responsibilities, through fulfilling which the women are likely to receive some degree of social credit. This dimension of experience has also made alliances with other workers' unions unlikely. VAMP women had also met with hostility from the trade unions when earlier they had thought of unionizing: the trade union leaders they encountered operated in a moral space, looking down on the women, and making it impossible to negotiate anything. One union actually threw VAMP members out of a meeting. Their lawyers wanted to know what the employee/employer relationship was, and couldn't get beyond these questions.

VAMP believes that sex work is definitely work. The problem is complicated by women who do not want the identity of a sex worker. So for them the argument that sex work is work holds, but the argument that all in sex work are workers does not.

Agendas for recognition

The ongoing struggle for VAMP is for sex workers to be recognized as persons who provide sexual services in a commercial context, as opposed to people engaged in an immoral activity. However, advocating this does not happen in a vacuum. The challenges facing sex workers are a complex web of interrelated issues. VAMP, together with the health and human rights umbrella organization, SANGRAM, has engaged with many players, with the overall goal of improving the quality of sex workers' lives.

While VAMP continues to assert and expand the rights of its membership, and strengthen the collective identity, SANGRAM works in other ways to build solidarity amongst marginalized communities more widely across other groups. Since 1997, SANGRAM – with the backing of VAMP – has conducted a District Campaign across western Maharashtra, working on HIV prevention, access to treatment and support with rural married women, adolescents and young men; later it also campaigned on violence against women and responsible safe sex amongst youth. The two organizations still work under a single banner during protests and direct action, and will continue to work hand in hand to raise skills levels of staff and membership to bring about policy changes that will ultimately have an impact on the lives of millions of sex workers.

Getting sex work accepted as a legitimate form of work can only be achieved when dignity is built amongst women who do sex work. With collective strength, the women attain courage. With the strategies of resistance outlined above, the chance of raising the status of, and reducing stigma around, sex work seems feasible. This is VAMP's current priority over fighting for specific benefits in terms of conditions. It is when such struggles are won that the road ahead will become clear for a debate on what part of the labour market they occupy and under what conditions they work.

Notes

1 This chapter draws on Meena Seshu's presentation at the conference on 'Organising Women in the Informal Economy: Lessons from Practice' (New Delhi, 20–21 October 2008) called by the Institute of Social Studies Trust and Pathways of Women's Empowerment RPC, a programme of DfID. It also draws on interviews with VAMP and SANGRAM in March 2011 and on literature produced by the organizations. Many thanks to Cath Sluggett for work on the first draft.

2 *Dhanda*/business is the term often used by sex workers in some parts of India to describe their work so as to mask their engagement with selling sex and thereby avoid social stigma.

3 See www.sangram.org (accessed 20 September 2011).

4 That is, in one of the seats allocated to lower caste representatives according to the reservation system.

5 A *malik* is a long-term lover/partner of the sex worker.

6 Interview by Cath Sluggett, 2009.

7 Interview by Cath Sluggett, 2009.

9
Gender, Ethnicity and the Illegal 'Other'
Women from Burma Organizing Women
across Borders
•••
Jackie Pollack

Introduction: the insecure work of the migrant worker

Migrants and migrant support groups work in a global environment that is increasingly anti-migration. Migrant journeys are often perceived as encroachment on the employment opportunities of local workers; as bringing in 'alien' values and ways of living; and, in recent years, as increasing vulnerability to terrorism and raising issues of national security. Migrant women live in a world where most women are still struggling to be able to exercise their rights, including the basic right to decent and productive work. Poorer migrant women workers enter a global environment that promotes temporary work and places more and more women in what is called the informal economy, a term which allows corporations and employers to evade their responsibilities to their workers but makes little sense to migrants who are subject to an intimidating array of rules and regulations governing all aspects of what they can and cannot do. Indeed, the only things that are 'informal' about the lives of poor migrant workers are the conditions under which they work and how they are paid.

This chapter deals with the experiences of the MAP Foundation in Thailand, an organization that came into existence in response to the precarious position and the accompanying rights violations experienced by migrants from Burma[1] working across the border in Thailand. MAP works with migrant men, women and children from Burma, but has a special programme for women that is the main focus of this chapter. About half of the two million migrants from Burma in Thailand are women and they work in almost every sector apart from fishing and mining. These women are located at the intersection of multiple forms of oppression: as women, as migrants, as informal workers and as members of persecuted ethnic minorities in their country of origin. As one of the founding members of the organization, in this chapter I reflect on what motivated the setting up of MAP and some of the tactics and strategies we have used to organize a highly vulnerable group of workers.

The first two sections of the chapter briefly explain the situation of migrants in Thailand, and explore the social and legal factors which frame their experience. The following sections give accounts of MAP's experience of enabling migrant women to come together: first as women, to increase their participation in decision making in the family and community, and improve their safety and security; and then as women workers, to improve their working conditions. The final section reflects on some important steps in liaising with organized workers and trade unionists.

Migration from Burma into Thailand: a brief account

In 2007, the National Statistics office of Thailand reported that of a total of 37.1 million people in the labour force, 62.7 per cent of workers (23.3 million), including agricultural workers, were in the informal economy. This percentage is increasing each year. However, it does not include the migrant workers from Burma, Lao PDR and Cambodia who, whether they work in the informal economy or not, are treated *en masse* as informal workers. As of December 2010, 932,255 migrants (812,984 from Burma)[2] were registered under the government's temporary amnesty policy and 98,386 migrants had verified their nationality and obtained a temporary passport from the country of origin. At least an equal number of migrants from the three countries had not been able to register under any of the schemes and have to live and work clandestinely.

The responses to migration into Thailand are governed at the national level by two key sets of actors: those engaged in national security and those in the business sector. The former perceive undocumented migrants as a threat to national security and attempt to document the whereabouts of migrants through amnesty-type temporary registration schemes, and then limit the movement of migrants through restrictions on travel and the setting up of checkpoints across the country.

The business sector, on the other hand, profits from the existence of a pool of labour that is transitory, disempowered and only partly covered by the panoply of rights applying to Thai citizens and workers. Many employers are reluctant to regularize the migrants who work for them, preferring a workforce that can be exploited easily with little redress. When migrants do register, the employers almost uniformly confiscate their documents, thus leaving the migrants vulnerable to police harassment, extortion or deportation. The employers, particularly in the border areas where large factories have been set up to benefit from migrant labour, encourage policies and practices that keep migrants in the area, blocking the workers' ability to experience better working conditions and pay in other provinces of Thailand.

Over the past three decades, political repression and economic mismanagement of Burma by the ruling military junta have forced large numbers of people from Burma, particularly ethnic groups, to cross the border to Thailand in search of safety and economic opportunities. Cut off by the isolation imposed on the country by the military junta, which is thus unable to provide awareness about migration or rights, people leave Burma without the information or preparation that could equip them to deal with their new environment. In the four years between 2006 and 2010 alone, the people of Burma had to cope, virtually unaided by outside assistance, with the devastating effects of Cyclone Nargis, an onslaught of crackdowns on anyone associated with the Saffron Revolution[3] or any other political activity, a famine in Chin State, a military offensive in Karen State, and chronic human rights violations across the country.

When families and communities are unable to pursue their lives and livelihoods in peace and security within a country, migration, either by the whole family or by some members of it, is a survival response. In the Burmese context, people do not have the means or the documents to migrate overseas, and so migrate across the borders to neighbouring India, China and Thailand, with some onward movement to Malaysia and Singapore.

The migration out of Burma is mixed migration, including forced migration due to human rights violations and armed conflict in ethnic areas, and migration for economic survival due to the economic mismanagement and social repression of the military regime. The migration patterns defy categorization because the element of forced migration is always present when a country is ruled by an illegitimate, undemocratic power. Individual migrants also experience different types of migration status, at times being in control of their migration and lives, and at others losing control to traffickers, abusive employers or authorities.

The people of eastern Burma have experienced armed conflict for over fifty years, as the resistance ethnic forces battled with the ruling junta for some autonomy over their lands. More recently, the junta made ceasefire agreements with some of the ethnic armies, but when it then tried to transform the resistance armies into their own border guards in the run-up to the military-sponsored election, the fighting resumed. The Thai Burmese Border Consortium estimates that at least 446,000 people[4] are internally displaced in the rural areas of eastern Burma alone.

Refugees from Karen, Karenni and Mon states who make it to the border are housed in refugee camps. In 2010, there were 140,000 refugees in nine camps[5] along the Thai–Burma border. Thailand offers no durable solution for refugees, and they live under the constant threat of being sent back to Burma. In the camps, the refugees organize the daily administration of the camps and international NGOs support schools, clinics and food supplies. Refugees are not allowed to leave the camps or mix with Thai society; they are not allowed to work or farm the land. The existence of the camps is temporary but protracted over the last twenty years. Refugees of other ethnicities, such as Shan or Kachin, are not recognized as refugees in Thailand and must survive by finding work in the labour market.

Work is available in Thailand for these migrants even if legal recognition and rights are not. Having crossed the borders illegally, migrants must make a choice between taking whatever work is available at the border, regardless of pay and working conditions, or risk using a broker to travel to work in other places in Thailand, without any guarantee that they will find better work. There are many tragic examples of the risks associated with illegal travel across Thailand. For example, in 2008, 54 migrants suffocated to death in a container because the driver was too afraid of being caught by the police to heed the phone calls from the migrants in the back of his truck telling him they had no air to breathe.[6] In 2010, three migrant children travelling in the back of a pick-up truck were killed and five adults were injured when the army shot at the truck to make it stop.[7]

While Thailand's policies on migrant labour have to some extent had to be reactive, responding to the particular situation in the Mekong and providing documentation for migrants once they are in the country, it is nevertheless quite ambiguous. On the one hand, the policy is said to desire the regularization of migrants' status, but, on the other hand, woven through the policies is a discourse of illegality and impermanence, warning the migrants annually that they are temporary and always liable to deportation. The policies clearly state that migrants may apply for a temporary work permit 'while awaiting deportation'. Each policy sets a date by which all migrants who entered the country illegally will be deported, and each policy states that this will be the last time that such a registration is allowed. In reality, the policies have been extended at the end of each year for the last nineteen years. Nevertheless, this warning of a final date serves a useful purpose for the government, ensuring that migrants who have been in the country nineteen years still feel like outsiders and are not integrated into the social fabric of Thailand.

The inception and aims of MAP

The MAP Foundation started out as the Migrant Assistance Program in 1996 in Chiang Mai. At the time, all migrant workers were undocumented and there were no organizations directly working with migrant workers. Only migrant sex workers had their own organization, 'empower', which catered to both Thai and migrant sex workers. When workers in other industries were in trouble, they contacted the sex workers for assistance. In turn, 'empower' networked with other organizations to respond to their needs. A network of concerned groups and individuals emerged to respond to the problems experienced by migrants from Burma, mostly Shan, working in Chiang Mai's construction and agricultural sectors, who were subject to dangerous working conditions, underpayment or no payment, periodic raids and regular extortion by the police, detention and deportation. The network groups – which included 'empower'; Images Asia, a human rights documentation centre; and Burma Relief Centre, which provided humanitarian relief to refugees and political exiles – pooled their resources in terms of language, skills and expertise in order to respond to the emerging situation of migrant workers.

When it became apparent that the work was too large for a diffuse network, a number of activists – I was one – set up the Migrant Assistance Program with the aim of promoting the rights of the migrant workers. Given the legally precarious status of these workers, we decided that health issues provided a relatively uncontroversial entry point through which to contact migrant workers. Our strategy was for outreach workers to visit migrant workers at their worksites and provide health education, with the longer-term goal of transforming groups of individuals who were undocumented and lived in constant fear into a community that could provide mutual support to each other. The fact that the organization was Thai-based was a major advantage. It gave migrants a greater sense of security, and with this the confidence to talk about health issues and share experiences about seeking health care, including going to the state hospital. As a result of these discussions, we began to provide interpreters to accompany migrants when they went to the hospital and to work with hospital staff to ensure acceptance of the workers.

Over the following years, the scope of MAP's activities expanded to focus on promoting labour rights, women's rights and increasing migrants' access to education as well as health prevention and care. After the 2004 tsunami in the south of Thailand, MAP set up the Tsunami Action Group (TAG), a response team, together with partner organizations to support Burmese migrant workers who were affected by the tsunami. Today MAP has two offices, one in Chiang Mai and one in Mae Sot; two community radio stations (FM99 in Chiang Mai and FM 102.5 in Mae Sot); a library/workers' resource centre in Mae Sot; numerous drop-in centres and community corners in migrant workplaces; and an emergency house providing care for up to 30 migrants in critical health and social situations. Our legal team responds to migrants' legal needs, particularly in cases of labour exploitation and violence against women from all over Thailand.

In 2003, we registered in Thailand as the MAP Foundation. We took the decision to register because we believed that it would give us recognition in the eyes of the Thai authorities and the public at large as a legitimate NGO working on the ground around a recognized set of issues. In turn, this would give greater credibility to our work, legitimacy to our advocacy efforts and a degree of security, given the nature of the work we were doing.

Imposed identities: migrant women as aliens and victims

Migrant women from Burma participate in multiple struggles for social justice. Closest to their hearts is the struggle in Burma for freedom and peace, but when they migrate across the border to Thailand, they must also deal with the injustices they face at the workplace and in society at large on the grounds of their poverty, their gender and their precarious legal status.

They are classified by their host society as 'alien workers' or as 'illegals'. As such, they are believed to bring with them diseases that were previously eradicated in the host country. They are said to commit crimes, to be dirty in their habits, to be people to be feared. In sum, they represent 'the other', the antithesis of the values to which Thailand aspires. Not surprisingly, this is not an identity that many migrants embrace for themselves. One rarely hears a migrant woman from Burma introducing herself, 'Hi, I'm Susu and I am an alien.' If aliens/migrants are not perceived as the dangerous other, they are perceived as the helpless other, that is, the victim. The US government under the Bush administration cast sex workers as a new category of 'victim' in need of US intervention. This was organized through moves to abolish sex work around the world, using an anti-trafficking framework and conditionality-bound funding. In this discourse, all sex work was exploitation and all sex workers were victims of trafficking. Not only has this encroached on the livelihood options available to women migrants who need to earn a living and support their families back home, but it has also undermined the kind of recourse they can seek to challenge exploitative working conditions. It transforms them from potential labour activists fighting for better working conditions into victims of traffickers. A trafficking victim seeks redress against individual traffickers for the criminal act of trafficking; but a labour activist through collective action would be able to seek justice against the exploitative conditions facing all workers.

None of these imposed identities relate to how people from Burma migrating to Thailand define themselves. For most people leaving Burma, their primary identity and sense of belonging is their ethnicity. They usually migrate with other people of the same ethnicity, flee shared forms of abuse in Burma which are directly related to their ethnicity, and arrive to work in occupations and areas with others from their ethnic group. Their particular histories, the languages they speak and the food they eat unite them with others who share the same ethnicity and separate them from other ethnic groups. Some of our first activities with these migrants involved finding ways to transcend these ethnic differences and unite around shared experience as women.

Organizing as migrant women

In the early years of MAP's work, we were offered a small grant by the International Women's Development Agency based in Australia. A rapid consultation led to a proposal by women from Burma that it should be used to create a space for women from different ethnicities to come together to discuss their experiences and to find ways of responding collectively to the problems they faced as migrants and as women. Essentially therefore it was a space to bring women from Burma together around what they shared rather than what divided them.

On International Women's Day 1999, the first Women Exchange was held. This idea of a 'space' for women gathered momentum along the border areas and Women Exchanges started in Mae Sot, then in Mae Hong Son and then in Ranong, gradually expanding to other areas over the years. By 2010, they were held monthly in thirteen locations along the Thai Burma border and other areas where there are many women from Burma. The space was open to women of all ethnicities, to refugee and migrant women, to women of all ages and in a wide variety of jobs. It was a space that tried to have no borders and to provide a new experience of inclusion to women who were everywhere facing exclusion.

When these forums started, the issue that came rapidly to the foreground was that of violence: the violence the women had faced in Burma as members of ethnic minorities, the subsequent violence they faced on their journey to Thailand, and then in Thailand itself. The nascent Burmese Women's Union was organizing workshops to raise awareness about violence against women within the community and MAP, as a Thai organization, complemented these workshops with trainings on how migrant and refugee women could use Thai law in cases of violence.

The opportunity to put this knowledge into practice came when a young woman and a girl from one of the refugee camps were raped by Thai rangers while they were collecting bamboo just outside the barriers of the camp. A witness took the woman and girl to the local women's organization and they determined together that they should seek justice through the Thai legal system. But at every step of the way, they encountered resistance. The UNHCR office was initially relunctant to assist, and the camp committee tried to persuade the women to remain quiet for fear it would upset the Thai authorities and result in the closure of the camps. When the women brought the case to MAP, together with the women's organization we bulldozed our way through the resistance, eventually bringing the other agencies on board to take this case to the military court, where the rapists were sentenced to nine years' imprisonment.

On the basis of this experience and the stories told at the Women Exchanges, we compiled a ten-step guideline on what migrant and refugee women could do in cases of sexual violence. The guidelines, referred to as ARM (Automatic Response Mechanism), took two years to complete as all the Women Exchange groups were consulted and changes made by one group had then to be checked by the other groups. All this took place in several different languages. But the final product was truly a product of the migrant and refugee women involved, walking women step by step through the process of providing support, counselling, medical care and legal assistance to victims of sexual violence. Once finished, we returned to each of the Women Exchange groups to train the groups on how to use the document. The trainings included visits to the one-stop crisis centres in the state hospitals and to the local police stations in order, on the one hand, to empower the women to dare to use these services and, on the other, to ensure that the local authorities were aware that migrant and refugee women were actively seeking to exercise their rights to medical assistance and to seek redress.

However, violence against women continues and the struggle to get justice remains a challenge. In Phang Nga in 2008, a Burmese couple, returning from their job of tapping rubber at night, were accosted by two Thai men. They killed the husband and raped the wife. The murderers and rapists have never been caught. In another incident in the same year, a taxi driver took two young Karen women to a motel, where he raped one of the women and then called the police to report illegal migrants. Despite having the registration number of the taxi, no one has been arrested in this case. While migrant women have more awareness of what they can do in cases of violence, and are increasingly trying to use the legal services and seek justice, in so doing they are challenging obstacles to access to justice for both poor women and migrant women. In many cases, justice is still evading them.

Nevertheless, the Women Exchange forum continues to be relevant and important in providing a space for women to develop self-confidence, to learn to speak out, to know our rights. We share our attempts to seek justice, our negotiations at work, our actions to stop domestic violence. Through the Women Exchange we learn of the experiences of women in the resistance movement, of political prisoners, of being part of the underground democracy movement.[8] Women from all over the world, including from Rwanda, Sri Lanka and Poland, have also come and shared their stories at the Women Exchange meetings. Women take this heightened consciousness back to their workplaces, back to their private households, to the factories and construction sites, back to the ethnic organizations and migrant support groups where they might be volunteering, and back to Burma when they return.

Organizing as migrant workers

While migrant and refugee women were quick to utilize and expand the space for them to come together under the identity of women, the process of finding commonality of interests and identities as workers took much longer. The work migrants are doing in Thailand is not work that they aspire to, it is not the job they dreamed of as a child, it is not their chosen career path. It is work that is available, that provides a wage, that they must do for the time being. The work that migrants do is largely determined by where they crossed the border, what the season was, and sometimes by their gender. Crossing into the north of Thailand, migrants – both men and women – are likely to work on orange or lychee orchards, flower farms, construction sites, craft factories, ice factories and as sales assistants. Women are also likely to enter domestic service. Crossing into Thailand in the south, migrant men will be taken to work as fishermen and seafarers, women as shrimp peelers, families will share work on rubber plantations and men and women will work on construction sites. Crossing at Mae Sot, the vast majority of women will go to work in the garment factories. Thus, with little agency or choice attached to the job selection, coming together under the name of their work was initially alien to the migrant workers. It was not an identity that they necessarily wanted to explore or to embrace.

The worker, whether Thai or migrant, is an identity which still commands little recognition or respect in Thailand. Only 2 per cent of the Thai working population is unionized;[9] most workers are employed in the informal sector, which is un-protected by labour laws, does not enjoy the full benefits of social security, and is transitory. But migrant workers face additional problems in promoting their worker status as their main identity. Demands for fair wages or better conditions are met with threats, harassment, violence, or arrest and deportation. The temporary work permits provide only precarious protection. Migrants with permits can still be arrested for being outside a designated area, for doing something different from the job designated on the card, or for working for a different employer. Any slight deviation can cause a migrant to lose their status of semi-legality, to become illegal and therefore liable to extortion or deportation. Since the main reason migrants from Burma have come to work in Thailand is to support their families back home, they are reluctant to take any action that would jeopardize their employment.

Furthermore, migrants from Burma have little experience of organizing as workers. Apart from brief periods of democracy since independence, their home country has been under a military regime. Trade unions have been banned in Burma since 1964. The military regime has routinely practised systems of forced labour. Gatherings of more than five people are forbidden by law. As a result, those who migrate to Thailand have no experience of organizing as workers. They only have the knowledge that any action can put labour activists at risk of arrest and long sentences of imprisonment.

All of these factors had created over the years nearly insurmountable barriers to migrants coming together as workers, risking livelihoods and safety for an identity to which they attach very little significance.

Turning to the law: women factory workers lead the way

As a result of these barriers, any attempt to organize migrants as workers has to start by strengthening the identity of worker and giving value to the work. Given the large concentrations of workers in one place, working under similarly exploitative conditions, it is not surprising that factory workers were among the first to claim their identity as workers and to engage in collective action.

In the late 1990s, migrant factory workers in Mae Sot, a town on the border between Thailand and Burma that has offered incentives to factories to set up their business there, organized spontaneous strikes in response to conditions that even migrant workers found impossible to tolerate. While workers had accepted poor wages and sub-standard living conditions, when this was combined with violence and threats the workers laid down their tools and went out on strike. But the moment they stepped outside the factory floor, the employers would call the immigration department and before sunset the workers would be arrested and deported. MAP, together with a partner workers' association, Yaung Chi Oo, started to provide workers with information about their labour rights and about the mechanisms for negotiations.

Gradually, workers started to present their demands to the employers instead of immediately going out on strike. Their demands were usually minimal: a few extra Baht a day, a little more meat or vegetables in the lunch provided by the factory (but paid for by the workers), some security in their living quarters (usually a dormitory sleeping up to 100 workers). These negotiations usually broke down quickly as the workers still had little bargaining power. The employer knew that he could dismiss the workers and quickly find others. If they are no longer working for the employer, registered workers have only seven days to register with a new employer – a process that involves making a legal complaint against the previous employer and securing his signature to release the workers, and then finding a new employer even though there is no system to help them do so. In areas such as Mae Sot, where the employers all club together, workers who have made demands of their employers find that they are blacklisted by all the factories, as the employers' federation shares information about activist workers, whom they call troublemakers.

In the face of these conditions, MAP continued to work with Yaung Chi Oo Workers' Association to offer workers training on Thai labour laws and policies, further develop negotiating and bargaining skills, and provide them with a broader perspective on their place in global value chains and their contributions to the profitability of the industry. With further trainings, the workers became cognizant not only about labour laws but also about the legal mechanisms for arbitration.

One group of workers from the Nut knitting factory decided to attempt to navigate these mechanisms rather than go out on strike. Their actions were based on what they had learnt about the rule of law and about the existence of mechanisms to protect their interests as workers. They also felt secure in the knowledge that they were acting within the law and had the support of a Burmese organization (Yaung Chi Oo) as well as a Thai one (MAP). Their struggle to take their case through the legal channels exposed the many barriers and obstacles that this pathway presented to migrant workers.

The Department of Labour Protection and Welfare was located one and a half hours away from the border town in which they worked – a drive through the mountains that entailed passing four checkpoints, none of which would let migrants through. Even when the Department was persuaded to provide services to this group, the official was Thai, could not speak Burmese, and therefore could not communicate with the workers. Meanwhile, the employer dismissed initially all the leaders of the group and then all the workers. Having lost their jobs, the workers lost their legal status and were harassed, arrested and deported. But they organized themselves to ensure that a group of leaders, mostly women, stayed on the border to return for the negotiations. Every time these women came to the court, they had to show border passes to indicate they were there legally. The case reached the court, because the employer had ignored the order to pay compensation to the workers issued by the Department of Labour Protection and Welfare. In the first court hearing, the employer offered each migrant 10,000 Baht (US$303) when the ruling was for 160,000 Baht (US$4,848) per worker. The judge said this was too little, but suggested it should be increased only by another 2,000 Baht (US$60).[10] When Ma Wai, the woman worker representing all her colleagues, was asked if the group would accept this, she said no. The judge said she did not believe that Ma Wai was speaking on behalf of the other migrants who were all in court. The other migrants were asked if this was the case. The group stood up without a moment's hesitation and in unison chanted a resounding 'Ma houk bu' (NO) that echoed through the court.

It was one of those historical moments when everyone present knew that an important barrier had been crossed, that there would be no turning back. Migrant workers could go to court; they could deliberate on the verdicts they received and make their voices heard. The court had to listen to migrants; the employers had to go through a legal process. The migrants in this case eventually received the equivalent of half the amount in the initial order, receiving lump sums of 70,000 Baht (US$2,121) each,[11] but their action had won a much greater victory: it changed the nature of all further negotiations.

Other migrants were given courage by the example of this group. Instead of spontaneous strikes, other workers in the area started to organize and negotiate. Each year since this case, around 1,000 workers in the area have taken cases forward with MAP's assistance and received compensation of between one and four million Baht (US$33,333 to US$133,333) a year. In addition, other NGOs have also followed the example of supporting migrants to make legal cases. While MAP and Yaung Chi Oo used to be the only groups doing this, now there are several NGOs around Thailand that provide legal assistance to migrants in cases of labour exploitation and occupational health and safety. The Department of Labour Protection and Welfare opened a branch in Mae Sot and provided translators. The spaces for migrants to embark on actions to seek remedy have thus increased greatly in the last few years, and the identity of worker has received more attention and acquired meaning.

Of course, just as the workers have become more organized and developed their strategies, so have the employers. When the workers took the employers at the Nut knitting factory by surprise with their unity and their daring, the only weapon the employer had ready was violence and thuggery. But now the realization that migrants can take complaints to court has led employers to develop new tactics. They close down the offending factory; they declare bankruptcy. The cases are more drawn out and the migrants end up with much less. There is still no real incentive for employers to pay minimum wages and give decent working conditions to migrant workers, despite the fact that they know they can be taken to court, because they also know that, even after a court case, even if they are ordered to pay the migrants, the amount they pay will total less than paying the minimum wage[12] – because the original order is calculated at the minimum wage, and then the figure is negotiated downwards.

In addition, taking legal cases against employers involves costs, particularly when the cases are not settled at the Department of Labour Protection but have to be taken to court. MAP has lawyers on its staff and coordinates with lawyers from the Lawyer's Council of Thailand, an organization which include a group that provides human rights advice and support. However, with many more workers taking up cases, MAP has also found it necessary to hire private lawyers.

When a factory owner in Chiang Mai offered to support some activities of MAP, this provided an opportunity to adopt a new strategy: setting up a fund which migrants could use for employing a lawyer and then reimburse the fund if and when they won their case. At first the migrants were reluctant to participate in what became known as the Re-Fund but after one group of workers used the fund and repaid into it, a group of 71 women factory workers who had not used the fund but who had received free legal counsel from MAP took the decision to donate some of their compensation money (around 71,000 Baht/ US$2,150) back into the fund. The Re-Fund has become one more aspect of the efforts used by MAP to promote the capacity of migrant workers to organize collectively against exploitation.

Building a membership organization

As migrant workers began to embrace the identity of worker, we set up a programme, modelled on the Women Exchange, for men and women workers called Labour Exchange. Here migrants could come together to exchange information about their working conditions and to share experiences of negotiating for better conditions. Labour Exchanges have also provided a forum for Thai and migrant workers to meet and exchange experiences. Labour Exchanges, like Women Exchanges, are held monthly in different areas.

In 2007, the original participants in the Chiang Mai Labour Exchange, men and women working in the construction industry, set up their own membership-based workers' association called the Workers' Solidarity Association (WSA). The association collects a small due from its 200 or so members and uses this revenue as welfare support for their members in case of illness, unemployment or arrest. The WSA has also organized petitions to local authorities regarding the level of restrictions imposed on migrants and access to justice. The local authorities now also recognize that the WSA is representing migrant workers in Chiang Mai and contacts them directly to assess the mood among migrants regarding upcoming policies.

The Labour Exchange groups are attended by both men and women migrants in more or less equal numbers, but once the Workers' Solidarity Association was set up with a formal structure and positions, all the leading positions were filled by men. This situation is being discussed within MAP as a manifestation of the strong culture of women's deference that characterizes gender relations and which gives legitimacy to male authority. As a result, while men have moved smoothly into positions of authority, women have withdrawn from them.

There is, of course, a practical side to this reproduction of gender hierarchies within the WSA. Men have far more time on their hands to participate in organizational activities than women, who have their domestic responsibilities in addition to their paid work. But given the deeply ingrained nature of gender roles, it will take a longer struggle to give women the self-confidence to take up leadership roles in the presence of men from their own communities.

Most of the workers who became members of the WSA are construction workers, and although their organizing is mainly around welfare issues, their existence is already proving to be a confidence booster to construction workers in Chiang Mai. MAP is now approached regularly by construction workers wishing to pursue action against under-payment or non-payment at work. In order to take such action, the workers have to agree to a united front so as not to lose their work immediately. Unlike amongst the factory workers, where the action is led by women, the construction worker actions are being led by men.

The case of domestic workers

Migrant women are at the bottom of the wage hierarchy, earning less than migrant men who in turn earn less than local men. Among migrant women, it is probably domestic workers who occupy the least well-paid and respected position. Domestic work is not protected by the labour laws, so there is no minimum wage, no legal obligation to give days off work, no limit on the number of hours worked.

Domestic workers represent a particularly difficult group to organize. They are isolated, often confined within homes, with little opportunity to interact with their peers or to learn the language and culture of the wider society. In some provinces, migrants have been restricted in their use of mobile phones, something which impacts particularly severely on domestic workers who are already so isolated.

MAP spent many years trying to reach out to domestic workers with little success. Occasionally our efforts – setting up booths at temple festivals, or providing a hotline or PO Box number – resulted in one or two domestic workers contacting us. Their stories only convinced us more that domestic workers desperately needed to be in contact with each other and to start organizing. We were inspired by one incident in particular. This was the case of a woman who told us how she used to watch her employer proudly display a plaque to all who came to the house. Not able to read or write Thai, she did not know what was written on the plaque but was convinced it held valuable information and copied down the letters.

When the employer refused to pay her salary for the last year, she left and contacted MAP. Since she had only ever left the house she had worked in once, she had no idea of who her employer was or the address at which she had worked, but she produced the slip of paper with her shaky handwriting. The plaque was an award to the president of a local club and had her employer's name and business on it, the exact information that was needed to pursue legal action.

The resourcefulness of this woman strengthened our determination to reach domestic workers. When we started a community radio station, we scheduled programmes targeting domestic workers and quickly felt we had made a major breakthrough. Domestic workers started to phone in. They often listened to the radio while they worked, sometimes on their mobile phones so as not to disturb anyone. We invited the listeners to come to a Domestic Workers' Exchange. Gradually, the number of women grew from five to ten, to fifteen, and so on upwards. Today, 80 women are a part of the Domestic Workers' Exchange. It is still a very small number compared to the approximately 200,000 migrant domestic workers working throughout Thailand, but it nevertheless is a group able to speak not just for themselves but also on behalf of other domestic workers who do not yet have a voice.

The major issue for domestic workers was the fact that they were not entitled to any paid leave. Most of the domestic workers worked for months without having a day off. They had no time to rest, to enjoy themselves, or study, or go to the movies, or go to the park, or come together with other domestic workers to talk about their lives, or to discuss their working conditions. MAP linked the domestic workers with a regional campaign, United for Foreign Domestic Workers Rights, which was calling for one day off and recognition under the labour laws. The migrant domestic workers in Thailand together with their Thai counterparts organized a postcard campaign, getting supporters to sign a postcard which would be sent to the Ministry of Labour on International Day of Solidarity with Domestic Workers, 28 August. Over 6,000 postcards were signed and handed to a representative of the Parliamentary Committee on Labour at a National Consultation on Domestic Workers. Two domestic workers and myself were then invited to visit Parliament and deliver the huge box of postcards personally.

It has taken many years to start any form of organizing among domestic workers, and it will always be one of the most challenging of our efforts. But as the small group of domestic workers gain experience of presenting their case to the authorities, of campaigning for their rights, of having the opportunity to be part of a regional campaign, and meeting inspiring domestic workers who have led the successful campaigns in places such as Hong Kong, there is a great deal of hope: we believe that domestic workers will be stronger in the future.

Domestic workers were excited that the International Labour Organization put the issue of domestic work on its agenda in its annual conference in 2010 and agreed to develop a Convention on Decent Work for Domestic Workers to be presented for a vote at the following year's conference. Before the Thai delegation left for the conference in 2011, the domestic workers handed them a petition calling for their support for the Convention and the recognition of their work as work. The domestic workers were very disappointed that the Thai government abstained from voting on the Convention. Nevertheless, they were excited that overall the Convention received enough votes to be adopted, and that there is now an international protocol, Convention 189 on Decent Work for Domestic Workers, that recognizes their work as work – which, of course, they have known for a long time.

Allying with the trade unions

Much of the organizing of migrant workers has been on an *ad hoc* basis, focusing on changing working conditions in particular factories and construction sites. Migrants are not allowed to form their own unions in Thailand, but they are allowed to join unions. However the majority of Thai unions are in-house unions based in Bangkok. Since migrants are not allowed to travel, this has posed a major problem.

In recent years, the Action Network for Migrants (Thailand), a network of fifteen NGOs and migrant groups, with a committee which includes both MAP and Yaung Chi Oo, has devoted time and energy to building links with Thai unions and labour groups, particularly with the Thai Labour Solidarity Committee, which represents twenty Thai unions and labour groups. The earlier position of Thai union leaders had been that migrants stole jobs from Thai workers and caused standards of working conditions to deteriorate. This attitude changed as these leaders found that Thai workers were themselves increasingly becoming employed on temporary contracts with fewer and fewer protections. With the realization that the same forces of globalization were leading to the deteriorating conditions of work among both Thai and migrant workers, a number of unions agreed to form a joint committee of migrant and Thai workers.

The Thai labour groups have on a number of occasions taken the migrants demands to the government or to international forums, thus providing a much needed voice for migrants. The challenge now is how to include migrant workers in Thai unions as active members, and how migrants can form their own associations and affiliate with Thai unions. And within both these challenges is the gender challenge of ensuring that women workers' voices do not get lost in these processes, which favour male participation.

Conclusion

There is a great deal of discussion today about the contribution that migrants make to the economy of their countries through their remittances. Women migrants from Burma are keenly aware of the importance of their efforts for the survival of their communities back home, but it is also clear that they are paying a heavy price to make these contributions. The relevance of migration to development is not only a matter of remittances. A developmental perspective on migration must also embrace gender aspects of the migration experience. Social justice demands that women should benefit from the development that they are contributing to, both in their host countries and in their countries of origin.

Through their experiences of tackling the intersecting inequalities of gender, class and ethnicity, migrant women in Thailand will be taking back valuable lessons in political organization to contribute to the future peace, development and democracy of their home country, Burma. One aspect of what they have learnt is succinctly conveyed in the words of Ma Wai, the woman leader of the workers striking at the Nut knitting factory: *'I have learnt what it means to win. It is not about the outcome. To win is to dare to start the fight for your rights.'*

Notes

1 The country is internationally known by two names, Burma and Myanmar, the latter being the name given by the military junta in 1989. We prefer to use Burma until the people of the country are consulted in the naming of their country.

2 See www.burmalibrary.org/.../IOM-Migrant_Info_Note_No_8 (en).pdf (accessed 23 July 2011).

3 In 2007, thousands of monks marched through Rangoon in response to rising prices, which were causing increased hardship to the population.

4 See www.tbbc.org/.../2010-10-28-media-release-idp-survey.pdf (accessed 15 December 2010).

5 See www.tbbc.org/whatwedo/whatwedo-news.htm (accessed 20 February 2011).

6 See www.mekongmigration.org/?cat=10 (accessed 9 March 2011).

7 www.hrw.org/node/88950 (accessed 10 March 2011).

8 Women's continued engagement with the struggle for democracy in Burma – and their resourceful use of their knowledge of their own culture to further it – was illustrated by a campaign carried out by Lanna Action for Burma, a group of women activists in Thailand. Playing on the fact that within Burmese culture, women's private garments have an emasculating effect on men, this group called on women across the world to send their panties in the post to the Burmese embassies in their country. The Panty Power campaign provided an outlet for women all around the world to vent their anger and outrage at the military regime in Burma, and in particular at its abuse of women. Women all over the world, including Brazil, Canada. Philippines, Australia and the UK, responded to the call

and organized Panty Power events.

9 See   www.solidaritycenter.org/content.asp?contentid=902   (accessed 14 May 2011).

10 At the time, the exchange rate was approximately US$1 = Baht 33.

11 Minimum wage at the time in Mae Sot was 133 Baht (US$ 4) a day.

12 All workers in Thailand, regardless of their legal status, are entitled to the minimum wage. This is around $US5 day, although it differs from province to province and is rarely received by migrants. On construction sites, migrant women are generally paid less than migrant men.

ENDNOTE
Looking Back on Four Decades of Organizing
The Experience of SEWA
• •

Ela Bhatt

Putting women at the heart of development planning

India has made remarkable economic progress in the past decades. It is one of the powerhouses of the global economy today. But inequality has been rising steadily as well. It is clear that India will be able neither to accelerate nor even to maintain its economic gains if it continues to marginalize the poor. It is only by investing in people and their economic potential that India can accelerate its economic growth more actively, effectively and democratically. Assessing our experience at the Self-Employed Women's Association (SEWA), I would say that poor working women are the key to this process.

We need to put poor women at the centre of economic reform and planning; we need to recognize their work as key to removing poverty. Focusing on employment will boost our economy at every level. When the poor come together on the basis of their work and build organizations that decentralize production and distribution, promote asset formation and ownership, build people's capacities, provide social security, and allow for active participation and a voice, they are the drivers of progress and need our full support. We need policies that encourage self-help, support local cooperative economic initiatives, and emphasize sharing and pooling of resources at every level. This strengthens the community and stops migration; it prevents alienation and exploitation; and it stems the spiralling freefall into poverty.

The vast majority of working women in India – and in much of the developing world – are in self-employment. Such self-employment represents the entrepreneurship and initiative taken by the poor. It has the potential to develop all aspects of the person – the social, the economic and the political. There is room for all kinds of development, and it is crucial to nurture the entrepreneurship the poor show in their fight to survive. By focusing their efforts on the dire need for credit among the working poor, the banking industry could potentially revolutionize our economy. How can one afford to ignore such a large, untapped, economically active client base?

Today we see that employment opportunities are shrinking in certain sectors: construction workers are losing employment due to mechanization and because contracts are going to large national and international construction conglomerates; handloom weavers have difficulty getting raw materials such as cotton and yarn because they are exported; many of the traditional economic activities of poor self-employed women are becoming redundant because of changing times and demand. At the same time, we see that the lifting of trade barriers presents opportunities to women in crafts, textiles, and perhaps even agricultural produce in the future. If organized, poor women can gain from these opportunities.

By focusing on women, there is potential for a different kind of change – a more integrated growth – and this occurs even at the family level. Women are resilient, hard-working, used to sharing and pooling and creating mutual support systems. They nurture and sustain the family unit under all circumstances. They need access to home-based work so they can care for their families as well; they need markets for their products, both locally and globally; they need credit and banking services; they need health care and child care; they need education, learning, and skill development; and they need a voice in the society in which they live. Investing in people and their living and working environments is true nation building.

We need to build cooperative economic structures around work. We need to invest in initiatives taken by poor women and provide sustained access to resources so that women can enter the mainstream economy and create a countervailing impact. We need to create a network of social security, so that health care, child care, housing, and insurance are universal. We need to build the capacity of poor self-employed women to enter global markets by strengthening their skill and knowledge base, individually as well as institutionally. Only a truly democratic process – of the people, by the people and for the people – will give birth to a democratic nation.

Work and the tyranny of classification

SEWA has been part of a larger process of organizing poor working women since 1972. The organization straddles the realms of union and cooperative. The union mobilizes and organizes the women to come together around their work issues. The women then form trade cooperatives in an effort to become owners of their labour. SEWA has nearly a hundred different cooperatives, rural and urban; some are built around products, others around services. There are vendors' cooperatives as well as midwives' cooperatives; rag pickers' cooperatives as well as weavers' cooperatives. There are as many trades as there are facets to a country's economy, and self-employed women can be found in every one of them. We also have SEWA Cooperative Bank which pumps 15 million rupees into the smallest levels of the city's economy each day through its women account holders. It helps poor women build ownership of productive assets to fight life's vulnerabilities. This way, our economy grows, woman by woman.

When asked what the most difficult part of SEWA's journey has been, I can answer without hesitation: removing conceptual blocks. Some of our biggest battles have been over contesting set ideas and attitudes of officials, bureaucrats, experts and academics. Definitions are a major part of this battle. The Registrar of Trade

Unions would not consider us 'workers'; hence, we could not register as a 'trade union'. The hard-working *chindi* workers, embroiderers, cart pullers, rag pickers, midwives, and forest produce gatherers can contribute to the nation's gross domestic product, but heaven forbid that they be acknowledged as workers! Without an employer, you cannot be classified as a worker, and since you are not a worker, you cannot form a trade union. Our struggle to be recognized as a national trade union has continued since then. It was not until 2007 that we finally succeeded.

The Registrar of Cooperatives would not register SEWA Bank because its members were illiterate women. Even though these women could earn an income, run their own businesses, save, borrow and repay, they could not form their own banking cooperative because they could not sign their names. Literacy, evidently, was more important to the registrar than the women's dynamic economic productivity. I've often felt that the real illiterates are on the other side of the table.

Similarly, we had trouble registering service cooperatives. Our rag pickers' cooperative was suspect because it did not manufacture any products; the midwives' cooperative was asked why delivering babies should be considered an economic activity; the video producers' cooperative was denied registration because the directors, the producers, and the sound and camera technicians were illiterate. Government officials had no concept of how much more powerful a visual medium is in the hands of those not enslaved by the written word. When vegetable vendors and producers wanted to form a joint cooperative, they were told that though both belonged to the same industry, they fell under separate category lists and therefore could not collaborate formally.

We had other problems with these classifications and categories. Since the income of poor women from any one type of work is usually not enough to make ends meet, they must have several income-earning occupations. In fact, 80 per cent of SEWA members are engaged in multiple types of work. Let me give you an example. A small farmer works on her own farm.

She may sell her vegetables. In tough times, she also works on other farms as a labourer. When the agriculture season is over, she goes to the forest to collect gum and other forest produce. Year round, she produces embroidered items, either at a piece rate for a contractor or for sale to a trader who comes to her village to buy goods. Now, how should her trade be categorized? Does she belong to the agricultural sector, the factory sector, or the home-based work sector? Should she be categorized as a farmer or a farm worker? Is she self-employed or a piece-rate worker? Should she be covered by a social security fund for home-based workers, given her embroidery work at home, or should she be entitled to a hawker's licence from the municipal authorities?

Because her situation cannot be defined and neatly contained in a box, she has no work status and her right to representation in a union is unrealized. She is denied access to financial services or training to upgrade her skills. The tyranny of having to belong to a well-defined 'category' has condemned her to having no identity. The livelihoods of millions of people are similarly not perceived as work and, therefore, remain uncounted, unrecorded, unprotected and unaddressed by the nation, conveniently 'invisible' to policy makers, statisticians and theoreticians. Dividing the economy into formal and informal sectors is artificial – it may make analysis easier, or facilitate administration, but it ultimately perpetuates poverty. Until the International Labour Organization (ILO) was forced to acknowledge the growing numbers of home-based workers, even international trade unions did not wish to recognize them as workers; instead, they considered them a threat to the organized labour movement. My point is this: when you are not officially classifiable, you have no official identity and you can be ignored; you are no longer subject to policy and you cease to be a citizen. If you ever come to official attention, it is only as an obstacle.

Classifications that are commonly used can exclude some workers. Work has many dimensions and meanings. It takes many forms. Meaningful work enables a worker to earn and live a balanced life. However, the world over, there is a tendency to promote only certain types of work – work that fits into the global market economy. Any work that falls outside of that narrow definition is either eliminated because it is 'unproductive' or is downgraded by reducing the price of its worth. This way of viewing work, backed by economic theories and adopted by our policy makers, manages to disenfranchise millions of workers around the globe every day. In India, where a majority of our workers fall outside of this current definition of work, perhaps it is time we asked, what is *Karma?*

Organization is power

During the 300 years of British rule, India witnessed its traditional social, political, and economic structures weaken, wither, or die at a steady pace. What replaced them were new structures that facilitated colonial rule – centralized governance, policy and bureaucracy, industrialization, to name but a few. They were never people-friendly, and they didn't need to be. But even after independence, these structures have remained intact. Gandhiji's effort to break them through *khadi*, *panchayat*, trusteeship, was a way of focusing our attention once again on building new structures that met the needs and faced the realities of our own people. He felt that India could be built on institutions that were small, local, democratic and dynamic.

Our political structure today is formally democratic but so riddled with vested interests that it increasingly marginalizes the poor masses. There is little accountability. Local self-government structures are weak and getting weaker. The arms of the government – the legislative, the judicial and the executive – when they reach the poor, seem to hinder rather than to help. Partly, it is the legacy of colonial rule, but perpetuating undemocratic structures and policies from the past has been convenient for the educated urban elite who hold so much power in the country.

Although it is accepted as general wisdom that politically decentralized bodies are essential to an active democracy, the economic decentralization of power and resources is largely ignored. It is unfortunate that centralized production, skills, technology and ownership of resources are seen as the most efficient way to progress in India, today. Decentralized political power with centralized economic power can be a dangerous mix. The working poor must be brought into the fold of the macro environment and given full support; they must not be controlled or removed from the economic scene as is being done with street vendors, cart pullers, marginal farmers, and their kind.

Change, to be real, has to come from the people; it cannot be trickled down, imported or imposed. As a country, we can create a climate for change if we can put our trust in the people. For that, everyone must have a voice. The poor, because they are in the majority, especially need to be heard. Today, SEWA with a membership of one million women spread across nine states of India, is a family of organizations, similar in structure to a banyan tree that spreads its branches. We have often been tempted to take on large-scale projects and implement them quickly by hiring professionals but we have tried to resist. Instead our policy has been to go through the long and difficult process of empowering grassroots-level people to run their own projects. It is not easy; progress is slow, sometimes frustrating, not always efficient, and full of seemingly avoidable setbacks. Yet it is in this process that groundbreaking change occurs. When women learn at their own pace through self-help and feel comfortable in their knowledge and actions, they change their lives and their environment for the better and for the long term.

Once, at a SEWA Bank meeting, I asked our board members if money was power. Some women categorically agreed. One woman said that money gave strength and that was power. But when asked who was the most powerful person in the room, the women pointed to the managing director of SEWA Bank. They felt she had the money power of the bank. Her power also came from the fact that she was educated, was efficient at her work and had the strong support of the women she worked for. I argued that since the money of the bank came from the women, why was it that they themselves did not feel the most powerful? They explained that while individual savings and capital give a sense of power to the self, it is only the collective strength of hundreds of thousands of women that really gave one 'big power'. In short, money is power, but collective strength is bigger power.

About the Contributors

•••

Ela Bhatt, a Gandhian, is widely recognized as one of the world's most remarkable pioneers and entrepreneurial forces in grassroots development. Known as the 'gentle revolutionary', she has dedicated her life to improving the lives of India's poorest and most oppressed women workers. In 1972 she founded the Self-Employed Women's Association (SEWA), a trade union that now has more than 1.3 million members. She founded SEWA Cooperative Bank in 1974; it now serves an outreach of 3 million women. She was a member of the Indian Parliament's Rajya Sabha (upper house) and subsequently a member of the Indian Planning Commission. She founded and served as chair for Women's World Banking, the International Alliance of Home-based Workers (HomeNet), Street Vendors (StreetNet) and Women in Informal Employment: Globalizing, Organizing (WIEGO). She also served as a trustee of the Rockefeller Foundation for a decade. She has received several awards, including Padmashree, Padmabhushan, the Ramon Magsaysay Award and the Right Livelihood Award, the George Meany-Lane Kirkland Labour Rights Award (AFL-CIO, US), the Légion d'honneur (France), the Madrid Creatividad Award and the CGAE Human Rights Award (Spain) as well as honorary doctorates from Harvard, Yale, KwaZulu-Natal and other universities. She is a member of The Elders, a global council brought together by Nelson Mandela (2007), Director of the Central Board of the Reserve Bank of India (RBI) (2011), and the author of *We Are Poor but So Many*, published by Oxford University Press (2006).

284

Poornima Chikarmane is an Associate Professor in the Department of Continuing and Adult Education and Extension Work at the Pune Campus of Shreemati Nathibai Damodar Thackersey (SNDT) Women's University. She has been closely involved in the Kagad Kach Patra Kashtakari Panchayat and SWaCH Coop through the Department's Programme for the Empowerment of Waste Pickers. Poornima is currently engaged in research and advocacy in occupational health and safety, social security and protection for waste pickers and informal waste collectors.

Andrea Cornwall is Professor of Anthropology and Development at Sussex University and has served as Director of the Pathways of Women's Empowerment programme since 2006. Trained as a social anthropologist, her work has focused on gender, democracy and sexuality. She is author of *Democratising Engagement* (Demos, 2009) and co-editor of *Feminisms in Development: Contestations, Contradictions and Challenges* (with Elizabeth Harrison and Ann Whitehead, Zed Books, 2008), *The Politics of Rights: Dilemmas for Feminist Praxis* (with Maxine Molyneux, Routledge, 2009) and *Men and Development: Politicizing Masculinity* (with Jerker Edström and Alan Greig, Zed Books, 2011).

Geeta Menon is a social activist working and struggling with the unorganized sector of women for more than two decades. She is part of a rights-based group building leadership among domestic workers. Geeta studied at the Tata Institute of Social Sciences (TIISS), Mumbai, and plunged straight into social and political activism. She is on the Sexual Harrassment Complaints Committee, active in various corporates and institutions. As part of her work she undertakes evaluations, short-term studies, and gender sensitization training.

Lakshmi Narayan is Founder-Secretary of the Kagad Kach Patra Kashtakari Panchayat. She has been working with waste pickers since she graduated from the Tata Institute of Social Sciences. Privatization and corporatization of waste management constitute a big threat to waste workers in the informal economy. Lakshmi is currently engaged in mobilizing around those issues to secure the livelihoods of waste pickers and to promote models of sustainable waste management. She is involved in national and international processes for improving the visibility and voice of waste pickers globally.

Anuradha Pande has been working with Uttarakhand Environment Education Centre (UEEC), Almora, since 1992. She has been a part of the team designing, testing and mainstreaming environmental education in government schools in the Central Himalayas. She is the founder and coordinator of Uttarakhand Women's Federation, a state-wide network of rural women's groups. Anuradha organizes and works with rural women on gender, environment, education, health and political issues. She conducts training for women and adolescent girls, and develops learning materials. Every year, she organizes about twenty women's conventions across the state, bringing rural women together to raise their concerns.

Jackie Pollock was there when two grassroots organizations were started in Thailand: empower, a sex workers' organization, in 1986 and MAP, a support group for Burmese migrant workers, a decade later. She is currently the Executive Director of MAP Foundation and continues to be involved in the work of empower. Jackie has also published articles on trafficking, migrant workers, refugees and gender. As well as developing a training course on labour migration management for government officials in the Mekong, she has undertaken international consultancies on trafficking, sex work and migration. Jackie graduated from the University of Sussex, UK.

Jesu Rethinam has worked with SNEHA (Social Need Education and Human Awareness), a federation of women fisheries workers' groups in Tamil Nadu, India, since 1984 and has been its director since 2004. She qualified and practised as a lawyer before becoming involved in social activism. She convened the

Coastal Action Network, which has worked to protect livelihoods and the coastal ecology since 1996, and has been a core
team member of the Tamil Nadu Women's Network for over
twenty years.

Ben Selwyn is a Senior Lecturer in international relations and
development studies in the Department of International Relations,
University of Sussex. He has conducted fieldwork in north-
east Brazil and is the author of *Workers, State and Development:
Powers of Labour, Chains of Value* (Manchester University Press,
2012). He has also written widely on development theory from
the perspective of labour, and is currently completing a book
provisionally entitled *Capitalism vs Development: Critiques and
Alternatives*, to be published by Polity in 2014.

Meena Saraswathi Seshu is General Secretary of Sampada
Grameen Mahila Sanstha, an organization based in Sangli, India,
which has worked since 1991 for the empowerment of people in
sex work, including mobilization for HIV-related peer education.
In 1996 this work broadened into the organization of a collective
of women in prostitution called VAMP (Veshya Anyay Mukti
Parishad). Meena has worked with marginalized populations,
particularly rural women, adolescents and people in sex work, on
HIV and AIDS, sexual and reproductive health, violence against
women, and gender and sexual minority rights through grassroots,
rights-based organizations in Karnataka and Maharashtra.

Colette Solomon is the Deputy Director of Women on Farms
Project, a feminist and human rights NGO that works with
women who live or work on commercial farms in the Western
and Northern Cape provinces of South Africa. Colette has a
doctorate from the Institute of Development Studies at the
University of Sussex.

Index

● ●